Based on the history and surviving records of German professional organizations, this work is the first to show how the learned professions in Germany emerged gradually in the nineteenth century from the shadow of strong state regulation to achieve a high degree of autonomy and control over professional standards by World War I. By studying professional groups collectively, it gives a more contoured picture of their fate under National Socialism than works dedicated primarily to the phenomenon of fascism itself.

The German experience of professionalization

The German experience of professionalization

Modern learned professions and their organizations from the early nineteenth century to the Hitler era

CHARLES E. McCLELLAND
University of New Mexico

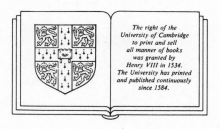

The right of the
University of Cambridge
to print and sell
all manner of books
was granted by
Henry VIII in 1534.
The University has printed
and published continuously
since 1584.

Cambridge University Press

Cambridge

New York   Port Chester   Melbourne   Sydney

Published by the Press Syndicate of the University of Cambridge
The Pitt Building, Trumpington Street, Cambridge CB2 IRP
40 West 20th Street, New York, NY 10011, USA
10 Stamford Road, Oakleigh, Melbourne 3166, Australia

First published 1991

Printed in the United States of America

Library of Congress Cataloging-in-Publication Data
McClelland, Charles E.
The German experience of professionalization:modern learned
professions and their organizations from the early nineteenth century to the
Hitler era / Charles E. McClelland.
p.   cm.
Includes bibliographical references.
ISBN 0–521–39457–0
1. Professions – Germany – History.   I. Title.
HD8038.G3M36 1991
331.7′12′0943 – dc20   90–21277
                                                        CIP

British Library Cataloguing in Publication Data
McClelland, Charles E.
The German experience of professionalization:modern learned
professions and their organizations from the early nineteenth century
to the Hitler era.
1. Western world.   Professions.   Role.   Social aspects
I. Title
305.553

ISBN 0–521–39457–0 hardback

Contents

v

Acknowledgments

It is a pleasure to acknowledge the help and encouragement of so many individuals and organizations without whom this work could not have been undertaken. An Alexander von Humboldt Fellowship enabled me to spend 1982 in Munich doing basic research for this volume, and the Institute for Advanced Study in Princeton provided another year of time and support for writing in 1987–8. The Research Allocations Committee of the University of New Mexico also provided support for additional travel and research.

The Bayrische Staatsbibliothek in Munich deserves a special word of thanks for tireless assistance, as do Thomas Nipperdey and his colleagues in the Institut für Neuere Geschichte at the University of Munich for their encouragement and conversations. The late Werner Conze, Jürgen Kocka, and their colleagues offered me a valuable forum for discussion of early hypotheses in the Arbeitskreis für Moderne Sozialgeschichte, as did Peter Lungreen and Hans-Ulrich Wehler in Bielefeld, Hartmut Kaelble in Berlin, Detlef K. Müller in Bochum, Wolfgang Mommsen in London, and Heinz-Elmar Tenorth in Frankfurt, as well as their colleagues. I am indebted for stimulus and criticism to the participants in several international conferences and workshops, including ones arranged at the University of Missouri by Konrad Jarausch and by Rolf Torstendahl at the Swedish Institute for Advanced Study (SCASSS) in Uppsala.

I would like especially to thank the many colleagues who read all or part of the manuscript and made many helpful suggestions, including Penelope Corfield, Christiana Eisenberg, Felix Gilbert, Harold James, Jeffrey Johnson, Henning Köhler, Daniel Moran, Peter Paret, and Moshe Zimmermann.

This book is dedicated to the memory of Felix Gilbert.

Abbreviations

ABA   American Bar Association
AMA   American Medical Association
ADB   Allgemeiner Deutscher Beamtenbund (General German Civil Servants League)
ADLV   Allgemeiner Deutscher Lehrerverein (General German Teachers Association)
ADLnV   Allgemeiner Deutscher Lehrerinnenverein (General German Female Teachers Association)
ADRV   Allgemeiner Deutscher Realschulmännerverein (General German Realistic Schoolmen's Association)
AVB   Akademischer Volkswirtebund (Academic Economists League)
BDA   Bund Deutscher Architekten (Federation of German Architects)
BDF   Bund der Festbesoldeten (League of Regular Employees)
BUTAB   Bund der Technischen Angestellen und Beamte (see BUTIB)
BUTIB   Bund der Technisch-industriellen Beamten (League of Technical and Industrial Officials)
BUDACI   Bund der Angestellten Chemiker und Ingenieure (League of Employed Chemists and Engineers)
CVDI   Centralverband Deutscher Industrieller (Central Association of German Industrialists)
DAF   Deutsche Arbeitsfront (German Labor Front)
DApV   Deutscher Apothekerverein (German Apothecaries Association)
DAT   Deutscher Anwalttag (Congress of German Attorneys)
DATSCH   Deutscher Ausschuss für Technisches Schulwesen (German Committee for Technical Schools)
DAV   Deutscher Anwaltsverein (Association of German Attorneys)
DAeV   Deutscher Aerztevereinsverband (German Medical Association)
DBB   Deutscher Beamtenbund (German Civil Servants League)
DCG   Deutsche Chemische Gesellschaft (German Chemical Society)

DEBV	Deutscher Eisenbahnbeamtenverein (German Railway Officials Association)
DHLT	Deutscher Hochschullehrertag (German University Teachers Congress)
DJnV	Deutscher Juristinnenverein (German Female Jurists Association)
DJT	Deutscher Juristentag (Congress of German Jurists)
DLV	Deutscher Lehrerverein (German Teachers Association)
DPV	Deutscher Philologenverband (German Philological Association)
DRB	Deutscher Richterbund (German Judges League)
DRV	Deutscher Richterverein (German Judges Association)
DVV	Deutscher Volkswirtschaftlicher Verband (German Economics Association)
KDAI	Kampfbund Deutscher Architekten und Ingenieure (Fighting League of German Architects and Engineers)
KLVDR	Katholischer Lehrerverband des Deutschen Reiches (Catholic Teachers League of the German Reich)
KVD	Kassenärztliche Vereinigung Deutschlands (Insurance Fund Physicians Association of Germany)
RDT	Reichsbund Deutscher Technik (Reich League of German Technology)
RHB	Reichsbund der Höheren Beamten (National League of Higher Officials)
RRB	Republikanischer Richterbund (Republican Judges League)
RTA	Reichsgemeinschaft der Technisch-wissenschaftlichen Arbeit (Reich Community of Technical-Scientific Work)
RVDV	Reichsverband der Deutschen Volkswirte (see DVV)
VALD	Vereinsverband Akademisch Gebildeter Lehrer Deutschlands (see DPV)
VAeWI	Verband der Aerzte Deutschlands zur Wahrung ihrer Wirtschaftlichen Interessen (Association of German Physicians for the Protection of their Economic Interests, or "Hartmann League")
VBDZAe	Vereinsbund Deutscher Zahnärzte (German Dental Association)
VCLn	Verein Christlicher Lehrerinnen (Association of Christian Female Teachers)
VDAIV	Verband Deutscher Architekten- und Ingenieurvereine (League of German Architect and Engineer Associations)
VDBV	Verband Deutscher Beamtenvereine (Association of German Officials Associations)
VDC	Verein Deutscher Chemiker (German Chemists Association)
VDDI	Verband Deutscher Diplomingenieure (German Diploma–Engineers Association)

VDEh	Verein Deutscher Eisenhütteleute (Association of German Iron-founders)
VDELV	Verband Deutscher Evangelischer Lehrer- und Lehrerinnenvereine (League of Protestant Teachers' Associations)
VDEP	Verband Deutscher Evangelischer Pfarrervereine (Association of German Evangelical Pastors)
VDET	Verein Deutscher Elektrotechniker (Association of German Electrotechnicians)
VDI	Verein Deutscher Ingenieure (Association of German Engineers)
VDMI	Verein Deutscher Maschineningenieure (Association of German Machine Engineers)
VDNA	Versammlung Deutscher Naturforscher und Aerzte (Congress of German Scientists and Physicians)
VDPSM	Versammlung Deutscher Philologen und Schulmänner (Congress of German Philologists and Schoolmen)
VDR	Verein Deutscher Realschulmänner (Association of Realistic Schoolmen)
VDT	Verein Deutscher Tierärzte (German Veterinary Association)
VDTe	Verein Deutscher Techniker (League of German Technicians)
VFD	Verband der Friedhofsbeamte Deutschlands (Association of Cemetery Officials of Germany)
VFS	Verein für Sozialpolitik (Social Policy Association)
VKDLn	Verein Katholischer Deutscher Lehrerinnen (Association of Catholic German Female Teachers)
VMRTB	Verband Mittlerer Reichspost- und Telegraphenbeamten (Association of Middle-level Postal and Telegraph Officials)
VWIC	Verein zur Wahrung der Interessen der Chemischen Industrie Deutschlands (Association for the Protection of the Chemical Industry of Germany)
WVDR	Wirtschaftlicher Verband Deutscher Rechtsanwälte (Economic League of German Attorneys)
ZVDZAe	Zentralverein Deutscher Zahnärzte (Central Association of German Dentists)

PART I

The problem of professions in Germany

1

Introduction

This work is an analysis of the creation and development of modern learned professions in Germany. It includes most, but not all, occupations requiring some kind of special or higher theoretical training (as opposed to the kind of training needed for manual labor, crafts, and trades). Specifically, such professions include "old" ones as physician, lawyer, and clergyman, as well as "new" ones such as engineer, teacher, and chemist. It seeks not only to show how such training came about, but also how the recipients of that training organized themselves into modern national professional groups to attempt to influence the conditions of professional life. It also seeks to gauge the successes and failures of those attempts.

The chronological boundaries of this work were chosen for two reasons. First, German learned professions were able to take on the contours of modernity only by the beginning of the nineteenth century. Like most other occupations, the traditional professions were not free. The weakening and widespread elimination of guild privileges by the first half of the nineteenth century had their counterpart in the opening of more scope for professional autonomy at the same time, but throughout most of the preceding centuries professions had been regulated from without. The conditions allowing for the creation of specifically *modern* learned professions will be explored in Chapter 2.

Second, the opportunity of professionals themselves to associate, organize, and attempt to shape the conditions of their occupations was severely restricted, if not made impossible, by the conservative German governments prior to the mid-nineteenth century and by the National Socialist regime beginning in 1933. Much as I would have liked to pursue the roots of modern professions backward in time and to write extensively about learned professions in the much-altered conditions since 1945, such an undertaking would have flown in the face of the realities of contemporary scholarly publishing and would require two additional volumes. The inhibition of professional autonomy in both the era of Metternich and that of Hitler also appear to set natural limits of roughly one century to the central experiment of professional development.

3

This work grows out of some specific interests of the author and is necessarily influenced by certain patterns of my experience and thinking, as well as scholarly debates about the meaning and importance of professions. It can only be fair to the reader to make these open and clear at the outset.

Born in the United States at the beginning of World War II, I grew up in a world dominated by the struggle against Nazi Germany. My interest in Germany was rooted from a very early age in the seeming contradiction between the great cultural achievements of the German *Volk* and the misery, even barbarism of other aspects of its history, usually those involving a misuse of power. Later, as a student of German history, the contradiction between the German "creation" of modern historical scholarship, based on textual authenticity and alleged value-free interpretation, and the wildly varying interpretation of another country's history by scholars increasingly obsessed with the power of the German state, led me to write *The German Historians and England*.

My mentor, Hajo Holborn, who gave so much fine impetus to a skeptical but sympathetic approach to German history in this country, pointed out that the discrepancies in German intellectual history should be sought, inter alia, in the structure of the educational system. I examined the contradictions of *Macht* and *Geist* in *State, Society and University in Germany, 1700–1914.* To my surprise, the contradiction was not as strong as has traditionally been supposed in the English-speaking world. Power and intellect sought not to destroy each other, but to reach a symbiosis.

Obviously the tendency for state and university to cooperate more often than they were adversaries did not square with the more romantic notion of universities championing pure spirit against the neanderthalic baseness of rigid bureaucracy, although there were some spectacular examples of the latter in the nineteenth century. Despite all the idealistic rhetoric (fostered, self-interestedly, by universities themselves) about the noble and selfless dedication to the unfettered life of the mind, universities continued to have, in an increasingly central way, the role of training Germany's civil and ecclesiastical servants, as had been the case at least since the Reformation. Particularly as the civil service came to be more and more professionalized, the links between university and state were, in the sense of personnel, an interactive continuum rather than a mere bond of hatred or suspicion.

The implication for this author, after studying the German higher educational system in its broader relationship with society and state, was to examine the products of that system, its "graduates." One of the many German myths about *alte Burschenherrlichkeit* (golden college days) reproduced endlessly in memoirs and even scholarly histories of universities was that students were at university for the spiritual experience, not for the grinding training that would make them into competent professionals. The ideal of Wilhelm von Humboldt in creating the "new model" University of Berlin as a place for quiet reflection, an institutional setting for a pristine "solitude and freedom," was little more than an aristocratic dream quickly dispelled by the cold day of reality. Berlin and all the other universities became not so much hotbeds of intellectual freedom, but seedbeds of disciplined professional behavior.

How could they not have? The state ran and funded the educational system, and it wanted competent, well-trained clergymen, teachers, physicians, and lawyers. The more successful German states learned from their western neighbor, France, and to a much smaller degree from England, that melding the energies and desires of the best of the *moyenne classe* and the service aristocracy with the welfare of the state produced good results − "the public welfare" − as well as higher tax revenues, greater prosperity, and public trust. The lesson learned by the German reformers of the Napoleonic era was that for subjects to become involved citizens, they needed autonomy in addition to discipline, self-actuating knowledge rather than rote learning, and rights as well as duties. A better-educated and more flexible, initiative-taking bureaucracy with admission and rewards based more on competence than birth had to initiate this revolution.

Authority based on intellectual achievement and individual responsibility − incidentally two attributes of modern professions − amounted to a dangerous proposition, as both Napoleon and his conqueror, Wellington, saw clearly by 1815. As will be clear in Chapter 3, Count Metternich agreed with them. "Ideologues," intellectuals, or the educated classes of society may have been perceived as a threat to the power classes, but they were also indispensable. The survival of the modern bureaucratic state depended on the mediation of its servants, bureaucratic, educational, military (and even medical, after the passage of some decades). And just as unfree agricultural labor and guild restrictions were increasingly abolished as a brake to the growth and prosperity of the economy, so strict bureaucratic regulation of many professions yielded to greater self-government.

The relative neglect of these "graduates" by critical historians until fairly recently has begun to yield to a variety of approaches to this special and important layer of German society. Excellent studies have appeared or will shortly appear about educated elites, as a part of "middle class" research. Others have examined individual professions at different times. "Mentality" studies, inspired by Paris, are also increasingly available. Social mobility studies exist at least for Germany. All this excellent research puts in question not only naive notions of what "graduates" did and were, but most received scholarly opinion.

What has not been much done is a critical examination of the "graduates" in terms of their later work-lives and their adherence to disciplinary communities that also took on the organizational forms of modern professional groups, eventually attempting to articulate the standards of the various "learned" professions and to advance their own interests. Histories of various professions emanating from within their own ranks exist in some profusion, but they are rarely critical. Furthermore, they are not systemic in approach and do not examine the whole range of professions in given epochs.

What I believe is needed, and what this work attempts to provide, is a system-wide analysis of the modern professionalization process itself, addressing the advance of standards deemed desirable by organizations of practicing professionals themselves, but incorporating the widest practical array of such organizations in order to seek common patterns of behavior. This novel approach not only facilitates a comparative analysis of the various professional disciplines in Germany but international comparisons as well. The focus here is not on medicine or engineering as such – for disciplinary history is only partly professionalization history – but on medicine and engineering insofar as they organized practitioners and tried to shape the parameters of professional life.

But why study professions at all? As Chapter 2 of this work will address in more detail, many twentieth-century students of modern societies have identified professions as a key concept in unlocking the structure and functioning of those societies. Other social theorists have all but ignored them or subsumed them under broader categories (e.g. "class" with Marx, *Herrschaft* with Weber). Even social theorists who have not bothered much with professions per se have perceived revolutionary implications in the "managerial" or "expert-dominated" essence of decision-making in contemporary societies. How are these experts chosen and trained? How, in social systems as diverse as the United States and the Soviet Union, can one plausibly argue that "convergence" depends on the rule of experts or "professionals"? Both the right-wing market philosophy of Milton Friedman and the "vanguard-of-the-working-class" justification of Communist Party rule deny the higher authority of professionals, but they seem to influence the parameters of decisions, whether by market or party, nevertheless.

All of this argument presupposes, of course, that there is some reality behind the concept of professions, and that it is not an "urban myth" or a complete fabrication of the information/entertainment industry of the late twentieth century. As we shall see in the next chapter, however, even those historians and social scientists who tend to deny the central importance of professionalism, let alone professional claims to monopoly, authority, special status, or social utility, do not deny the reality of professions, at least not in the English-speaking world. Assuming that reality, one further purpose of this work is to clarify the extremely vague connotations current in the English language about "profession," "professional," and "professionalization." Comparison is still one of the best ways to clarify concepts; in the case of this work, comparison between English usage and the empirical reality of another culture.

Traditional nineteenth-century liberal beliefs in Anglo-American political culture, still current under different political labels today, hold that the private sphere of life should be left unmolested by the state as much as possible. Liberals on the continent of Europe often had a more accepting view of state intervention as such, seeking rather to shape and control that intervention by a process of advice and consent of those involved. This belief may indeed be only that, flying in the face of evidence to the contrary, as Magali Sarfatti Larson argued in her brilliant and controversial work, *The Rise of Professionalism*. If professional organizations in the English-speaking world actually used the power of the state to reinforce their monopoly of services and control their market, older assumptions about the "freedom" of the liberal professions from government "intervention" in the English-speaking world must be rethought.

And in that case, too, so must the history of professions on the European mainland. They may instead be viewed as just as interactive with state power as their sister professions in England and America. Such a view calls into question the widespread (if rarely examined) assumption of Anglo-American social theory that professions were fundamentally different on the European continent.

The study of German professions is important for other reasons as well. Other historians in the English-speaking world, notably in England, have since underlined the notion that there was no German "special path," or *Sonderweg*. Power and cultural elites cohabited quite well in England, and as some American social scientists and historians have also been arguing, in that country as well.

One disturbing implication of such arguments is that Hitler is a perfectly understandable link in the continuity of German history. The state and the educated elite, also the middle class, always seek and usually find accommodation, even if it is in distortions of the "historical processes" described by Hegel and Marx. As the reader will find, I am skeptical of this "continuity" argument as it applies to the National Socialist regime. Otherwise, I see a great deal of continuity between educated elites and government. International debate about a "special path" stands and falls on the place of the Nazi regime and its crimes, including those carried out by "professionals."

Many excellent works on the crimes of professionals under National Socialism have appeared since World War II. To mention only two widely read studies in the field of medicine, those of Alexander Mitscherlich and Robert Jay Lifton, appearing, respectively, shortly after the end of World War II and nearly forty years later. Both authors are scrupulous in documenting the decay of professional ethics under Nazi rule.[1]

But can such evidence of decay be transposed to all members of the profession, and not just the small number who participated in inhumane experiments? Many scholars have gone so far as to identify the "failure" of German professionals to "stop" Hitler, if not a professional culture saturated with National Socialist ideology, as contributing elements to the nightmare of 1933–45. The assumption is often *pars pro toto*. A great deal more empirical research

1 Alexander Mitscherlich, *Doctors of Infamy: The Story of the Nazi Medical Crimes* (New York, 1949) and Robert Jay Lifton, *The Nazi Doctors: Medical Killing and the Psychology of Genocide* (New York, 1986).

will be needed to back up such assumptions, for thus far (and this work will argue mostly in this direction) what is known appears ambiguous.

Although I hope the meaning of such terms as "profession" will gain in contour through this work, the reader should be assured that this work does not proceed along semantic lines or employ the techniques of "deconstructionism." The techniques of Gadamer, Derrida, their predecessors, and their followers undoubtedly have their place in expanding the interpretation of "texts." But my purpose is to synthesize an interpretation of the rise of modern professions in Germany, not to call into question their meaning. I have usually assumed actors meant and understood what they wrote, said, read, and heard. This does not mean accepting the objective veracity of all such statements or discounting self-interest behind them. But in a work of reconstruction, one must begin with the assumption that such statements have clear meaning.

I hope it is also evident from the body of the work that I am not a follower of either classic functionalists or critical interpreters of professions in general (more will be said about those antipodes in Chapter 2). Historians need neither glorify nor belittle professions, or rather their driving collective motivations, to analyze and understand them. I have drawn on arguments used by both sides in the debates about professionalization over the last few decades.

This consultation of primarily Anglo-American theoretical work on professionalization was all the more necessary because there is no extensive corpus of theoretical literature on professions by German scholars. As Chapter 2 suggests, this corpus reveals sharp disagreements about the nature of professions even in England and America, let alone continental Europe. Nevertheless, this corpus of scholarly literature must necessarily remain a point of reference in examining continental professionalization. Even if there were a unified Procrustean bed of the sociology of professions, it would be methodologically misguided to try to force continental experience into it. The important differences of the continental experience, can, however, be illuminated better by keeping the parameters of Anglo-American theory in mind.

Aside from their importance as a subform of the organization of labor or, in the German case, of that influential stratum of the middle class that derived its legitimacy largely from education – the *Bildungsbürgertum*, why should professions interest historians at all? By its barest definition, a profession is just another occupation, and it often becomes confused with others, as in "professional hairdresser." But if the term is to have any clear meaning, it must apply to those occupations that require a high degree of usually theoretical training as a precondition and a high degree of responsibility as a practitioner. Guilds, before their decline in the eighteenth century, may have served this purpose often, but their eclipse before the free labor market in the nineteenth century served to accentuate the differences between skilled laborers and professional men.

A "profession" is more than a special kind of occupation, however: the term also applies to the entirety of a discipline (e.g. medicine) or more narrowly to the organizations that represent significant portions of its practitioners (e.g. a medical association). Thus, studying professions, singly or collectively, can shed much light on the development of disciplines in practice (as opposed to the theoretical side evident in research and teaching within the discipline). Professional organizations also serve the useful function of articulating the self-image and wishes of the members of the profession and thereby of the primarily middle-class aspirations of its members.

How learned occupations became professions, one of the main themes of this work, might be broadly termed "professionalization." It was not always a "project" carried out by the "external" dictates of disciplinary necessity (e.g. advances in medical knowledge) or at the behest of government bureaucracies (as the tenor of current German professionalization theory holds), nor always a Whig-history tale of triumph by disinterested, well-organized professional groups against ignorance and superstition (as the tenor of much older Anglo-American literature, especially that of the professions themselves, has held). There seems nothing inevitable about professionalization, about this process of discipline communities becoming better organized, more self-regulating, more exclusive or difficult of entry. The German case helps us see how dialectical the process was, with decades of "progress" being washed out in a few short years. But the very process itself, seen from the angle of professional people and the organizations they helped build (or in some cases opposed), can shed new light on German domestic history as well.

The chief foci of this work are the great national professional organizations that began to form in the 1840s and were mostly expunged or co-opted by the Nazis during the 1930s. Their interactions with public bodies (governments, bureaucracies, universities) and even private groups (e.g. industry) formed the core of research. The focus on national organizations was dictated in part by logic, since their views and officers tended to be more representative of the professions as a whole than regional or local associations (a few of which were even older than national bodies). But the records of regional and local bodies proved in almost all cases to be ill-preserved or not very helpful in shedding light on major issues of professionalization in the time period under consideration here. Not that the records of the national organizations were always complete or helpful, quite the contrary. But national professional journals and publications managed to preserve much important information that was destroyed in its archival form.

Within the major learned professions, some seemed more appropriate for inclusion in this study than others. The choice was often made by the professions themselves: some, such as the clergy and military officers, created national professional organizations very late, or these were rather quiescent, or both. Some, like journalists, were never really able to agree on what criteria defined their occupation or that higher theoretical training was necessary to it. Much the same could be said of many very skilled occupations, such as the arts or publishing, in which often unstandardizable attributes such as talent or imagination complicated the search for professional identity and homogeneity, in which external certification had given way to market forces for validation of success, and where the self-taught often proved to be the great innovators.

It is precisely in such areas that the application of categories such as profession and professionalization can be helpful and shed new light on German social history. Artists, journalists, and officers all belonged, in German parlance, to a Stand (estate), as did doctors and lawyers; but they did not all belong to learned professions in the way doctors and lawyers did. Insofar as they found it difficult or impossible to organize their Stand to press for more uniform standards of admission (usually through higher educational qualifications and certification procedures), they might be said to have been "nonprofessionalizing" or "late professionalizing" occupations. Some were unquestionably already professions (e.g. the clergy) or part of a profession (e.g. the upper civil service as a part of the legal profession), but since they organized late or feebly, they might be called even "late professionalizing (old) professions." The process of organizing, agitating, demanding altered access to the occupation, higher economic rewards and security, and other "lobbying" features are precisely the hallmarks of the professionalization process in the modern world; but not all professions or would-be professions made use of these features in equal measure. This work concentrates especially on those that did.

If it is fair to say that the difference between Germany today and the same territory two centuries ago is that a *Leistungsgesellschaft* (achieving society) has replaced a *Ständegesellschaft* (society of estates), then the principles espoused by modern German professions must reflect more than those of other groups in this transition. Yet German academic professions and their organizations have never been seriously studied as a group. The "graduates" of the German higher educational system confronted the adult world at least as much *qua* graduates of law, philosophy, medicine, theology, and later other technical faculties as *qua Bildungsbürger,* and thus their behavior in discipline-oriented, modern professional organizations must be of interest to historians.

More universal reasons for studying professions, including the increasing centrality of expertise in the management of the modern world (or put negatively, the "tyranny of experts"), will be discussed in the following chapter. Yet the German experience of professionalization, with its complicated tangle of private sphere and bureaucratically controlled dimensions, may prove more typical of professionalization throughout the twentieth-century world than the Anglo-American "model" from which much of the social-science theory of professions has been derived. Let us now turn to that body of theory.

2

⌀⌀⌀⌀⌀⌀⌀⌀⌀⌀⌀⌀⌀⌀⌀⌀⌀⌀⌀⌀

Problems and methods in the history of modern German professions

Social scientists and social historians have been aware of the importance of professions for some time, at least in the English-speaking world. Some of the earliest serious studies date back to the period between the world wars. Not coincidentally, academic interest in the professions followed closely on the heels of the rise to prominence and influence of such professional bodies as the American and British Medical Associations and a parallel emergence of "professionalization" of more and more occupations.

For reasons intrinsic to both modern society and sociology, furthermore, professions have come to be more and more prominent objects of social-scientific study. As one observer recently put it:

How expert knowledge is deployed in different institutional forms, how it is controlled, how it is used as a resource of power and a basis of privilege, and how in turn different institutional forms of deployment, social control as well as collective and individual advantage, are affected by other and wider social structures and processes – inquiries into these questions tell us much about the structure and the dynamics of society as a whole. That, furthermore, the subject is closely related to a – perhaps the – central theme of classical sociology, the emergence of modern society and culture, becomes clear once we identify increased rationality in the pursuit of pragmatic goals as one of the major characteristics of that process.[1]

Although Max Weber had little directly to say about professionalization or the *Berufsstände* organizing in Germany during his lifetime, he did point to the rationalization of life and the demystification of the world as signs of modernization. Following that lead, Talcott Parsons has been even more insistent on the importance of professions:

It is my view that the professional complex, though obviously still incomplete in its development, has already become the most important single component in the structure of modern societies. It has displaced first the "state," in the relatively early modern sense

---

1 Dietrich Rüschemeyer, "Professional Autonomy and the Social Control of Expertise," in Robert Dingwall and Philip Lewis, eds., *The Sociology of the Professions* (New York, 1983), p. 38.

11

of that term, and, more recently, the "capitalistic" organization of the economy. The massive emergence of the professional complex, not the special status of capitalistic or socialistic modes of organization, is the crucial structural development in twentieth-century society.[2]

Although few today share such a high-flying view of professions, Parsons' "functionalist" approach long dominated Anglo-American sociology of professions. Recently it has come under increasing fire from diverse quarters, most significantly for its assumptions that the privileges accorded to the learned professions are justified by their unique base in knowledge or science, their autonomous self-reliance, their altruism, their expertise, or some other "objective" and disinterested measurement. Against the functionalist or "structure-oriented" sociology of professions there is now a solid body of "power-oriented" analyses that also happen to be closer to critical historical methods than the functionalists.[3]

Declaring the sociology of professions to be in "turmoil" or even a "shambles," these power-oriented analysts look more to strategies developed by professional groups to dominate or monopolize the market in the services they offer, to employ the power of the state in achieving such goals, and to strive for self-interested improvements in income and status, exclusivity, and independence from legitimate societal control.[4]

Much of the interest in and literature about professions among social scientists has remained confined largely to the English-speaking world, a problem to be addressed more fully below. Interest in professions in Europe and elsewhere is, however, a much more recent phenomenon. Possibly because of the persistence of older conceptions of the proper object of historical study (e.g. diplomatic and political events) or, in the case of Marxist analyses, a tendency to study the "productive" forces rather than service elites, interest in the history of professions and professional people has emerged only fairly recently.

Such an interest goes beyond mere historical curiosity. As historians and social scientists come to terms with such secular trends as the demographic shift from agricultural and industrial to service predominance in advanced societies, they naturally will scrutinize more carefully the "experts" and elites in that sector of the economy, just as they previously studied manufacturers and laborers.

A number of questions must be raised concerning the professions and the ongoing process of professionalization. How were professions defined or re-

2 Talcott Parsons, "Professions," in D. Sills, ed., *International Encyclopedia of the Social Sciences* (New York, 1968), vol. 12, p. 545.
3 John Cullen, *Structure of Professionalism* (New York, 1978), p. 58.
4 For critiques of the recent state of the field, see Rüschemeyer, "Professional Autonomy," pp. 38–58; Eliot Freidson, "Are Professions Necessary?", in Thomas L. Haskell, ed., *The Authority of Experts* (Bloomington, Ind., 1984), pp. 4–27, esp. p. 5; in the same volume, Magali Sarfatti Larson, "The Production of Expertise and the Constitution of Expert Power," pp. 28–80, as well as her *The Rise of Professionalism. A Sociological Analysis* (Berkeley, 1977).

cognized and set apart from other occupations? How did their members acquire the special knowledge needed, and how was their adequacy certified? By what process were old occupations turned into professions, or new ones established as such? Through what mechanisms did the professionals enforce control and discipline on practitioners of their particular skills? To what degree were they subject to control by outside social, political, and economic forces? What methods were employed to impose what M. S. Larson calls the "professionalization project"[5] on an often unwilling society (and even reluctant practitioners)? How were the professions organized, and how did their organizations behave?

Functionalist sociology of professions has often answered such questions as these using ideal types and contemporary empirical data, rather than with historical information. Partly as a result of this ahistorical orientation in the social sciences, historians find insufficient analytical tools there that work satisfactorily in the context of European historical developments. If it is true that most sociologists today regard the problems raised (and disagreed upon) by Parsons and Hughes as the beginning of a real sociology of professions,[6] it is nonetheless important to note the very American environment of these perceived problems. This theoretical deficit is something with which all historians using social science models must struggle. This introductory chapter will point out some of the theoretical problems of applying an inadequate and limited corpus of social science theory to continental historical processes, especially as exemplified by Central Europe. Better empirical studies of actual development of professions there, in turn, may stimulate modifications in the theory of professions. That is one of the goals of this work.

One natural reaction to the weaknesses of Anglo-American theories about professions among more recent social scientists in Central Europe has been to move to an opposite explanatory extreme: if the Anglo-American assumption of professional autonomy cannot be made to fit continental reality, then the opposite assumption might be worth exploring. Hence, the concept *Berufskonstruktion,* as first used by H. E. Hesse,[7] implying the "professionalization project" but with the image of the professions "constructed" from the outside, for example to serve the interests of social or economic forces extrinsic to and more powerful than the practitioners. This idea has some merits in explaining certain phases of German professionalization, but not all; and it underestimates the degree of self-actualization present in the empirical history of many individual professions. It is a suggestive analytical concept produced by the study of only certain professions (e.g. chemistry) at certain times.

5 Larson, *Rise of Professionalism,* p. 50., views professionalization as a "collective project which aims at market control," the core of which is "the production of professional . . . practitioners."
6 Dingwall and Lewis, *Sociology of the Professions,* p. 1.
7 See Hans Albrecht Hesse, *Beruf im Wandel. Ein Beitrag zum Problem der Professionalisierung* (Stuttgart, 1968).

One of the most neglected tasks of both social scientists and historians up to now has been the comparative study of professions. Here a usually parochial concern with purely local or, at best, national professional systems over the past half-century has led to some fundamental problems of defining what constitutes a profession, with historians and sociologists from different countries even going so far as to dispute whether professional systems other than their native land's really deserve the name at all. As Elliot Freidson has recently argued, professionalism is an "Anglo-American disease," just as the concept of profession "is intrinsically bound up with a particular period of history and with only a limited number of nations. . . . "[8] These nations implicitly do not include those of continental Europe, according to Freidson, because there "primary identity was not given by occupation, but by the status gained by elite education no matter what the particular specialty."[9] Thus, even a sociologist severely critical of traditional Anglo-American theory of professions nevertheless tends to deny significance to European professions. Freidson also makes a distinction without a difference, because most professions depend to a large degree on elite education.

One of the major residues of older social science debate about professions is a catalogue of characteristics that distinguish the professions from other occupations. Typically these lists include at least the following: (1) highly specialized and advanced education, (2) a special code of conduct ("ethics"), (3) altruism/public service, (4) rigorous competency tests, examinations, licensing, (5) high social prestige, (6) high economic rewards, (7) occupational career pattern or ladder, (8) monopolization of market in services, and (9) autonomy. Naturally many of these characteristics, taken singly, may also be typical of other occupations, but taken together they may be said to serve as a sort of ideal type of a profession. One must also add that many of these characteristics have been individually disputed for one profession or another.

It has been the tendency of "functionalist" analyses (and, for obvious reasons, of self-evaluations emanating from professional groups themselves) to regard these characteristics as inherent in or as the legitimate goal of professionalization. But even critics of the functionalist view (as well as segments of the public skeptical of the self-evaluations of professional groups) tend to discuss the same catalogue of characteristics. The important difference is that critics turn them upside down or question their reality, legitimacy, or desirability as attributes of professional practice. This skeptical attitude is certainly fruitful for understanding the historical development of professions. But to throw out the "characteristics" embedded in these ideal types as mere camouflage and propaganda would be equally self-defeating, because much of the debate about professions historically has been couched in these or similar terms. Indeed, each term can have positive as well as negative values. The notion of altruism and public

8 Eliot Freidson, "The Theory of Professions: State of the Art," in Dingwall and Lewis, *Sociology of the Professions*, p. 26.
9 Ibid., p. 24.

service, for example, can and does exist in the professions (although it clearly is not the chief motivation for professional practice), yet it can and does bring with it its "shadows," patronization and arrogance.

These characteristics can thus be used as a framework of discussion without their becoming a straitjacket on historical analysis and without involving those who use them in largely sterile definitional debates. Expanding empirical historical investigation beyond the temporal and spatial boundaries of those debates should indicate the reasons for their sterility and of "essentialistic" definitions of professions and professionalization.

Let us confine ourselves for the present to a further scrutiny of those characteristics which, in toto or in clusters, appear to have been at least arguably appropriate to describing professions.

That highly specialized training is a component of professions is hardly disputed, even though it is not unique to them. Carpenters, politicians, secretaries, auto mechanics, hairdressers and farmers all require special learned skills to do their job. The professions share this need for particular skills with most other occupations.

The chief difference lies in a host of prerequisites for obtaining these skills, in their theoretical or esoteric nature, in the institutional arrangements designed to impart them, and in the usually high cost of acquiring them (including foregone income, to mention a major difference between apprenticeship and preparation for the learned professions). In most cases it means advanced education lasting several years beyond the normal school-leaving age or, in the Anglo-American system, the first university degree. Whether this training needs intrinsically to be so complex, expensive, and therefore exclusive, as "functionalists" have usually argued, or exists mostly as a mechanism to shore up monopoly, (as "power-oriented" critics maintain), all agree it is central to professions.

Not too many decades ago, the "professions" were commonly set off from other occupations by underlining this educational qualification, so different in quality and level, by the predicate "learned." In German and French this qualifier is essential *(gelehrter* or *akademischer Beruf, profession liberale)*, because *Beruf* and *profession,* without qualifiers, simply mean occupation. (As we will see below, another meaning of the English "profession," the collectivity of practitioners, has no exact German equivalent, although *Berufsstand* was a common, if vague, alternative.) The old learned professions were usually held to be those of clergyman, doctor, and lawyer, with perhaps military officers and professors included in some countries. In the case of the English term, "liberal professions" implied that the chief qualification for entrance into them was a liberal, or a classical, education, "that is, the education of a gentleman, not of a trader or an artisan."[10]

10 W. J. Reader, *Professional Men* (New York, 1966), p. 10.

As educational qualifications mounted and new occupational roles emerged, "new" learned professions such as scientist, engineer, dentist, and architect were added. In all cases, it was the upgrading of educational qualifications to the university level that transformed an artisan's trade into a learned profession and, for example, changed the humble barber with a sideline in tooth-pulling into the modern dentist and dental surgeon. Generally speaking, this process was chronologically more advanced in France and Germany by the beginning of the nineteenth century than in Britain or the United States, particularly in the latter, where proprietary "medical schools" and self-taught lawyers were common.

The second characteristic mentioned above, a special code of conduct or "professional ethics," is also not exclusive to the learned professions. But there are good reasons why it is essential to them. Many learned professions deal in existential problems of their clientele: the health of the patient, the rights, liberty, and property of the legal client, or the salvation of the parishioner's soul have long been recognized as concerns requiring a high degree of special responsibility. The scientist who fakes experimental results or the civil engineer who designs structures that collapse requires more than the usual market forces to prevent his doing further harm. Beyond careful education and competency testing, lifelong peer-review processes by qualified experts are necessary to see that he conforms to the ethics and standards of the profession.[11]

Close empirical examination of the workings of professional review has been a rarity, but some studies indicate it may work imperfectly at best.[12] Still, the major function of professional ethics is to guide the practitioner rather than to serve as a legal code that is actively policed. Insofar as policing is required, a central question is who does the policing? Self-regulation of abuses within professions has often constituted one of their demands, even if in practice such "watchdogs" may be more attentive to unethical competitive practices than malpractice.

Some sociologists of professions, notably in the Anglo-American world, have stressed the altruistic nature of learned professionals. This may be nothing more than a misplaced subcategory of professional ethics. It shows itself most clearly in the traditional sense of extraordinary obligation of the physician abandoning normal working routine to help a patient, of the doctor or lawyer aiding clients who cannot pay for their services, or the professor who lectures to community groups without fee. Although all professionals depend on remuneration, it is sometimes argued that they have a higher "calling," that they are not engaged in a trade for profit only. Martin Luther and other Protestants certainly underlined this aspect of *Beruf* as a service to God and, indirectly, to mankind. The language of professions reflects this: a "public service" is offered rather than a "product"; many receive "fees," others "salaries" (often augmented by fees), but

11 Deborah A. Stone, *The Limits of Professional Power* (Chicago, 1980), pp. 12–15; Charles L. Bosk, *Forgive and Remember. Managing Medical Failure* (Chicago, 1979).
12 Bosk, *Forgive and Remember*, p. 178.

nobody receives "wages." Lawyers, for example, "counsel" their clients or "give" (not "sell") legal advice.

Yet, one suspects the centrality or even essentiality of this characteristic of professions. Traditional semantic distinctions aside, large parts of the working population are engaged in public service without being regarded as professionals. The opportunities for individual altruism, even among professional people, are increasingly limited by organizational and even legal constraints, yet nobody will suggest that professionalism has disappeared or shrunk along with altruism.

Tests of competency, such as examinations, and licensing of successful examinees constitute a fourth characteristic mentioned in most of the literature on professions. These are of course shared with many other occupations. As with education, however, professional examination and licensing procedures theoretically involve very high demands on the practitioner. Probably more than with other occupations, they can be used to manipulate the contours of the profession in many ways. Not only the quality but the quantity of practitioners can be controlled by changing examination and licensing standards. This phenomenon has apparently been more common in regard to the professions than with most other occupations. The reasons for this are understandably complex. Restricting competition (and thereby income loss), fears of a flood of unemployed and potentially discontented professionals, changing the social-recruitment pools of a profession, as well as a desire to improve professional performance have acted as motives in modern times.

Who creates and administers examinations and who licenses practitioners? Should this be left up to the profession itself, on the grounds that its members alone have the expertise necessary to judge competence? Should it be left to a state agency, on the grounds that professional competence is of public concern? The Anglo-American practice has tended to favor the former solution; the continental one, the latter. But elements of both have been mixed to one degree or another in much of the practice.

The professions in modern times have been associated with high social prestige. In many cases, this prestige may derive from the associations between professionals and their high-status clientele, in addition to respect for learning and expertise. The proximity of lawyers to the court, of prescientific medicine to wealthy and influential clients, or university professors to small elites are examples of reflected social prestige. Such has not everywhere been the case with other professions, however. Many clergymen and elementary teachers have not shared in the professional esteem of other callings. In some cases, as with medicine in the Soviet Union, even traditional high-status professions have not always been held in high regard. New professions, such as engineering and chemistry, have normally faced a struggle for social recognition and status.

Another widely assumed characteristic of modern professionals is their favorable economic position. Clearly there have been many prosperous physicians, attorneys, architects, and others, but this characteristic is by no means universal enough to warrant more than a relative value. Indeed, some professions at some times (for example teaching and the priesthood) have been more noted for their relative poverty. Certainly membership in a profession, practice by itself, does not at most times appear to have guaranteed high economic rewards. A great span of incomes appears to be as characteristic of members of the professions as of other, mostly bourgeois, occupations.

The existence of a career "ladder" is supposed by some theorists to be a further characteristic of professions, at least of modern ones. In general terms such a ladder presupposes ascending levels of training, testing, experience, and responsibility, much on the model of modern civil services. The presence and temporal extension of such "rungs" tend to preclude switches in and out of professions or the concurrent practice of two or more of them, as was common two centuries ago. The progressive differentiation and specialization of professions also played a role in creating these ladders, which have really come to resemble something more approaching a rail switchyard than a simple vertical set of steps.

Monopolization of the specific market for services is a characteristic (or perhaps an ultimate) goal attributed to professionals. Some recent authors (e.g. Freidson and Larson) have argued that the drive to such a dominant or exclusive right to offer services lies at the heart of the professionalization process. Clearly competition with "nonprofessional" practitioners (and attempts to limit or destroy their activity) has a long history. The fortunes of quacks, herbalists, midwives, hypnotists, and hosts of others may be regarded as an index to the success of the medical profession in advancing its claim to exclusive therapeutic knowledge, for example, but all professions suffer at least the threat of competition from similar unlicensed practitioners. The professions themselves, as well as both sympathetic and critical sociologists, have placed considerable weight on this feature of market strategies: without a valid claim to the exclusive ability to perform professional services (and one backed by social and political authority), the professions would cease to exist as such.[13]

A central defining point of professions, particularly modern ones, is their much-debated autonomy. Of all the characteristics of modern professions, this is the one most often cited in theories of professionalization. Autonomy, it is mostly simply stated, is essential to the existence of a profession. By the same token, a lack or diminution of autonomy reduces the vital preconditions for the existence of professions to the vanishing point. Without autonomy, professional work is indistinguishable from skilled wage labor. The most common form of

13 For a dispassionate critique of Larson's method and approach, see Cornelis W. R. Gispen, "German Engineers and American Social Theory: Historical Perspectives on Professionalization," *Comparative Studies in Society and History* 30 (1988): 553–6. Freidson, "Are Professions Necessary?" demolishes the arguments of the Milton Friedman school concerning "unregulated" professions.

diminution, in the view of many sociologists, consists of bureaucratization, or external control of the professions' vital functions. Thus, according to the view widespread at least in the English-speaking world, such phenomena as state control or regimentation by the bureaucracy are inconsistent with professional activities. Although some Anglo-American sociologists have perceived no conflict between autonomy and bureaucratization,[14] this is far from the norm.

The difficulty with this line of argument lies in its tendency to exclude the professional systems of much of modern continental Europe, not to mention the rest of the world, from the history of professions and professionalization. Another difficulty with this argument is that it makes little allowance for the ongoing recent process of bureaucratization of the professions so apparent in all societies. If one carries this argument to its extreme conclusion, one might conclude (as many conservative professionals themselves contend) that by definition the professions are disappearing. As important as autonomy is, however, it need not be irreconcilable with certain kinds of societal control.

To avoid confusion, it is useful to break down the concept of professional autonomy into two types or "faces." The first may be called autonomy toward the client, in which professional expertise and judgment logically must be given a considerable latitude. The second consists of autonomy in face of other reference groups, such as the state, churches, pressure groups, insurance companies, and so on. It is the second kind of autonomy that is really at issue here.

The second kind of autonomy has its natural limits. Furthermore, as professional groups have organized themselves into associations to advance what Larson calls "the professionalizing project," the autonomy of the individual members is necessarily reduced in the name of collective professional solidarity.[15] Because such collective conformity is, however, often voluntary, historians and sociologists have not usually looked upon it as a threat to autonomy. If the professional associations are able to determine or influence the general standards of admission to and practice of the profession, they have been content to see themselves as defenders of an autonomous profession. Indeed, as one sociologist has claimed, they should be content, for a "profession" is not so much an occupation as "a means of controlling an occupation."[16]

More serious has been a running conflict between the rising professional organizations and the modern bureaucratic state since roughly the middle of the nineteenth century. As Larson and others have begun to point out, however, the historical model of the noninterfering state and the vigorously autonomous professions in England and the United States from the mid-nineteenth century onward is partly myth. "Far from being in conflict with the model of profession,

14 Everett C. Hughes, *The Sociological Eye* (Chicago, 1971), pp. 364–96; Celia Davies, "Professionals in Bureaucracies: The Conflict Thesis Revisited," in Dingwall and Lewis, *Sociology of the Professions*, p. 177.
15 Larson, *Rise of Professionalism*, p. 49.
16 T. J. Johnson, *Professions and Power* (London, 1972), p. 45.

the 'bureaucratic phenomenon' creates the structural context of successful professionalization."[17] The professional groups were quite often willing and able to use the power of the state to promote their own ends, and many have complained loudly in the twentieth century only when the state has intervened uncongenially to them. In other words, if state intervention in the affairs of the professions has been welcomed and tolerated when done with the approval of the professions and is consistent with "autonomy," then intervention against the will of the professional groups is bureaucratization, a development to be resisted.

This is too simplified, of course: much bureaucratization of the professions has come about internally or in response to other pressures than those emanating from the state. But the state has been the most resented and feared agent. And because professional organizations themselves have shaped the understanding of their own role more than anybody else, the notion of a conflict between state and professional autonomy has entered not only the public consciousness but even the scholarly literature, at least in the English-speaking world. As one sociologist put it, his colleagues have often become "the dupe of established professions (helping them justify their dominant position and its payoff) and arbiters of occupations on the make."[18]

This summary of widely accepted characteristics of modern professions can help us grasp the dilemma of the sociohistorical student of professions in Europe. Being largely derived from analysis of contemporary Anglo-American empirical reality, they are culturally biased and throw into doubt the general validity claimed for them as soon as tested against continental reality. They are also a static catalogue, not a part of a dynamic concept of the evolution of professions over time.

In fact, it would not be too exaggerated to say that the only "characteristics" mentioned above which seem consistent at most times with professions in Europe since about 1700 are educational requirements and the notion of public service. Even if one adds the adjective "modern" to include changes made in the nineteenth century, the catalogue is still of only relative and limited use. In some cases, one sees an actual decline of prestige and income correlating with increases in educational and examination requirements, or a loosening of monopolistic rights correlating with greater autonomy. Indeed, in the matter of autonomy one can see the difference between Anglo-American theory and continental reality highlighted most sharply.

Both the historical situation and the analysis of professional autonomy versus bureaucratization have been different on the continent of Europe and elsewhere. In Europe, the long-standing control over professional education and in many cases professional practice by the state preconfigured the relationship of profes-

17 Larson, *Rise of Professionalism*, p. 145.
18 Julius Roth, "Professionalism: The Sociologists' Decoy," *Sociology of Work and Occupations* 1 (1974): 17.

sions to state and society differently. Compared to the U.S. and Britain, the methodical study of professions by sociologists and historians is currently in its infancy on the continent, but it is already clear that attempts merely to import and translate Anglo-American concepts are not fully equal to describing continental realities. [19]

A recent American social science study of German medical systems, itself a major step forward in this genre, managed to sum up the difficulties in mutual understanding (while also telescoping the historical development in Germany):

> In the United States, the medical profession and other private associations have been granted political autonomy largely because their affairs are not thought to be of great political significance either to their individual members or to the state as a whole. In Germany, the medical profession has been allowed to regulate itself because the dominant ideology holds that all important social and economic functions are best performed by self-regulating corporative groups. Thus, in the United States the basic question in the relationship between physicians and government is whether there should be any government control over medical affairs at all. In Germany, the question has always been what kind of government regulation is appropriate for the medical profession. [20]

A brief preview of professional development in Germany may help to illuminate some of these generalizations. In the early nineteenth century, Germany, unlike the Anglo-American countries, did not experience vigorous growth of professional organizations, certainly not on a national level. This was not because attendance at a university was sufficient to identify one as a member of one of the old-line "status professions," as Freidson seems to believe, but rather because of hostility to such organizations by the arch-conservative German states. By the Napoleonic period at the latest the German states had all assumed control of the universities and thereby controlled what was taught in professional preparatory courses. They also created and administered state examinations in most of the professional fields.

When at last professional organizations were tolerated under Bismarck and his successors, the former initially pressed for and achieved a partial disengagement of the states from professional affairs, for example, for the free practice of law and medicine. As professional organizations proliferated and grew through the rest of the pre-World War I period, however, the initial impulse toward professional autonomy began to yield perceptibly toward greater cooperation with the reliance on the state. In many important areas this tendency centered on questions of education and certification for the professions, and in some cases on government policies, such as health insurance, that had a growing impact on the professions.

Unable to control access to the professions directly, professional groups turned to pressure tactics to influence the number and quality of practitioners.

19 Hesse, *Beruf im Wandel;* Marc Maurice, "Propos sur la sociologie des professions," *Sociologie du Travail* 13 (1972): 213–25.
20 Stone, *Limits of Professional Power,* p. 163.

From the professional organizations' viewpoint, the problem of overcrowding worsened steadily from the end of the nineteenth century into the 1930s. The number of students in almost all fields increased dramatically during this time, and German governments refused to impose restrictions on the number of professionals. Many professional organizations demanded in vain a *numerus clausus*, or enrollment limit. A more successful tactic was to call for the raising of curricular and examination requirements. In other areas, too, German professional organizations called upon governments to intervene in professional life, usually with the object of protecting incomes and limiting competition. The medical profession went so far as to request a new law regulating the practice of medicine in Germany, a total reversal of its stance in the 1860s, when it had lobbied successfully for the free practice of medicine. Such a law was not passed either under the Kaiser or the Weimar Republic, to the disgust and alienation of many doctors.

The point of this historical sketch is to suggest that autonomy from state intervention not only seems to have been a relatively weak characteristic of modern German professional life, but that many professional organizations, when faced with higher competition and lowered incomes, actively sought to surrender some of their autonomy in return for state protection; or, to use Larson's concept of the "professionalization project," an increase in state control and bureaucratization, not in autonomy, became central to the "project" of several German professional groups. It is indeed this type of interaction among the professions, on the one hand, and political and social forces, on the other, which must be addressed by historians of professions and professionalization in order better to understand their subject. Static lists of characteristics used to define professions, such have typically been found in social science literature of the past half-century and more, simply exclude the dynamics of the developing situation. They are also the product of certain cultural biases, an ahistorical approach to the problem, and of a certain willingness to accept self-descriptions by the professional groups themselves.

Self-description and self-evaluation certainly enter into the characteristic of social status, particularly in the German case. Much of the notion that the professions stand by definition in a relatively elevated social niche comes from the assumption of increasingly fluid social barriers of the United States and Britain at the time theories of professions were being formulated. (The reality of such fluidity may be another matter still, even in those countries.) To speak at all of "German society" is to overlook the heterogeneity of a country encountering national unification, rapid industrialization and urbanization, modernization and resistance to it, and wide differences and rivalries among the various regions and states. A country doctor in East Prussia obviously faced a different professional reality from that of a specialist in Cologne; and a doctor of engineering employed in a large Rhenish factory faced a different set of challenges than did a mechanic who had learned his engineering in a small shop in Chemnitz.

Furthermore, German professional thought persisted to some extent in the premodern self-assessments common to other social groups. Even down to the Nazi seizure of power in 1933, the most common term used to designate a professional group was "Stand," reflecting the "estates" of the premodern era. One of the major challenges to the emerging professional organizations consisted of recruiting the maximum number of members of the Stand into the organization or, in other words, to translate the passivity of ascribed status (Stand also means status) into the activity of professional engagement.

Ironically, the increase in both the number of professions and the number of professionals may have had a deleterious effect on the status of all the professions; at least this was a widespread complaint among contemporaries. If one relies on the perceptions of contemporaries, the dynamics of professionalization in Germany may have meant a decline in traditional status for the old professions and a consequent organization of forces to counteract it. Many of the new professions aspired to forms of statutory recognition of status comparable to those of the old professions. The very notion of statutorily defined status among the various professions is one so alien to Anglo-American traditions that striving for it might seem to some social theorists to be contrary to nature, and certainly contrary to the autonomy of professions from state control that by definition they consider vital to professional life. Yet, many an acrimonious debate about professional status was solved precisely in this way in Germany and elsewhere on the continent.

Another characteristic of German professionalization that does not conform to the Anglo-American sociological model is high economic status. It is not possible, given the current state of knowledge, to determine precisely the income levels of the German professions over the past two centuries, the relative value of such incomes, or reliable figures for comparisons abroad. Scattered evidence, however, indicates that German professionals with few exceptions began by the turn of this century to consider themselves less well-off than they thought they should be or in comparison to their English or American colleagues. This feeling intensified in the economically critical period after World War I, when first raging inflation and later the Great Depression disrupted the market for professional services.

But did economic deprivation lessen the status or blur the definitional lines of the profession? The evidence seems equivocal, suggesting that high economic status may not be a very important characteristic of professions after all. Nor did the poor economic prospects of many professions deter a flood of students preparing for them, despite dire warnings about the oversupply of professionals in the 1920s as well as various earlier periods.

The existence of career ladders was certainly an early component of professionalization in Germany, but not for all professions. The tendency was always in that direction, with the model being that of the various German civil services. In one degree or another, all the old professions underwent this type of professionalization even before the middle of the nineteenth century. The clergy, physicians, and that part of the legal profession not directly employed as *Beamte*[21] stood under some kind of state regulation and an indicated, if still weak, pattern of career moves. Starting in the 1860s, however, state-imposed restrictions began to be lifted with the more fluid policies of the liberal era. It later became incumbent on the professional organizations to attempt to restructure and expand career ladders.

By the same token, monopolies in the market of services were at first generally imposed or upheld by the German states in the early nineteenth century, only to yield in some cases to a more laissez-faire attitude later. To be sure, such areas as public administration, schooling, and clerical ministrations remained monopolistically controlled by the states. In addition, many public functions carried out by private professionals in America and England, such as architecture and many areas of engineering remained de facto under German state authority because the states were the main patrons and hired their own bureaucratic staffs.

Two of the old professions (law and medicine) and most of the new ones, however, found themselves in anything but a monopoly position after the liberal era. Academically trained physicians and attorneys complained constantly about competition from a congeries of "quacks" and untrained legal advisors. Members of the new professions complained, too. Characteristically, German engineers were unable until the early 1960s to restrict the title "engineer" to academically trained members of the occupation.

It should be mentioned in this context that the history of many professions in America demonstrates the weakness of the criterion of monopoly over services to the public as essential to professions. The American Bar and Medical Associations, both far more successful than their German counterparts, were helpless against similar forms of competition in the nineteenth century. Furthermore, given the very unequal quality of American medical and law schools at the time, it is highly questionable whether even duly trained and licensed practitioners could always claim a legitimate superiority over their competitors. American proprietary medical schools were already notorious in Germany in the 1880s, when medical degrees were in effect being sold for money by some American "medical colleges," even to Germans.

One may still agree with "power-oriented" analysts that the drive toward monopoly is one of tendency – a part of the professionalizing project – rather than an achieved reality. But the behavior of German governments nevertheless appears to have stood in stark contrast to that of American and, to some de-

---

21 *Beamte* are civil servants, but under German practice as developed in the nineteenth century, they acquired certain rights of tenure; upper civil servants generally had to have advanced education in the law and, because of years of poorly paid or unpaid work, to have some private means. Some *Beamte*, such as university professors and (later) schoolteachers, had further special rights and/or disadvantages in comparison to the "immediate" civil service.

gree, British governments. There are also many anomalies. What German states considered essential to the cohesiveness of the community – for example control of the clergy and schoolteachers – was not left to the free market. What monopoly the American Medical Association (AMA) and American Bar Association (ABA) achieved by the twentieth century in their fields of endeavor is still, in the view of many German physicians and attorneys, lacking for them.

The dimension of education and certification was perhaps much more important in the construction of modern professions in Germany than in Anglo-American countries. Although not sovereign in setting the parameters for professional activity, German professional organizations were sufficiently independent, well-organized, inclusive, and influential to have a large potential for influencing those parameters. This appears to have been especially true of influence on educational and examination systems, which were more uniform and central to professionalization in Germany than in the Anglo-American world.

Any history of professions and professionalization in modern Germany must carefully scrutinize the relationship between professional organizations on the one hand and such state institutions as universities, examining (licensing) boards, and disciplinary courts on the other. Not only formal influence, such as was brought to bear through legislative and administrative regulatory lobbying, but also informal influence must be scrutinized. For example, the disproportionate presence of leading university professors on the boards of directors of several professional organizations points toward a sort of back-door control of the organization over curricular and examination matters as well as the possibility of government influence on "autonomous" professional organizations. Similarly, the growing influence of leaders in private industry over both governments and professional organizations must be studied, especially in relationship to the sciences and engineering.

My research points toward a tendency, especially after about 1900, of a growing interaction of economic, political, and professional entities in many fields. To give one brief example, the chemical profession was given its shape through the interaction of the *Verein deutscher Chemiker,* captains of the chemical industry such as Carl Duisberg (who became head of the VDC for several crucial years) and the leading academic chemists of late Imperial Germany. The interactions of these groups with each other and government education ministries produced a uniform training and examination of the majority of German chemists.

These examples of "peculiar" German historical variations in the "characteristics" of professions are cited here merely as a preview of the great complex of deviations they show from the Anglo-American "model." There does not appear to be a fixed or absolute boundary on the definitional characteristics of the professions if one looks at them over time. What is apparent, however, in the German and, more generally, continental European history of the establishing of modern professions is the persistently important role of higher education and the degree to which it provided the key to shaping professions. To relegate higher education to a role equal with or inferior to other "characteristics" of modern professions, as has been the tendency in Anglo-American sociology, is to misunderstand continental professionalization. By the same token, artificial distinctions such as that made by Freidson between "profession as a very broad, educated stratum" and as "a distinctive form of organized occupation" (the latter being more concrete and precise) merely tend to absolutize the Anglo-American model once again.

If we recognize the central role of higher education in continental professionalization, we shall naturally wish to raise the question: who influenced education and subsequently tested its efficacy in professional socialization? Such questions are hardly peripheral, but are rather central to the understanding not only of the evolution of professions in Central Europe, but, in a broader sense, of the evolution of society there.

One might rather relativize the whole debate and ask such questions as: why did Anglo-American professions take the organizational and dynamic roles they did, whereas German professions both accepted less autonomy and pursued a strategy of influencing training and licensing, resulting in a much more cohesive and uniform set of professions? Or, to ask a similar question, why did American professions carry on the professional project as closed, autonomous organizations while the Germans preferred a certain fluidity of interaction among organizations, state bureaucracies, and institutions of higher education?

Thus, the study of other cultural situations over the entire period of the rise of modern professions and their representative associations promises to yield new perspectives even for social science theory. The study of Germany should be particularly valuable in this respect, because the German states appear to represent a sort of middle ground between the conditions of professionalization prevalent in the Anglo-American world and many East European and non-European countries. Compared to the former world, and arguably even to France, Switzerland, and Italy, the German situation was characterized from the eighteenth century and even earlier by the tradition of state intervention. Compared to Czarist Russia and the Soviet Union, however, Germany's professional associations were relatively strong, autonomous, and effective. Compared to the rest of Eastern Europe, Germany had a relatively homogeneous society, in which ethnic, class, and religious questions played a comparatively small role. In Eastern Europe, by contrast, the smooth integration of the few modern professionals into the indigenous society was often encumbered by local conditions, so that Jews were disproportionately represented in the medical profession, and, as in Hungary, the impoverished lower nobility flocked into the law.

Certainly German professions, in their emergence into modernity, confronted very different historical conditions from others. As we shall see in the next chapter, a crucial element in the early part of that history was the modern bureaucratic state.

Indeed, the modernization, scientificization, and homogenization of learned professions in Germany owed much to interactions with state authority and its living administrators, the civil servants. The upper levels of bureaucracy were themselves among the first occupations to become *modern* learned professions. These required, in contradistinction to honorific or part-time occupations so typical of the eighteenth century and earlier, continuous and practically exclusive work in the service sector, based on extensive, specialized education on the tertiary level and the demonstration by an examination/licensing process of adequate cognitive knowledge.[22] Under modern conditions, starting in the early nineteenth century, previous practices in learned professions, such as second occupations or switching occupations, became increasingly rare, as we shall also see in Chapter 3.

22 For a further discussion of this and other definitions, see Charles E. McClelland, "Zur Professionalisierung der akademischen Berufe in Deutschland," in Jürgen Kocka and Werner Conze, eds., *Bildungsbürgertum im 19. Jahrhundert,* pt. I (Stuttgart, 1985), pp. 234–7.

PART II

The transition to modern professions in the early nineteenth century

3

The beginnings of modern professions
in Germany

There were professions in eighteenth-century Europe, as there had been for centuries. There were also learned people – *savants, Gelehrten* – a few of them professionally engaged in learning and science, but most of them not. Training for a *profession*, as the Germans and French called it, had little direct connection with advanced knowledge of a theoretical kind. Because *Professionen* were in fact trades, some of them skilled, education for them was readily carried out by the venerable system of apprenticeship or some other form of what today is called on-the-job training. The connection of high theoretical knowledge with practical occupations, a hallmark of modern professions, had not yet been made.

There were, to be sure, a few occupations that required higher education, but they were not easily classified as economically productive. Religion, law, and medicine were the three traditional callings requiring higher education. But there are two significant points about these three ancient professions. First, their objects were not of a concrete but rather of a highly abstract nature. Second, although higher education was a prerequisite, it did not necessarily prepare the professionals for the practice of their art.

Eighteenth-century England illustrates this paradox. So far ahead of the rest of Europe in commerce and empire-building, the English still maintained very varied and ad hoc methods for creating professionals. With the exception of the clergy, for which universities had been in large part created in the Middle Ages, practitioners of learned professions (e.g. law and medicine) got further training in extrauniversity institutions, such as the Inns of Court. Even so, only a minority of physicians was trained or licensed by the Royal College of Physicians. Ad hoc arrangements predominated.[1] Where university education was a presupposition for the "liberal professions," it still rested chiefly on the classics, and more for social than functional reasons: parsons, barristers, and physicians were to a large degree dependent on the patronage of the gentlemen who ran

1 Geoffrey S. Holmes, *Augustan England. Professions, State and Society, 1680–1730* (London, 1982), esp. chaps. 6–7.

31

England and achieved a certain social acceptance by virtue of their liberal education.[2] University education was expensive, so it is no surprise that most members of the learned professions came from comfortable circumstances.

The situation in Germany was already somewhat different in the eighteenth century. There universities actually taught law and medicine in addition to theology and the classics. But, as in England (and everywhere in Europe), physicians were not expected to undertake surgery (that was still a trade practiced by barbers) or, indeed, even to cure patients. Lawyers had to undertake further training after university in an already highly bureaucratized legal system. Clergymen quite normally had to practice some other occupation (such as teaching) while waiting for a parish.

Nor were these learned professions held in especially high respect. As in England, lawyers were perennial fair game for satirists. The king of Prussia ordered his lawyers to wear black robes so that, he joked, the people could "see the scoundrels coming."[3] One of the founders of the University of Göttingen (among the most advanced of the age) grudgingly agreed in the 1730s to create a medical school only "so that the dead can be conveyed to the cemetery in an orderly fashion," speeded on their way by the young medical "angels of death."[4] Even the clergy fared badly under the spread of enlightened and anticlerical thinking by the end of the century. Some German spreaders of enlightened ideas called for the abolition of universities because they produced nothing of social utility – presumably meaning clerics spouting an outworn and illogical theology, lawyers endlessly squabbling about outworn and contradictory laws, and physicians doing more harm than good to their patients.

The ethos of the Enlightenment had at its core an idea subversive to the traditional learned professions. Expressed in many different ways, it espoused the essential rationality and educability of man, personal independence, and concomitantly the need to rid the world of obfuscation, irrational authority, superstition, and prejudice. Any man, freed from these shackles, could live in a utopia of natural simplicity. Lawyers would not be required if law were a matter of simple, readily understandable codes based on the observation of nature. Pastors and priests were unnecessary and even harmful intermediaries for the German Pietist movement and the Catholic Illuminati. Although physicians were few and their clienteles very small, their therapeutic aid was widely regarded as negligible compared to the healing powers of nature. There was little room for the traditional learned professions in the rationalists' universe.

By the time of the French Revolution, however, one learned profession had begun, ever so haltingly, to become the instrument of the rationalization of life for which the Enlightenment called. The civil service, or *Beamtentum*, began to

2 Reader, *Professional Men*, pp. 10–12.
3 Adolf Weissler, *Geschichte der Rechtswissenschaft* (Leipzig, 1905), p. 310.
4 J. G. von Meiern, as quoted in Götz von Selle, *Die Georg-August-Universität zu Göttingen, 1737–1937* (Göttingen, 1937), p. 27.

apply the precepts of rational public order they had learned in the law *Fakultäten* of reformed universities. Having committed themselves one after another to the principle of legitimation by utility, the hundreds of German states could no longer dispense with legally trained bureaucrats. It is quite significant that the German bureaucracy, trained in the law, founded the very model of the leading German modern profession by the turn of the nineteenth century. (Quite incidentally, and perhaps owing more to the decline of their profession than its resurgence, many members of the Protestant clergy contributed to the reestablishment of a German national literature and culture.)

Why the German civil service, based on academic study of the law, came to have such a decisive controlling influence on German life by this time is too complex a story to tell here. Suffice it to say that a form of learned "professionalism" began to enjoy a legitimating sway in many German states at a time when traditional aristocracy still ruled England and, for a brief time at least, pragmatic talent, rather than Napoleon's despised "ideologues" ruled France. It is of no small significance in explaining the further development of professions in Germany that its experiences in the quarter century of the French Revolution and Napoleon were stamped by the decisions of professionally trained lawyers rather than gifted amateurs (as in the case of England) or a brilliant dictator-general.

Also significant was the survival, in a tougher and modernized form, of the German university system and the synthesis of aristocratic values and professional training attained by such new model institutions as the University of Berlin (1810).

By that time, many German universities had closed their doors in the face of declining enrollments and Enlightenment-utilitarian criticism of their uselessness. The score of survivors and new foundations may have come in time to owe some of their ethos to the newly formulated concepts of humanistic *Bildung* and *Wissenschaft*, but they owed their pragmatic justification largely to their production of professionals for the civil service, the bar, the parishes, the newly reorganized humanistic *Gymnasium*, and medicine.[5]

So well did the German universities recover from their slump of the eighteenth century that by the mid-1830s German governments were taking steps to limit enrollments. The reasons had to do with fear that too many unemployable professionals were being turned out and that they might become resentful opponents of the conservative political and social order. From then until the foundation of the German Empire in 1871, enrollments (and the production of

5 These terms are not easy to translate simply. *Bildung* refers to "cultivation" through (normally) advanced education, but in terms of the school system almost always referred to having a classical *Gymnasium* education. The latter consisted of up to nine years of training in classical languages, history, and some in more modern subjects, and was the privilege of a tiny percentage of German youth, which however initially enjoyed the sole right to attend universities. *Wissenschaft* is "science," but in a broader sense than in contemporary English, which usually restricts the word to natural science; *Wissenschaft* also includes "organized knowledge" and "scholarship."

professionals) remained relatively stable at under fifteen thousand per year, despite a near doubling of the population.

Another important change at the universities in the first half of the nineteenth century was qualitative in nature. The spirit of *Wissenschaft* gradually suffused the teaching bodies. Professors came increasingly to view their task as one of advancing the frontiers of knowledge rather than merely passing along a glacially changing body of information. As the universities came to be the centers of scholarly and scientific research in Germany, the professional training they offered came to be *verwissenschaftlicht* ("scientificized"), linked to the idea of evolutionary improvement of professional knowledge. Not only was this true of such obvious fields as chemistry and physics (still hardly "professions"), but of philology, history, and medicine. Even theology and law, disciplines hardly conducive to being placed on a "scientific" basis, began to take seriously the research ethic.

This process did not reach its full development until the second half of the nineteenth century. It did, however, begin to have a peculiar effect on preparation for the professions. Students (and they were probably the large majority) who resisted the research ethic and merely wanted to get on with preparing for a career came to be labeled with the sobriquet *Brotstudent*, bread-student or careerist. At the same time, no graduate wanted to admit to having been a *Brotstudent*; at least the posture of being cultivated and au courant with the latest discoveries in one's field became more common among the professional elites. Although many professors undoubtedly welcomed as many fee-paying students as possible, they did not declare so publicly. Instead, it came to be good tone to decry *Brotstudenten* and make life difficult for them by raising standards.

Such a process was not, to be sure, easy for the professors. Because they received student lecture fees as an important supplement to their rather low state salaries, economic self-interest worked against drastic increases in requirements demanded of students. Thanks to the principles of *Lern- und Lehrfreiheit*,[6] a form of academic freedom that benefited students as well as teachers, German teachers did not have many formal means to compel students toward higher achievement. Nevertheless, through their influence with the German state bureaucracies, they were able from time to time to put through (or resist) higher standards of preparation for the professions, tougher postgraduate certifying examinations, and higher entrance standards to the universities themselves, as we shall see in the following sections.

6 *Lehrfreiheit* was the traditional right of the professor to speak (and by extension to publish) on his subject (but not necessarily on "political" themes) without undue government interference, and was guaranteed further by the system of outside chair offers usually available to a noted professor in case of persecution in his own state. The freedom to study (*Lernfreiheit*) implied that students could move freely from one institution to another, appear or stay away from classes, generally not be bothered by frequent examinations, and take rather full responsibility for their course of studies.

In this respect the state was often quite willing to accede to the wishes of a minority of the professoriate. The former had a quantitative, the latter a qualitative reason for limiting the production of professionals. The *Ordinarien,* or full professors who governed the universities, and who increasingly were drawn from the ranks of the leading scholars and researchers in the universities, and who finally had the best contacts with the government, were also usually the most economically secure lecturers. It was widely understood by the students that their success in passing state qualifying examinations for the professions depended on attending (or at least registering for) the standard courses of the *Ordinarii.* This system worked to the income disadvantage of the other professors, the so-called *Nichtordinarien*; but the ranks of these mostly unsalaried, fee-dependent teachers were still comparatively small before the second half of the nineteenth century.[7]

1. PROFESSIONS AND THE STATE

If state supervision of the professions was closer in Central Europe at the beginning of the nineteenth century than in England or America, one can point to at least four historical reasons for any differences.

First, the triumph of the Erastian principle in church–state relations between the Reformation and the reform era through the Napoleonic period assured state regulation of clerical training. Such regulation remained lighter in the Catholic states, but it nevertheless existed.

Second, the accommodation between absolutist princes and aristocratic elites since the Peace of Westphalia had produced bureaucratic rather than parliamentary forms of government in most of the larger German states by 1815. The upper echelons of administration were as a rule reserved for the *Gross- und Kleinadel* (nobility and gentry) down to the end of World War I. But the higher civil service increasingly required university and subsequent on-the-job training since the eighteenth century. A statistically significant number of German law students was drawn from the aristocracy in the early nineteenth century.

Third, efficient government was necessary in order to carry on the main business of the state in the eighteenth century: warfare. The military orientation of German life required not only competent soldiers (another occupation that became professionalized rather early in Germany), but competent surgeons as well, to see what could be saved from the carnage of the battlefield. The welfare of soldiers was a serious concern of the larger German states by the eighteenth century, so that the competence of *Wundärzte* (military surgeons) became a state concern long before anyone thought to regulate mere M.D.s.

---

7 The *Nichtordinarien* included associate professors, honorary professors, *Dozenten* or lecturers, and other irregular or "out-of-plan" (*ausserplanmässge*) staff, who received either no regular salary or a small one and relied principally on student lecture fees for their income. Although they became increasingly indispensible for university instruction, their legal and financial rights always remained very precarious.

Fourth, many German states rediscovered the citizenry in the course of the Napoleonic wars and began to take the task of educating that group into its own hands. Although not entirely new, this concern led to different forms of supervision (not to mention different forms of schools and educational initiatives) than those already common since the Reformation. Out of it, the *Gymnasium* and the *Gymnasium* teacher were born by the early nineteenth century. That much of this educational effort was motivated by the state bureaucracies' appalling experience of the apathy of the citizens to the potential of their overthrow during the Napoleonic period is merely accidental.

Against all these generalizations one must also point out that "Germany" did not clearly exist as a political entity when England and the United States unquestionably did. There was little economic and social cohesion within the Holy Roman Empire (to 1806), the Rhenish Confederation (1807–14), the Germanic Confederation (1815–66), or even the German Reich of 1871–1918. The organization of labor, including the professions, would require a separate volume to describe.

It would suffice for this volume to say that the control of the German states over professions even in the early nineteenth century was as diverse as the landscapes, dialects, and forms of government of Germany. Princely absolutism may have existed in many German states, but it is difficult to say that government control of professions was more effective than in England, for example, when a doctor, lawyer, clergyman, or professor who had violated some real or imagined professional canon could simply move on to another sovereign German state, let alone talent-hungry Russia or eastern Europe.

Before the invention of the telegraph, the railroad, and the German Empire itself, much of this "control" had to be local. Certainly the professions were not expected to regulate themselves through their own collegial bodies: such would have meant a continuation of old-regime practices most states were now determined to eradicate. The "liberal" or learned professions were thus not "free" or autonomous. The clergy was regulated, as in all state–church systems, by church hierarchies. Lawyers, even those who did not work in the civil service or sit on the bench, were "officers of the court" and subject to its control. The medical profession was more variegated, but large numbers of licensed practitioners were in state employ or were regulated by the guildlike orders. One can surely not yet speak of teaching as a profession at all by the end of the eighteenth century (or far beyond), when its practitioners were often career transients, ranging from theology graduates waiting for a parish to retired army NCOs (as in Prussia).

It is often difficult to see any universal and consistent trends in the relationship between the German states and the professions in the early nineteenth century. One definite trend, although not touching all professions equally, was toward greater governmental regulation. This trend was a part of the modernization resulting from the Napoleonic reforms, which placed unprecedented power in the hands of most larger German states. Still, even though there were only thirty-nine states in the post-1815 Germanic Confederation, a reduction from hundreds under the Holy Roman Empire, neither the rationalization of professional standards decreed by the states nor the growth in the number of professionals led to general satisfaction. Although again not a universal phenomenon, another trend was a call for further unification of the professions by their members, preferably with more autonomy or at least greater consultation of them by the state authorities.

The reaction of German governments to such countercurrents in an era of relative economic stagnation and political arch-conservatism was, on balance, negative. It is thus not surprising that the reformers in various professions became, along with the rest of the German bourgeoisie, increasingly restless and grasped the opportunity of the 1848 revolutions to press for sweeping changes. Their aims, like those of the broader German revolutionary movement, remained largely unachieved but left an agendum for future changes.

A few more generalizations can be safely made about trends affecting the professions in the first half of the nineteenth century. Although standards and expectations were clearly on the rise, rewards were not. The economic position of professionals was not a happy one. To be sure, the social prestige of being a university graduate and (still in most cases) a state or church *Beamter* offset some of the suffering of financial distress. At the same time, professionalization came increasingly to mean that professionals could no longer earn income from a secondary occupation, as had been common in the eighteenth century, or readily change occupations from profession to trade or commerce. Farmer-doctors, wineseller-professors, and even barber-surgeons began to disappear from the professional landscape.

The general rise in mandated university entrance requirements, length of study, standards of qualifying examinations, and other regulations had the effect of raising the costs of qualifying for a profession at a time when the financial rewards did not necessarily increase to cover such an investment. This trend had the effect, at least after the mid-1830s, of decreasing the proportion of students from less affluent levels of society entering the universities and therewith the professions.

Finally, it should be mentioned that the early nineteenth century witnessed not only a redefinition of most of the traditional professions, but the virtual creation of a new one, the *Gymnasiallehrer*. As the classical-humanistic *Gymnasium* became a standard feature of German urban life, its teachers became professionals in the sense of being placed on a primitive career ladder, and higher school teaching ceased to be a transitional career.

Examples of these generalizations are in the following sections, in which we examine the structure and change of the traditional professions in the early nineteenth century.

2. THE MEDICAL PROFESSION

If the medical profession was the classic model on which others patterned themselves in the Anglo-Saxon world, as has often been said, it was far from being
that in the German states. As one historian of German medicine put it point-
edly, "the concept of a German physician was unknown during much of the
nineteenth century."[8] Most officially recognized "medical personnel" were in
fact not licensed doctors (*approbierte Aerzte*) but "surgeons" (*Wundärzte*) of many
different classes and with little or no academic training.

This lack of a uniform profession was complicated by the standards of training that differed widely from one German state to another. It became an issue
for mounting concern to the medical establishment and the German states only
in the early nineteenth century, and the issue remained prominent far into the
twentieth. Prussian doctors could not practice in Bavaria. Medical men had to
struggle with five different systems of medical weights and ten different
pharmacopias.[9]

The Prussian system, as regulated in the *Medizinalordnung* of 1825, decreed
three classes of licensed medical personnel. Licensing had been transferred to the
state from the universities in 1725, at a time when their reputation of rigor and
scrupulousness was under a cloud of doubt. The first class, *approbierter Arzt* or
doctor, required four years of university study and a qualifying examination. A
doctor could practice internal medicine and, with a special course of study,
surgery or gynecology as well. The second was "first class surgeon" (*Wundarzt
erster Klasse*), requiring three years of training in a special seminar, several years
of apprenticeship, and a qualifying examination. Generally first-class surgeons
were restricted to minor surgery but, like doctors, could prescribe drugs.
Second-class surgeons (*Wundarzt zweiter Klasse*), who were prominent in the
countryside, had less formal training, a longer apprenticeship, and as a rule
were not supposed to prescribe drugs (in fact they often had to).

Prussia had also sought to regulate dentistry in its 1825 reform. It had attempted to stamp out unauthorized dentistry (typically performed by "market
hawkers" at fairs, much like itinerant self-proclaimed dentists on the American
frontier). Still, dental medicine was considered only at best a low variant of the
activities of the least qualified second-class surgeons.[10]

Bavaria had doctors, country doctors, and licensed *Bader* (literally "bathers").
Württemberg had ten classes of licensed medical personnel, with further subdivisions for *Wundärzte* who did or did not have the right to practice gynecology,
to treat broken bones, or to inoculate, to mention a few.[11]

8 Kurt Finkenrath, *Die Organisation der deutschen Aerzteschaft* (Berlin, 1928), p. 3.
9 Ibid.
10 Walter Lafrenz, *Die Geschichte des zahnärztlichen Unterrichts in Deutschland* (Erlangen, 1936),
  pp. 3–6.
11 Finkenrath, *Organisation*, pp. 4–6.

To be sure, even scrupulous recent research has been unable to determine to what degree regulations governing medical practice were really carried out.[12] The Prussian government's attempts to raise standards of education, examination, licensing, and discipline after 1825 failed in any case to solve one of the most pressing health-care problems it perceived, the delivery of medical treatment to the vast majority of the population, located chiefly in the countryside.[13] The number of doctors practicing outside cities was always negligible, and the number of *Wundärzte* declined absolutely over the first six decades of the century.[14] Although the Prussian *Allgemeines Landrecht* of 1794 and subsequent laws prohibited medical practice by unlicensed persons (or persons unlicensed for a particular kind of practice), it nevertheless continued.

A telling index of professionalizing trends in the first half of the nineteenth century was the shifting numerical relationship between doctors (*Aerzte*) and other kinds of medical personnel (e.g. military surgeons). Whereas the class of "surgeons" continued to decline in numbers, that of academically trained doctors increased; the number of the latter who also qualified for surgery also increased dramatically. The number of graduated doctors (*promovierte Aerzte*) in Prussia rose from under 2,200 in 1833 to over 2,800 in 1842 and nearly 4,200 in 1858 – increases of 27 percent and 48 percent against 1833. Population growth in the same periods had been eight and 35 percent. Whereas doctors had comprised just under half of licensed practitioners of all three classes in 1833, they represented 71 percent by 1858.[15]

Another interesting phenomenon was the high proportion of "independent" to "employed" medical practitioners. Most bigger German states employed a large portion of medical personnel in bureaucratic or military positions. Municipal and county (*Kreis*) medical employees, military surgeons, and similar licensed physicians in government employ made up 36 percent of the medical personnel in Prussia in 1833, for example. By 1842 this proportion had not changed significantly.[16] But the number of academically trained doctors (*Aerzte*) employed by the authorities had sunk from a bit under one-half to a little over one-third. Such employment was, in many cases, not full-time, but even so the trend toward doctors being a part of an overwhelmingly "free" profession was clear.[17]

This "freedom" was not, however, absolute. Even doctors in private practice were subjected to a host of government regulations that made them, in effect, partial (and usually unremunerated) agents of the state. Some of these requirements included supervision of local pharmacists, writing periodic reports on the medical situation in their localities, and treating indigent patients gratis. The freedom to move one's practice was severely restricted.[18] Medical ethics

12 Claudia Huerkamp, "Aertze und Professionalisierung in Deutschland," *Geschichte und Gesellschaft*, 6 (1980): 353.
13 Ibid., pp. 354–5.   14 Finkenrath, *Organisation*, pp. 32–3.   15 Ibid.
16 Ibid, p. 19.   17 Ibid.   18 Ibid., pp. 20–8.

questions were not supervised by the "free" doctors themselves, but in many states (including Prussia and Austria) by some type of medical *collegium,* or committee, staffed by civil service medical personnel.[19]

3. THE LEGAL PROFESSION

If the medical profession lay under considerable state control in the early nineteenth century, the situation with law graduates was even more tightly controlled and state-dependent. As with medicine, the legal profession was not uniform. The study of law continued throughout the century to be considered the most *vornehm* (distinguished) academic discipline, because it was required for the higher civil service as well as the bench and the bar. Sons of noble and gentry families, intent on a government career, were present in much higher proportions in the law faculties than in the other three. Thus, if the legal profession enjoyed a higher social status than the medical, it owed this to its nearness to the state, the administration of which was still largely entrusted to the aristocracy.

At the same time, legal education was less carefully organized than medical and certainly less tied to advances in science and scholarship. Law students were notorious for their laziness and absence from lectures throughout the nineteenth century; law was widely regarded as a subject best gotten through with memorization rather than intellectual penetration; and in no other field was the post university "cram school" for exam preparation so widespread. The response of the states to these perceived abuses was resort to ever-sharper and more elaborate state examinations from the eighteenth century onward, about which more later.

The structure of the legal profession showed a number of peculiarities in the German states, not least of which was the difference from one place to another. By the early half of the nineteenth century, students trained in law could choose to go into the higher levels of administration or into the court system. Requirements for the two basic divisions of government varied. In some places the prestige and qualifications for administration were higher than for the bench; in others the reverse was the case. Administrators, judges, and attorneys all had to pass a series of examinations before and after unpaid trial periods. Their number was usually fixed by ordinance, so that free competition for clients among attorneys was usually very circumscribed. Indeed, there were generally fewer attorneys than judges at any given time: Prussia in 1849 allowed roughly one attorney for every two judges in its courts; and the number of attorneys actually sank slightly between 1837 and 1858, but remained in the range of 1,100 to 1,200.[20]

19 Ibid., p. 21.   20 Weissler, *Rechtswissenschaft,* p. 529.

Compared to the Anglo-Saxon world, Germany already had a highly disciplined, bureaucratized, and proportionally smaller legal profession before 1850, at a time when civil service was only a reformer's dream in Britain and America. On the other hand, the "profession" of law was rather sternly divided among its two major parts; and even in the courts lawyers and judges did not often change places. Thus starting from a common training, Germany's lawyers developed three different subidentifications following the nature of their offices. Furthermore, ordinary attorneys appear to have been less inclined until the very end of the century to emulate their Anglo-Saxon colleagues in acting as general agents for business, agriculture, or politicians.

If attorneys constituted a distinctive minority in the totality of legal practitioners in the early nineteenth century, they at least were not always divided, as in Britain, France, and Italy, into two classes of practitioners. This division had begun in the medieval courts of canon law and created different roles for the "barrister" (*avocat, avvocato*) and the "solicitor" (*avoué, procuratore*). The latter could advise a client but not represent him before the court.[21] Also in German lands the distinction between *Advokatur* and *Prokuratur* had existed or (as in the formerly French provinces west of the Rhine) continued to exist well into the nineteenth century. The trend, beginning in Prussia in 1748, however, was to eliminate the "solicitor" (*Prokurator*) and create a unified class of attorneys (*Advokaten*), after about 1850 called *Rechtsanwälte*.[22]

The legal and administrative reforms of the late eighteenth and early nineteenth century, particularly in trailblazing Prussia, are too complex to be described in full here. The general trend was toward a greater bureaucratization of the legal profession and a victory for the principle of a codified, state-run legal system, to the gradual exclusion of legal jurisdictions representing feudal and particularist interests, for example, that of the aristocracy.[23] To be sure, these trends would not be fully consolidated until well after the unification of Germany in 1871.

Suffice it to say that by the middle of the nineteenth century, most of the larger German states had transformed the legal profession into a rationalized system of bureaucratic administration, royal courts operating under clear written rules and codifications of law, and attorneys enjoying, if not the privileges and autonomy of their Anglo-Saxon counterparts, a high degree of respect and state indulgence in return for submission to educational and examination standards that clearly represented an advance over the previous century. The situation of attorneys was enhanced not only by their restricted numbers but also by the requirement that they be trained to be capable of assuming a judgeship. Indeed, in Prussia at least, judges sometimes sought to change their positions

21 Julius Magnus, ed., *Die Rechtsanwaltschaft* (Leipzig, 1929), p. 3.   22 Ibid., p. 6.
23 Dietrich Rüschemeyer, *Lawyers and Their Society. A Comparative Study of the Legal Professions in Germany and the United States* (Cambridge, Mass., 1973), chap. 5.

and become attorneys, partly because practice was relatively lucrative under then-prevailing circumstances.[24]

Legal training by the middle of the nineteenth century came under the same kind of regulation as medical training: a minimum number of years of university education, an average of three followed by a first state examination as prerequisites for entering one of the several initial "training" paths. In the bureaucracy, this path was accompanied by the title *Referendar* or some equivalent. After several years of mostly unpaid service, a second state examination could be taken, with the usual result of becoming an *Assessor.*[25] From this point on, attorneys were free to apply to a court to practice and aspiring judges to obtain their first appointment to the bench. In Prussia, through much of the nineteenth century three exams were required for this process. A great deal of discretion by the courts or administrative bureaucracy could determine which candidates were invited into the civil service, and means-testing to show the candidates could survive through all the years of waiting and training were common.

Despite the imposition of a framework on the legal profession by the mid-nineteenth century, it would be misleading to think that there were firm career ladders. For example, nobles obviously still possessed many advantages in the civil service and upper judiciary in Prussia.[26] Thus, status depended still to some degree on personal or family social position as well as hierarchization inherent in the civil service ladder. As for the simple attorneys, many of them continued to derive much of their income from administrative functions, such as estate management or sitting on municipal councils, through the greater part of the nineteenth century, and thus cannot be said to have become strictly professionalized as practitioners at the bar.

Similarly, lawyers' incomes in the early nineteenth century varied widely. Those on a career ladder in the administrative service or the judiciary enjoyed more or less steady incomes from salaries, although these were hardly adequate for a comfortable life-style except at the very highest reaches. Average salaries of 500 thalers annually (roughly $500 or 100 pounds sterling) were about all the majority of Prussian or Bavarian judges could expect before 1848; this was considered insufficient for maintaining a family of four. To be sure, salaries in some states, such as Saxony, were as much as double this much.[27]

Judging by the wish of some magistrates in Prussia to quit the bench for the bar, and the relative decline in the number of attorneys allowed to practice in

24 Weissler, *Rechtswissenschaft,* p. 530.
25 *Referendar* was the lowest grade of the upper (university-trained) civil service or court system, regarded by the bureaucracy as a form of on-the-job training (hence the virtually negligible income paid to these young men). Assessors were regularly appointed civil servants after completing the training and all required examinations, and from this pool the higher ranks might be filled after several further years of low-paid work and waiting.
26 Erich Döhring, *Geschichte der deutschen Rechtspflege seit 1500* (Berlin, 1953), p. 74.
27 Ibid., p. 86.

the first half of the century, attorneys were probably on balance a little better off financially; but no generalizations encompassing all German attorneys can safely be made on the basis of available evidence. One statistic indicating that attorneys in the early nineteenth century, and even down to the 1870s, may have enjoyed some degree of prosperity is that their numbers on a per-capita population basis appear to have declined. In Prussia, at least, after reforms of the 1790s and subsequently, the number of attorneys was controlled by the bureaucracy. In contrast to a ratio of one attorney for every 2,000 people around 1700, Prussia had only one for every 10,000 by 1850.[28]

On the other hand, early nineteenth-century lawyers were much more rigidly controlled by the state than in the previous century, and one can hardly speak of autonomy of the profession. Thanks to this and the increasingly rigorous educational requirements of the same period, however, the reputation of lawyers for diligence, probity and neohumanistic *Bildung* probably placed them in much higher public esteem than had been the case a century before.[29]

4. THE CLERICAL PROFESSION

It has often been said that clergymen constitute the oldest and, indeed, the original learned profession from which all others flowed at least since the founding of Europe's medieval universities. All professionals, not just the clergy, were originally clerics, and theology was still held to be the queen of sciences, officially if not in fact, at German universities in the early nineteenth century.

In Germany as elsewhere in Europe, the clergy had many hallmarks of professionalization long before its secular rivals in the professions. Mastery of a specialized body of knowledge, a respected social standing, a rigorous ethical code, altruism, and a market monopoly of services, coupled with a certain kind of licensing and some possibilities of a career ladder, make the clergy appear partly professionalized long before the nineteenth century.

Yet, like military officers, the clergymen were certainly not autonomous in their practice: they worked in a distinct hierarchy. Their economic rewards varied not so much with their competence in their tasks as with their personal and family connections, much as was still the case with the military and civil service at the beginning of the century. The gap in education, family background, and wealth between a village priest and an archbishop (not to mention a prince-bishop) in pre-Napoleonic Catholic Germany was far too wide to allow placing both ends of the spectrum under any meaningful title of "profession." If the gap was smaller in the Protestant lands, it was nonetheless striking. Preferment and patronage still played a far more important role than professional

28 Rüschemeyer, *Lawyers*, p. 147; Magnus, *Rechtsanwaltschaft*, p. 5.
29 Rüschemeyer, *Lawyers*, pp. 150–3.

competence in a clerical career and can be said to have continued to do so throughout much of the nineteenth century.

Still, the clergy was an academic calling, perhaps the learned profession most open to young men of small means. A large part of the Protestant clergy was recruited from the homes of pastors, a fertile bed from which so much of Germany's philosophical, literary, and general intellectual revival sprang from the eighteenth century onward. Many of the new scholarly disciplines drew their founders from such backgrounds, and many others had initially studied theology at Protestant universities. Catholic Germany did not, of course, have the family relationship of the *Pastorenhaus* to draw upon, but theological study was still an attractive route of social mobility, if not financial security, for poor young men.[30]

Despite an upturn in the fortunes of theological faculties after 1815, however, the secularization of teaching (one of the main occupations of younger clergymen) and the diminishing importance of domestic tutors in the face of expanding public schools had the long-term effect, in the early nineteenth century, of reducing the scope of careers for clergymen. The rise of *philosophische Fakultäten* (schools of arts and sciences at the universities) accompanied the expansion of humanistic secondary schools. Theologically trained men were able to hold their own in school appointments against the secularly trained graduates of the philosophical faculties in heavily Catholic parts of Germany down to the 1848 revolution (e.g. in Bavaria), but the trend was toward restricting theology graduates (and the less well-trained pupils of seminaries) to offices within the churches. As this trend became increasingly obvious, theological enrollments in universities began to dry up in the latter half of the nineteenth century.

If we take as our example the parish clergymen, who comprised the largest component of "professionals" trained in theology, we can say that their education and qualifications undoubtedly improved overall in the early nineteenth century. The critical and historical methods introduced in the eighteenth century became widespread in theological faculties by the mid-nineteenth century. Catholic Germany certainly lagged behind in this development, but it was not wholly excluded from it.

Theological disputes and factional struggles within the main churches were, indeed, very lively in the early nineteenth century. The firm alliance between throne and altar after the defeat of Napoleon also insured that such disputes became political ones, closely followed by most educated people.

But precisely the firm ties between the German churches and the conservative thrones virtually guaranteed that the parish clergy, unlike some of their eighteenth century forebears, were disinclined or prevented from taking up a

---

30 Anthony La Vopa, *Grace, Talent and Merit. Poor Students, Clerical Careeres, and Professional Ideology in Eighteenth Century Germany* (Cambridge, 1988), passim. The *Pastorenhaus*, or Protestant pastor's house, had a long tradition of learning, cultivation, and producing the next generation of pastors (or secular intellectuals).

critical stance toward their own hierarchies or those of the state. Thus clergymen were unable to organize themselves, or even attempt to, outside the confines of authority. The parish clergyman was, from a professional standpoint,
under such severe discipline and constraint that this autonomy was perhaps
more limited than that of any of the other "old" professions.

This should not be too surprising. As we have seen, the medical and legal
professions were concentrated in largely urban areas, as were members of such
"new" professions as schoolteachers and, a bit later, engineers and scientists.
The clergymen were still concentrated where the vast majority of Germans
lived, in smaller communities widely dispersed across the land. If they were
among the last to join the wave of modern professionalization, the reason must
be sought in the fact that their "profession" for centuries had tied them to the
land, to its peasant people, and to the local grandees whose favor was still more
powerful an influence than the decrees of consistories and episcopal sees.

5. THE TEACHING PROFESSION

The comments above concerning the occasional teaching functions of the traditional clergy might have alerted us to the continued preprofessional status of
one of the world's oldest occupations – that of teachers – in the early nineteenth
century.

Teaching encountered a number of impediments to becoming a modern profession. Before and even during the various educational reforms of the nineteenth century, this occupation was even more disunified than the traditional
professions discussed so far. Educational qualifications varied immensely, from
the bare literacy of retired soldiers in elementary schools to the learnedness of
university professors. The upper and smaller end of the occupation, comprising
university professors and teachers at urban Latin schools or classical *Gymnasien*,
were normally university graduates; the lower and larger end comprised a be-
wildering welter of teachers not specifically trained for the task plus an increasing number of graduates of special teachers' seminaries at various levels. The
upper end of the profession enjoyed a certain status by virtue of university training and proximity to the economic and social elites they instructed. Members of
the lower end were often socially despised even by the illiterate peasants who
grudgingly sent their children to the village school and even more grudgingly
paid the fees to support instruction.

Dependence on patronage, whether of the rude rural parents who paid fees,
the village parson or priest who was the first instance of supervision, or of
urban school authorities greatly circumscribed the autonomy of most schoolteachers. Ironically, teaching is one of the occupations that became professionalized largely through the instrument of increasing state control – and not only
in Germany. Before this occurred, the supply of potential teachers was limited
only by the poor prospects of the occupation, and schoolteachers, singly or collectively, could exert little influence on the conditions of their work.

If the profession was not uniform, neither was it usually a career. Opportunities for advancement were severely limited. If professors and *Gymnasium* teachers had to be at least full-time practitioners of pedagogy, without the need to carry on secondary occupations, they also were driven to supplement their incomes by writing or giving private tutoring. Lower schoolteachers were not so lucky. Sometimes they doubled as church sextons or, in rural areas, spent the vacation (i.e. growing and harvesting) periods as agricultural laborers – on plots attached to the school, if they were fortunate, as hired hands when they were not. Or they might be artisans who also taught school (tailoring was a favorite combination in the eighteenth century because its quiet nature did not disturb the children's concentration).[31]

The reform of the school-teaching occupation initiated by Prussia and other German states in the first half of the nineteenth century produced a growing cadre of trained and licensed teachers designed to correct this situation. By 1834 Prussia had thirty main teachers' seminars spread around the provinces, each offering a two- to three-year course to fifty to one hundred pupils; and Prussia required after 1826 that nonseminarists pass the same examination as seminarists, which "insured that the seminars would assume a virtual monopoly over training."[32]

Specialized training and licensing did not, however, insure an adequate living standard for most teachers. At the beginning of the nineteenth century, when common day laborers might earn 50 to 100 thalers per year, only a small minority of elementary teachers earned more than 100. A very modest livelihood might have cost 200 thalers a year. Even by the 1840s, a period of inflation, and despite some gains at the lower end of the teachers' income scale, Prussian elementary teachers were still thought to earn less than artisans.[33] Not only their incomes but their privileges were less than that of *Gymnasium* teachers and professors.

The introduction of the examination *pro facultate docendi* by Prussia in 1810 was a milestone in the professionalization of the higher school-teaching corps. A comparatively stringent examination in the subject matter of classical humanism, it virtually forced attendance at a university, for which in turn the school-leaving diploma or certificate of maturity (*Abitur*) normally achieved by attendance at a *Gymnasium* became a requirement in 1834. The Prussian system gradually triumphed in North Germany, although such Catholic states as Bavaria still gave licensing advantages to theological seminarians over secular teachers down to 1848.[34] Classical philology was the basis of training and examination.

31 Anthony J. La Vopa, *Prussian Schoolteachers. Profession and Office, 1763–1848* (Chapel Hill, N.C. 1980), pp. 14–16.
32 Ibid., p. 54.   33 Ibid., pp. 17, 34, 44, 83–4
34 Helga Romberg, *Staat und Höhere Schule. Ein Beitrag zur deutschen Bildungsverfassung vom Anfang des 19. Jahrhunderts bis zum 1. Weltkrieg* (Weinheim, 1978), p. 487.

Finally, the rise of the classical *Gymnasium* left more practical types of secondary education in a certain limbo. Mathematics and natural sciences received only secondary attention in the *Gymnasium*, and most "philologists" scorned the *Nutzlichkeitsanstalten* ("utilitarian schools") that emphasized them. The early nineteenth-century teachers at these *Realschulen* came to feel so insulted and undervalued by their classical school colleagues that they broke away and founded their own *Verein Deutscher Realschulmänner* (Association of Realistic School Men, or VDR) in 1843.[35] German governments did give some grudging recognition to technical education before mid-century, but their teachers and pupils did not enjoy the privileges of the classical secondary schools.

Other teachers were also feeling the effects of professionalization in the early nineteenth century, without however showing signs of agitating for radical change. The occupation of university professor could by now be called a clear career, with educational and "licensing" requirements not so much invented as revived from earlier centuries and filled with the new meaning of *Wissenschaft*. Already by 1848, however, university professors began to relate more to their disciplinary community (e.g. law, medicine) than their collegial one (the university as self-governing corporation), and their needs for professional affiliation were largely met elsewhere.

One final group deserves a mention here, but perhaps not much more. Military officers, like professors, had a very special relationship to the German states and were even less critical of their masters. And although the base in specialized knowledge for officers was undoubtedly higher in 1830 than in 1730, formal knowledge and tested competency clearly did not count much after the fading away of the reform era by 1820. Formal educational requirements for officers continued to exist, but such characteristics as birth, "character," and loyalty seem to have outweighed them in practice. Much like the priesthood, military officers showed little sign of desiring any professional activity or even change until very late.

6. PROFESSIONAL ORGANIZATION

Organization of learned professions, especially on a large scale, faced many difficulties in the early nineteenth century. Travel and communications, while improving steadily, remained slow and expensive. The sheer numbers of "professionals" remained relatively low. In Germany, many of the concerns and functions of modern professional organizations – educational and professional standards, discipline, working conditions, and even income – lay still under the control of government, and most professionals were dependent on the state directly or indirectly.

35 Paul Mellmann, *Geschichte des Deutschen Philologenverbandes* (Leipzig, 1929), pp. 2–3.

Even in other parts of the Western world, the first half of the nineteenth century was not notable for rapid organization of the emerging modern professions. England had only about 400 members of the Royal College of Physicians at the beginning of the century, and a slowly growing number of surgeons (5,200 in 1832; a little over 8,000 in 1843). There were only about 800 barristers in 1814.[36] Because most barristers and physicians lived around London, and were in easy communication, the need for organization came more from the lower orders of medical and legal men spread around the country, resentful of the airs of the London physicians and barristers. The Apothecaries Act of 1815 was a major breakthrough in professional organization launched by Parliament, and some new professional groups were founded before 1850. But traditional rivalries persisted and foiled much progress in unifying the old professions; even the forerunner of the British Medical Association, when set up in 1832, was founded as a provincial medical society in opposition to the dominance of the traditional London physicians.[37] The Le Chapelier Law of 1791 prohibited the free organization of French medicine, which was finally regulated by the state; and French lawyers worked under conditions somewhat comparable to German ones, even if they seem to have been freer and probably more prosperous.[38] Medical and legal organization did not fare very well in the young United States, either, where laissez-faire thinking dominated discussions of the role of professions.

Locally and regionally, relations among members of the same profession, it should be recalled, were not inevitably warm and fraternal. As one of the later organizers of German doctors in the 1870s, H. E. Richter, commented looking back on an earlier period: "Doctors in general lived like spiders, each in his nest; and they richly manifested the legendary mutual enmity of these insects."[39]

Organization of the German professions suffered from a further difficulty that was largely absent in Anglo-Saxon countries and, after 1830 to some degree, France: hostility from the state. A jealous desire by the bureaucracy to maintain and increase its regulatory powers – in which probably a large part of the professionals tacitly acquiesced before the 1840s – was but one reason. The fledgling opposition to the political settlement of 1815 drew much of its leadership from the professions and university students bound for them. Nationalist, constitutionalist, liberal, and even democratic reform programs appeared to the nervous conservative governments to lurk around every corner. The Karlsbad Decrees of 1819 and their renewal in 1834 were symbolic of this nervousness.

36 Reader, *Professional Men*, p. 48.   37 Ibid., pp. 50, 64.
38 Matthew Ramsey, "The Politics of Medical Monopoly," in Gerald Geison, ed., *Professions and the French State, 1700–1900* (Philadelphia, 1984), pp. 235–41; Hannes Siegrist, "Gebremste Professionalisierung," in Conze and Kocka, *Bildungsbürgertum*, pp. 303–5.
39 H. E. Richter, *Aerztliches Vereinsblatt* 1 (1872): 66, quoted in Eduard Graf, *Das ärztliche Vereinswesen in Deutschland und der Deutsche Aerztevereinsbund* (Leipzig, 1890), p. 3.

Free citizens' associations, even ostensibly professional ones, were widely regarded as subversive to public order and authority.

Some regional professional organizations nevertheless were founded, but they did not thrive. National organizations appeared even more dangerous, as vaguely subversive to the sovereignty of the nearly forty German states joined together in the loose Germanic Confederation. Although the efficacy of the *Bund* has long been underrated by historians, it is true that its only memorable acts of a domestic nature consisted of suppression of liberal and nationalist dissent.

On the other side of the coin, however, many German states were eager to benefit from the prestige of the rapidly developing *Wissenschaften* at their universities. Thus, national organizations with the avowed sole purpose of scientific and scholarly information exchange and dissemination could establish footholds. One was the *Versammlung Deutscher Naturforscher und Aerzte* (1822) and the *Versammlung Deutscher Philologen und Schulmänner* (1837), encompassing scientists and doctors and classical philologists, respectively. Such organizations did not, however, attract more than a small fraction of practitioners to their national congresses and generally refrained from taking a strong advocacy role in pressing demands for professional improvement.

More typical of voluntary organizations were local associations, usually with some "scientific" purpose, but sometimes carrying on other functions, such as mutual aid or even professional control. In the medical profession, some larger cities or regions had medical societies, such as Berlin's *Hufelandsche Gesellschaft* (1810), the *Gesellschaft für Natur- und Heilkunde* (1810), and the *Kollegialer Verein für Natur- und Heilkunde* (1832). The three Hanseatic republics each had a medical society by 1832, and before 1848 such larger cities as Hannover, Frankfurt, Dresden, and Leipzig, and a number of Prussian, Hessian, and Bavarian cities. A few of these had over two hundred members (Dresden and Munich, for example), but the rest had under a hundred, and a few dozen was the typical membership.[40]

The chief impetus for organization of the professions in Germany came from mounting dissatisfaction with the current situation in the 1840s. Economic hardship, including a palpable inflation, gnawed at the security of professional practitioners in most fields of endeavor. Doctors, lawyers, teachers, clerics, engineers, and others began to write the word "reform" on their banners and began, in their own spheres, to lock horns more boldly with conservative governments, replicating a broader mood of reform wishes among the educated middle class. A new, younger, and restless generation of professionals had graduated from the much-improved German universities, imbued with the high aspirations of *Wissenschaft* and an often zealous wish to apply its findings to professional practice. The timidity, smugness, and *Schlendrian* (routine) of the

40 Graf, *Vereinswesen*, pp. 2–4, 139–60.

older generation (and, undoubtedly, that generation's seemingly unwarranted hold on the power to improve conditions) stood as a constant barrier to better careers.

As we shall see in the next chapter, the desire of German professions for change and a greater autonomy to carry it out was not simply absent. It required only the collapse of nerve by German governments and the opportunity to vocalize long-standing complaints during the 1848 revolution to reveal the depth of professional dissatisfaction.

4

Professions between revolution and unification

During the upheavals of 1848, the Berlin doctor and reformer Rudolf Virchow wrote in his new weekly publication that "medicine is a social science, and politics is nothing more than medicine writ large."[1] Many doctors may have disagreed, but Virchow's statement captures something of the engagement of professionals in the efforts to cure the German body politic of its long-standing illnesses. At the same time, they tried to exploit the mood of change to bring about reforms closer to their immediate interests and to found organizations to formulate their demands.

It could hardly be expected that professionals as badly splintered and unhomogeneous as those of the German states could, in a bare few months, smoothly bring together unified organizations capable of presenting unanimous sets of demands to state and society, and of course they were unable to do so. But the demands of disparate groups do adumbrate, in their aggregate, some of the issues that would recur constantly in the rest of the century and beyond. For this reason alone they deserve some attention in this chapter.

No matter how interesting regional and local professional organizations might be for the development of individual disciplinary professions (showing as they do tendencies toward individuation and interest-group conflict), the former are difficult to use for generalizations about the German professions as a whole. For these, only the arguments and resolutions of national organizations will serve fully. Thus, it is important to begin the history of modern German professions on the national level, and it was just before during the 1848 upheavals that they began to reveal their awakening sense of professional identity that, like national identity, transcended the centuries-old provincialism of German life. (Naturally this "national" orientation could also be a "cosmopolitan" one and did not exclude international contacts; but the latter were more scientific in nature and, aside from arguments that could be used from foreign experience, largely irrelevant to the "professionalization project.")

1 Rudolf Virchow, editorial in *Die medicinische Reform*, no. 18 (1848).

51

Whether moderate or radical, national or regional, however, German professional groups failed in their organizing efforts and demands, simply because the failure of the revolution by 1849 and the vengeful hostility of the restored conservative authorities to the idea of change undid most of their gains. From the viewpoint of the political reactionaries, professionals had been mixed in the front ranks of revolutionary leadership and were to be trusted even less than before.

It is true that a large percentage of the Frankfurt National Assembly as well as the local revolutionary assemblies came from the ranks of Germany's professional groups. The Frankfurt government was not, as myth maintains, a "parliament of professors,"[2] but it certainly contained enough of them, not to mention teachers, lawyers, judges and prosecutors, professional civil servants, physicians, and clergymen. Together these professional groups constituted nearly 75 percent of the elected delegates, the rest consisting chiefly of businessmen, landowners, and journalists.[3] Equally obviously, only a minority of the professionals who served as delegates were political radicals.

But the treatment meted out to activists in the time of reaction filtered down to moderates and even to professionals who had not participated directly in the revolutionary events. All organizations that had arisen nationally in 1848 were either suppressed outright or harassed into silence and moribundity. If such organizations were allowed to continue to meet in some of the remaining German states with more open official attitudes, most of the larger states forbade their teachers and other public officials from attending meetings or maintaining membership. Reform agenda from 1848 were simply shelved in most cases; in some sensitive cases, for example in the area of education, reform suggestions even provoked a counterrevolutionary agendum. The Stiehl Regulations of 1854 in Prussia may be viewed as the high-water mark of this type of reaction.

Gradually and piecemeal, however, the reaction ebbed a bit and professionalizing projects were able to resume, albeit very cautiously. One notable feature of the official reaction against the revolution was its Janus-faced policies toward liberal or democratic political initiatives, on the one hand, and economic revitalization, on the other. Pragmatic conservatives could admit that economic stagnation had been a major spur to discontent before 1848 and that growth might serve to prevent recurrences.

In this spirit, it is perhaps not surprising that the major national professional organization founded in the 1850s – and in conservative Prussia at that – was one dedicated to the advancement of industrial prosperity. The *Verein Deutscher Ingenieure* (Association of German Engineers, or VDI) took a strictly apolitical

2 Charles E. McClelland, "Die deutschen Hochschullehrer als Elite, 1815–1850," in Klaus Schwabe, ed., *Deutsche Hochschullehrer als Elite, 1815–1945* (Boppard, 1988), p. 50.
3 Frank Eyck, *The Frankfurt Parliament, 1848–9* (London, 1968), p. 95; see also Heinrich Best, "Recruitment, Careers and Legislative Behavior of German Parliamentarians, 1848–1953," *Quantum Information*, 23 (1982): 26.

and "scientific" stance, but one tinged with a quasimessianic faith in the benefits of technology for German society. This and the fact that most of its members originally came from the private sector and thus could not be suspected of organizing government employees undoubtedly account for the survival and growth of the VDI in an environment otherwise hostile to professional organizations during the 1850s.

Another organization founded in the 1860s to represent a rapidly modernizing occupation (chemistry) was much more circumspect. The *Deutsche Chemische Gesellschaft* (German Chemical Society, or DCG), founded in 1867, was in fact a scientific body, although it would much later have an indirect impact on professional chemists.[4]

Two other national professional organizations of the 1850s might be contrasted to the VDI. The first, the *Verein Deutscher Tierärzte* (German Veterinary Association, or VDT), was founded in 1841; but it held its last national meeting in 1851 and fell apart subsequently in the climate of repression, not to reassemble again until the 1870s. The second, the *Allgemeiner Deutscher Apothekerverein* (General German Apothecary Association, or ADAV), grew out of a regional North German Apothecary Association (1821) which, during the 1848 revolution, tried to incorporate regional South German professional associations. The marriage, formalized in 1850, was however never consummated, because the organization continued to exist in two semiindependent organizations – again in reaction to official hostility to national professional leagues. The German apothecaries did not found a genuine national association until 1872. Both cases merely prove how difficult it was to found or maintain such associations in the 1850s.

A "new era" emerged in Prussia with the regency and then accession of King William I. Nationalism and liberalism were once again tolerated in Prussia, where a liberal parliament was elected. Abroad, first Russia, then Austria, the pillars of reaction in Europe, were shaken by defeats in the Crimean and Italian unification wars, respectively.

It was thus not entirely a coincidence that one further national organization emerged in Berlin in 1859 – the *Zentralverein Deutscher Zahnärzte* (Central Association of German Dentists – ZVDZAe). That was also the year when the German unification movement began to get new wind in its sails. Like the engineers, veterinarians, and apothecaries, the dentists practiced an occupation that had traditionally been a specialized trade rather than a learned profession. The perception by members of these occupations that they needed to organize and improve their standing vis-à-vis the traditional professions explains in part why they, rather than their more prestigious rivals, sought to band together in the 1850s.

4 Walter Ruske, *Hundert Jahre Deutsche Chemische Gesellschaft* (Weinheim, 1967), passim; "Constituierende Versammlung vom 11. November 1867," *Berichte der Deutschen Chemischen Gesellschaft*, 1 (1867): 1–12.

Of the traditional professions, only one – the legal profession as a whole – took tentative steps toward some form of nationwide forum with the first *Deutscher Juristentag* (Congress of German Jurists, or DJT) in 1860. This organization cannot, however, be regarded as a true representative of the whole range of professional interests of German attorneys, magistrates, government officials, and law professors who constituted its variegated membership. Its main purpose – and the founding date is here significant – was to prepare the way for the reform and codification of German law that a unified nation-state would require. Indeed, its first meeting, held in Berlin, was heavily subsidized by the Prussian king, and the delegates were invited en masse to a reception by Crown Prince Frederick, a sure sign of its political usefulness to Prussian's maneuvers in the "German Question."[5]

Thus the DJT was to the law what the Society of Scientists and Doctors was to medicine – a relatively neutral and multiprofessional organization dedicated to the advancement of legal reform.

But even if the older professions began thinking again of organizing nationally in the less stultifying climate of the 1860s, the sharpening rivalry between Prussia and Austria, between the *kleindeutsch* and *grossdeutsch* idea, made the very term "national association" an object of acrimonious debate. Only after Prussia's victories over Austria, which led to the founding of the North German Confederation in 1867, and of France, which resulted in the addition of the three South German states of Baden, Württemberg, and Bavaria to transform the Confederation into the German Reich in 1871, was there a "nation" around which to organize professions.

The history of failures, frustrations, or even tiny successes makes for tedious reading. Thus, it should suffice to discuss in this chapter principally the efforts of large and vocal occupational groups to reform their professional structure before, during, and after the 1848 Revolution. Two of the older professions – medicine and law – and two emerging ones – teaching and engineering – may exemplify the developments in the quarter century before German unification.

1. THE MEDICAL PROFESSION

One of the groups most vocal in its demands for change in professional standing and regulations in the 1840s was that of physicians. As noted in the last chapter, the typical division of officially sanctioned medical personnel into at least three groups and the continued existence of unlicensed practitioners hardly made for common interests in the "profession of medicine," if it can be called that.

The catalogue of complaints was a lengthy one, and in the course of the last half of the 1840s it became increasingly public. Anonymous pamphlets circu-

5 Thomas Olshausen, *Der deutsche Juristentag. Sein Werden und Wirken* (Berlin, 1910), p. 20.

lated with greater and greater frequency, calling for (or resisting) a host of particular changes. German doctors, particularly in the heavily urbanized areas of the Rhineland, were inspired by an unusual voluntary congress of French physicians in Paris in 1845. This had proposed a series of desiderata to the French government as it faced reforms in the laws regarding medicine. German doctors did not necessarily agree with all the demands of the French, but they emulated their foreign colleagues' example by calling for regional or even national congresses to discuss similar problems.

The question of *Medizinalreform* (medical reform) was neither simple nor purely an expression of the professionalizing needs of the leading physicians. It was not simply a clash between doctors and benighted governments; quite often the latter recognized the problems addressed by the physicians. Older doctors frequently resisted calls for congresses and organizations, remembering the constraints of guildlike regulations that had disappeared only decades before. Liberal physicians called for more freedom and autonomy; social reformers called for more government intervention to assure better distribution of health care. Indeed, most accounts agree that the low social esteem of the medical profession, coupled with radical doctors' despair at the mounting health problems of the masses, produced a distinctly "democratic" tinge in the whole issue of *Medizinalreform*.[6]

As mentioned in Chapter 3, one thing most reformers agreed upon was that the medical profession needed to be unified, and that the already declining division into *Aerzte* and *Wundärzte* should be abolished.[7] Not only should all physicians have the same high level of university training and examination, but "empirical" medical practitioners, ranging from village herbalists to shepherds, should be forbidden. Most physicians in private practice wanted to be treated as the equals of government-employed doctors, who often enjoyed unusual rights and privileges. (Government doctors, for understandable reasons, did not call for reforms nearly as much, presumably fearing for their positions.) Most also agreed that doctors in military service ought to have officers' rank, a significant issue when one considers that 15 percent of Prussian doctors served in the army.[8]

In other areas, however, opinions were divided. A perennial problem – lack of adequate medical care outside large cities – would be made worse if a monopoly were granted to university-trained physicians. These already congregated in large numbers where paying customers were, and – incredible though it seems in comparison to later times – some local medical associations

---

6 Kurt Finkenrath, *Die Medizinalreform. Die Geschichte der estern deutschen ärztlichen Standesbewegung* [*Studien zur Geschichte der Medizin*, Heft 17] (Leipzig, 1929), pp. 2–3.
7 Hans G. Wenig, *Medizinische Ausbildung im 19. Jahrhundert* (Dissertation, Medizinische Fakultät, University of Bonn, 1969), p. 68; Erwin Heinz Ackerknecht, "Beiträge zur Geschichte der Medizinalreform von 1848," *Sudhoffs Archiv,* 26 (1932): 113.
8 Finkenrath, *Medizinalreform,* pp. 11–15; Ackerknecht, "Beiträge," 119.

complained in the 1840s of an oversupply of doctors.[9] The logical solution seemed to be government restrictions on *Niederlassungsfreiheit* (which many German states in fact had), that is, on the physician's freedom to settle and move his practice anywhere. Yet other physicians called for the opposite.

Liberal physicians tended to request an end to most forms of government regulation.[10] But the cutthroat competition, principally in the cities, that would result from deregulation obviously frightened many established (and protected) doctors. To some degree, this clash reflected a generation conflict. In Bavaria, for example, young physicians had to wait an average of four to five years for a practice, and they were naturally eager to abolish limitations on their freedom to practice wherever and whenever they chose.[11]

Some social reformers correctly foresaw that liberalization would not solve the massive public-health problems of rural Germany. Even urban doctors complained about the difficulty of collecting fees from their patients; poor peasants were even less likely to be able to afford medical attention. A number of writers suggested in the 1840s that all doctors be made state officials with guaranteed incomes, and that a district doctor be appointed to treat the poor.[12]

Another area of lively discussion was educational reform. Most German doctors supported the requirement of a *Gymnasium* education as a prerequisite for medical study, and many criticized a too one-sided emphasis on merely medical study in universities, holding that a good doctor should also be a good humanist. University medical schools were sometimes criticized for hideboundness and nepotism, and some doctors went as far as to demand influence over professorial appointments by the wider profession.[13] The duration and consequently costs of a medical education were also a concern. One reformer calculated the minimum cost for obtaining an M.D. was 3,000 thalers, an amount that contradicted the high-minded claim of many reformers that medical education should be open to talent.[14]

If, before 1848, governments usually left brochures, petitions, and letters unanswered, they were nevertheless sometimes contemplating reforms of their own. This process was accelerated by the revolution in 1848. Throughout Germany, local medical societies called for statewide or national medical congresses to prepare a reform agendum. Despite some opposition from within the profession, most doctors apparently believed that some kind of permanent organization of the medical profession was necessary, although a tiny minority favored a mandatory, state-controlled *corporation* rather than a voluntary *association*.[15] Although there was no medical equivalent of the Frankfurt Parliament, a very lively periodical press sprang up with the abolition of censorship and devoted its columns principally to questions of reform.

9 Finkenrath, *Medizinalreform*, p. 35.   10 Ackerknecht, "Beiträge," 126–7.
11 Finkenrath, *Medizinalreform*, p. 38.
12 Ibid., pp. 38–41; Ackerknecht, "Beiträge," 138–47.   13 Wenig, *Ausbildung*, pp. 79–89.
14 Ibid., p. 85.   15 Ibid., p. 77; Finkenrath, *Medizinalreform*, pp. 43–4.

Prussia resisted the doctors' demand for a democratically elected Prussian medical congress, but it did hold one consisting of medical personnel appointed by the *Regierungspräsidenten* (regional governors) in June 1849. Despite careful selection of delegates, the congress occasionally voted against the wishes of the government officials who had summoned them. They resisted, for example, the suggestion that medical education be extended to five years and regulated by a minutely detailed study plan.[16]

Among other reforms, this congress proposed the elimination of all classes of doctors below those trained in universities, hiring of civilian doctors by the army, paid district physicians for the care of the poor, and the election of "honor councils" by all physicians for the purpose of resolving disputes and applying sanctions for unethical practice.[17] In most other respects, the existing system was retained.

The triumph of the counterrevolution in 1849 left the medical reform movement in abeyance. Many doctors were among the leaders of the last resistance and were subjected to harsh prison terms, including the later founder of the German Medical Association, Dr. Hermann Eberhard Richter.[18] Richter was not the only one to see in the failure of German physicians to unite a key weakness in the whole medical-reform movement. Virchow, in the last issue of his journal in 1849, wrote, "Nothing remains for doctors but to construct a system of associations on the greatest possible scale."[19]

The main reform to emerge was the unification of the medical profession in Prussia (by 1852) and the closing of schools for *Wundärzte*. Other states followed suit only later.

2. THE LEGAL PROFESSION

As mentioned in the introduction to this chapter, German attorneys had tried unsuccessfully to organize themselves before and during the 1848 Revolution. A first attempt in 1844 to hold a German Attorneys' Congress (*Deutscher Anwalttag*) in Mainz came to nought, partly because several large governments, including those of Prussia and Bavaria, forbade participation by their subjects. A second attempt in 1846 did take place, but it had to be held in the Freemasons' Lodge in the free city of Hamburg, after most other states had refused it hospitality. Hamburg was also host to a meeting of some one hundred and fifty delegates in 1847. A third was held under more auspicious circumstances during August 1848 in Dresden, and here a *Deutscher Anwaltverein* (Association of German Attorneys, or DAV) was formally founded. This and further national meetings were submerged in the post-1848 reaction, however. As one lawyer later wryly put it, the successful suppression of a national lawyers' association at

16 Wenig, *Ausbildung*, pp. 100–1.   17 Finkenrath, *Medizinalreform*, pp. 47–8.
18 Ibid., p. 57.   19 Virchow, *Die medicinische Reform* 52 (1849): 1.

this time proved "that German disunity was a myth: Germany was completely unified against the dreadful danger of attorneys' congresses."[20]

The program of these early meetings was liberal and national in tone, if not particularly radical. Points under discussion referred to the state of the profession, but in a broader sense, the central aim was a thoroughgoing reform and unification of the German legal system. Among the major reforms discussed were the introduction of press freedom, public court sessions, juries, and oral rather than written court proceedings. Opinions were divided on such practical questions as whether the office of attorney should be made independent of state regulation and open to free market competition. But clearly the notion of the *freie Advokatur*, or independent legal profession, had many powerful spokesmen.[21]

As in so many other areas, the conservative governments of the post-1848 period, having persecuted and reviled the activists, proceeded to introduce many of the demands of the attorneys piecemeal before 1870. The widely admired cornerstone of Anglo-American justice, the jury system, made serious inroads into German courts through reforms of the various states' curial codes down to 1870. Presenting evidence and arguments to juries required abandoning to some degree the ancient practice of purely written briefs and made the old office of *Prokurator* increasingly superfluous. More and more states allowed the *Advokat* to plead directly before the court and thus undermined the distinction, still present in the English courts today, between barrister and solicitor. The new word *Rechtsanwalt* or, simply, attorney came to replace the older terms for the various court functions.

A further problem was that many "advocates" under the old systems had not been required to undergo the same training as the "procurators," since they did not formerly appear before and were not required to match knowledge of the finer points of law with the sitting magistrates. If the *Rechtsanwalt* was to appear in court, however, many argued that he would have to have the same university training and examinations as future judges.

Although these reforms of the 1850s and 1860s satisfied many of the demands of German attorneys, the particularistic and piecemeal way in which they were carried out state by state pointed to a remaining central deficiency that was addressed by the failed Congress of German Attorneys of the 1840s: the lack of a unified legal system for Germany.

This lack, plus the relaxation of government disapproval, called into being the *Deutscher Juristentag* mentioned in the introduction to this chapter. Beginning in 1860, under the official patronage of the Prussian crown, this organization of judges, attorneys, and law professors met every year or two to debate, resolve, and present to German governments principles for legal reform.

20 Weissler, *Rechtsanwaltschaft*, pp. 514–22.   21 Ibid., pp. 520–1.

Typically, the DJT was dominated by judges, high officers of the juridical bureaucracy, and law academics. The three presidents of the DJT in the 1860s were all law professors (C. G. von Wächter, Leipzig; J. C. Bluntschli, Munich and Heidelberg; and R. von Gneist, Berlin), and no mere attorney presided until 1931.[22] Perhaps because of its distinguished leaders, however, the DJT had a considerable influence on the shaping of the German law system.

In the first decade of its existence, the DJT debated and resolved a long series of reforms that need not concern us here, but the tenor of which was broadly in keeping with contemporary liberal thinking – for example, the independence of judges and states' attorneys, the validity of civil marriage, improvements in the property rights of minors and women, and the abolition of the death penalty. Resolutions concerning the legal profession as such were less prominent at this time.

Still, the DJT called for a number of measures affecting the professionalization of the law. These included combining procuracy and advocacy, making attorneys into a "free profession" (*freie Advokatur*), creating *Anwaltskammern* (attorneys' chambers) to regulate the resulting private practitioners of law, and the right of lawyers to settle and move where they wished.[23]

A series of resolutions in 1863 took aim at legal education and certification. These sought to assure the freedom of teaching and learning law, including the right of students to study at any German university and take whatever courses they wished. They sought to guarantee that examinations would be stiffened and administered by parity commissions representing practitioners – judges and attorneys – in addition to government officials.[24]

All these resolutions pointed toward emancipating the lawyer from the restrictions of a closed training, certification, and employment system. Departing from such a system of course threatened the fairly secure incomes of the existing attorneys, who had been used since the early nineteenth century to a kind of monopoly in their judicial districts. But as Rudolf von Gneist, one of the leading men of the DJT, argued in an influential 1867 pamphlet, Germany had far too few lawyers for the development of a free society.

Gneist pointed out that Prussia in 1867 had only one attorney to roughly 12,000 inhabitants, a figure that had not changed significantly for thirty years. At the same time, the ratios in Britain, France, and Belgium were 1:2,500, 1:1,970, and 1:1,800, respectively.[25] Even if the lawyers' emancipation

---

22 Ernst von Caemmerer, *Hundert Jahre deutsches Rechtsleben* (Karlsruhe, 1960), vol. 2, pp. 45–7.
23 Olshausen, *Juristentag*, pp. 24–9.
24 [Oberlandesgerichtsrat Thomsen, ed.], *Gesammtbericht über die Taetigkeit des Deutschen Juristentags in den 25 Jahren seines Bestehens. 1860–1885*, (Berlin, 1885), pp. 41–2; *Verhandlungen des Deutschen Juristentages* 4 (1863): 152–87.
25 Rudolf von Gneist, *Die freie Advokatur* (Berlin, 1867), pp. 18–22, 67–70.

from restrictions might cause intense competition, Gneist argued, that would be limited in scope; and even if some attorneys had to become municipal officials, journalists, etc., it would be good for the nation.[26]

It is worth noting that the free-market approach advanced by German liberals, and their confidence that liberty was best for the profession, would not have been greeted with complete accord by American lawyers at the time. Democratic pressures since the Age of Jackson had placed American lawyers under great strain, so that the organized legal profession had crumbled apart. American lawyers called for a national legal organization as a way out of their problems, and the American Bar Association was thus founded in 1878.[27]

Even as Gneist wrote, the North German Confederation was becoming a reality. A new constitution was being forged in a tug-of-war between German liberals and the older principles of German statehood represented by the Prussian bureaucracy and Count Bismarck. The capacity of the newly born German *Rechtsstaat* (state based on laws) to integrate all classes in a dynamically developing community was doubted by few of Gneist's liberal contemporaries. The task of unifying a millennium of particularistic Germanic law with a half millennium of generalizing Roman law, creating a national system of penal, property, business, and constitutional jurisprudence, and harmonizing the rights of the citizen with the duties of the bureaucracy did not seem insuperable to Gneist or the DJT in the 1860s. In all of this, a free and independent judiciary, open courts, clear written laws produced by an elected parliament, and a large and active body of attorneys seemed the wave of the future.

3. THE TEACHING PROFESSION

The general hostility faced by organizational efforts among German professions before and immediately after the turbulent years of the 1848 Revolution was, if anything, mild when compared with government reactions to similar efforts by teachers.

A reform movement among teachers was, to be sure, a matter of greater worry to state officials than almost any other group of public employees. First, there were so many more schoolteachers by 1848 than senior civil servants, doctors, or attorneys that any effective organization, particularly one transcending sovereign frontiers, would be a sizeable force. Second, effective organization might accelerate one of the main reform demands of all teachers – higher pay – and make a difficult fiscal situation impossible. Perhaps most importantly, however, most German governments in the 1840s demonstrated a remarkable fear of the ability of schoolteachers somehow to stir up enough oppositional sentiment to being on revolutionary upheavals, an attitude that was only reinforced by the 1848 Revolution.

26 Ibid., pp. 88–90.
27 Roscoe Pound, *The Lawyer from Antiquity to Modern Times* (St. Paul, Minn., 1953), p. 254.

Not even regional teachers' leagues were exempt from the suspicion of the authorities. Bavaria's teacher associations were dissolved by government decree in 1832, for example, as "neither appropriate nor permissible."[28] A decade later, the conservative Prussian education minister Eichhorn used the crude, if effective, circular argument that teachers' associations would only want to discuss their low pay, and such discussions would have a negative effect on government officials like himself, who were in the process of thinking about raising teachers' pay; thus *in the teachers' own interest*, such associations were forbidden![29]

Even in some of the more liberal German states, where schoolteachers' associations were tolerated, their complaints rarely fell on fruitful ground. The Württemberg Elementary Schoolteachers Association (*Württembergischer Volksschullehrerverein*) was founded in 1840 (not atypically, by a number of young teaching seminar graduates) and had 1,700 members by 1846. Their pleas were quite typical for those of other German elementary schoolteachers, as reflected in a petition to the royal government in 1844: salary increases, a right to a pension, abolition of sextons' duties for teachers, and representation on the local church council (i.e. school board).[30] Such pleas earned them only the scorn of the government; the king himself high-handedly cancelled a planned salary raise weeks before the 1848 Revolution because some of them had shown a lack of loyalty during elections. Members of the state diet argued against salary increases because schoolteachers were already getting above their station and "losing touch with the pupils" because of their exalted seminar training.[31]

The schoolteachers in Prussia, to take another example, were still 79 percent rural in 1848; their reform program, implying a rapid increase in the social and professional level of school teaching (but also by implication of the peasant masses to be taught), was often misunderstood or even considered "absurdly ambitious" by nonteachers.[32] To conservatives, the message of Adolf Diesterweg, the great agitator for school reform from the late 1830s on, was not only the emancipation of the teacher, but of the masses as well. (It might be added that some recent historians have, somewhat unconvincingly, argued that such reformers as Diesterweg were really attempting to achieve the "integration of the proletariat" into a budding industrial system.)[33]

Not all schoolteachers saw themselves as missionaries with the goal of raising up the ignorant and suffering masses through better education – the Enlightenment agendum – and many indeed stood loyally by the conservative principle

28 Robert Rissmann, *Geschichte des deutschen Lehrervereins* (Leipzig, 1882), p. 7.   29 Ibid.
30 Gerd Friedrich, *Die Volksschule in Württemberg im 19. Jahrhundert.* [*Studien und Dokumentationen zur deutschen Bildungsgeschichte*, vol. 6] (Weinheim/Basel, 1978), pp. 103–4.
31 Ibid., p. 200.   32 LaVopa, *Schoolteachers*, pp. 81–2.
33 See Hartmut Titze, *Die Politisierung der Erziehung* (Frankfurt, 1973), passim; in rebuttal, Kenneth Barkin, "Social Control and the Volksschule in Vormärz Prussia," *Central European History* 16 (1983): 31–52.

that a firm grounding in Christian doctrine was the basis of all good teaching. But virtually all teachers felt underpaid and unrecognized. On these points, and not on philosophical ones, they could rally around a common cause by the 1840s.

As one early sociological study of Saxon schoolteachers concluded, by 1845 they had an idea of the profession, a virtually universal professional education, a concept of a minimal common living standard, a professional press, and a consciousness of the value, dignity, and need for solidarity of their profession. They only lacked organizations and leadership that would press the professionalizing project.[34] They also lacked a career ladder, any serious degree of professional autonomy, a professional monopoly (de facto is not de jure), or even a full-time occupation, because schoolteachers often still had to scrape by with nonpedagogical jobs on the side. But teachers were beginning to clamor for those things, as the 1848 Revolution made clear. The realization of these increasingly articulated demands constituted their professionialization agenda.

Low incomes naturally did not attract the best and brightest into teaching, and the social recruitment into the field was almost exclusively from the peasantry and artisanate, if not from schoolmasters' families themselves.[35] Even though training courses and examinations had become more rigorous and salaries (not adjusted for inflation) may have improved a bit in the decade before 1848, the increasingly vigorous schoolteachers' press complained more bitterly than ever about their low pay and low respect in the community. Neither condition was likely to attract gentlemen into the profession; and the perceived status gap between community leaders (such as university-educated civil servants, doctors, lawyers, and clergy) and the *Volksschullehrer* (elementary schoolteacher) remained wide throughout the rest of the century.

There remained also a considerable gap between the schoolteachers and their academically trained colleagues in the "higher schools," for example, the *Gymnasium* and similar schools requiring university training of their teachers. Better unified in their educational and social background than schoolteachers, and generally less restive in the 1840s, higher schoolteachers nevertheless suffered economic privation and a nagging sense of being second-class citizens in a privileged world of civil servants.

The first national organization encompassing higher schoolteachers, the *Versammlung Deutscher Philologen und Schulmänner* (Congress of German Philologists and Schoolmen, or VDPSM, 1837), was, as mentioned in Chapter 3, principally a scholarly organization. Even it broke apart in 1843, when the teachers at *Realschulen* were accused of "materialism" because their institutions emphasized such crass subjects as mathematics and modern languages. If recapitula-

---

34 Alfred Zieger, *Schulmeister, Schullehrer, Volksschullehrer: das Werden des Lehrerstandes in Sachsen* (Langensalza, 1933), pp. 158–9.

35 For examples from Prussia and Württemberg, see LaVopa, *Schoolteachers*, p. 71; Friedrich, *Volksschule*, table 8.

tions of the battle of the "ancients" and "moderns" could shatter even a scholarly association, one can well imagine that mere elementary schoolteachers were welcomed by neither of the successor groups.

Teachers at *Gymnasien* often had reason to be relatively satisfied. Their schools were usually state (as opposed to municipal) institutions with the possibility of mobility (promotion or transfer); and even if salaries (500 to 1200 thaler per year in Prussia in the 1850s)[36] were lower than for other state employees with university training, they were at least paid regularly, something not guaranteed in municipal schools. Even so, the urban *Gymnasium* of the pre-revolutionary era was probably much closer to serving the educational needs of all urban social groups than it would be half a century later, when it was much more an "elite" school.[37] Perhaps because of this, the idea of a teachers' organization embracing all types of pedagogues was not as illusory at the time as it would seem to later generations.

The revolution of 1848 brought a whirlwind of demands for school reform and professional organization. One of the most interesting organizational steps was the foundation of the *Allgemeiner Deutscher Lehrerverein* (General German Teachers Association, or ADLV), the first such national body, and regional teachers' associations where they did not yet exist or had been suppressed. The ADLV represented chiefly the interests of schoolteachers, although it was founded as an organization for instructors in all types of schools.[38] Putting forward the more radical demands of the Diesterweg "liberators," it called for an educational system under state control from top to bottom, implying a "nationalization" of all schools and the "liberation" of teachers from local parental and community controls. It also pushed the idea of the *Einheitsschule,* or unified school, an idea that would not be taken up again until after the collapse of the German monarchy in 1918 and then again in the 1960s. This unified and comprehensive school would, in the view of Diesterweg's followers replace the hierarchical and class-riven one that had grown up organizationally in the nineteenth century.

One recent study has estimated that less than one percent of schoolteachers took an active part in the revolutionary events of 1848, and certainly the ADLV's program went far beyond the more modest wishes of a very large part of the profession.[39] The coolness of higher schoolteachers to such unified organizations, doubts of pious Christians about trends toward de-emphasizing religious instruction, timidity and geographical isolation in the countryside were all good reasons for the ADLV to have failed. But government hostility in the

36 Mellmann, *Philologenverband,* p. 5.
37 Margret Kraul, *Gymnasium und Gesellschaft im Vormärz [Studien zum Wandel von Gesellschaft und Bildung im 19. Jahrhundert,* 18] (Göttingen, 1980), pp. 147–52.
38 Ilse Gahlings, *Die Volksschullehrer und ihre Berufsverbände* (Neuwied, 1967), p. 63.
39 Ibid.; Douglas R. Skopp, "Auf der untersten Sprosse: Der Volksschullehrer als 'Semi-Professional' im Deutschland des 19. Jahrhunderts," *Geschichte und Gesellschaft,* 6 (1980): 400.

period of reaction hobbled it with further disadvantages. It led only a shadowy existence thereafter and may have done as much by its positions to split the schoolteachers' movement as to strengthen it.

In addition, the reactionaries of the early 1850s used the carrot-and-stick technique to discipline any remaining teachers who might think of resorting to joining independent teachers' professional associations. On the one hand, teachers (and especially the training "seminars" that had produced so many lively young spokesmen for teachers' demands) were accused of being virtually the seedbeds of the revolution; on the other hand, good behavior was rewarded with promises and sometimes even actions toward improving individual salary and other working conditions.[40]

The further professionalization of the German teachers could and did emanate from the state. Small reforms were carried out even before 1870 that reduced the wide gaps between one man and another calling himself "teacher." In Bavaria, for example, the privileged position of theology students wishing to enter higher school teaching was abolished; henceforth they had to take the same *Lehramtsprüfung* (examination for the office of teacher) as other university graduates.[41] Steps amounting to the same result were also taken in Württemberg in 1865.[42]

On another front, the legal position of at least higher schoolteachers as *Beamte* became clearer; Prussia began the process of defining them so in 1852.[43] Far from seeing in "bureaucratization" a step toward lessening their autonomy, most teachers evidently viewed such a process as desirable and liberating. Although this was not achieved by the (elementary) schoolteachers, who resented chiefly clerical supervision, it was achieved by most higher schoolteachers, who wished to escape from the control of the communities in which they lived. "The higher schoolteachers unreservedly recognized the state of the nineteenth century as much as the guarantor of educational freedom that a serious conflict of loyalties, an unbridgeable difference between service to the state and to education, did not seem imaginable."[44]

Here and there attempts were made to raise teachers' salaries modestly, as in the Prussian *Stellenetat* ("position budget") of 1863. This resulted in considerable increases for some *Gymnasium* directors, but only modest ones for their teachers, and it had no effect on the urban *Realschule* teachers.[45] To be sure, such half-hearted efforts could divide teachers against each other. As one remembered, the new budget system allowed for promotion only with the death (or in the absence of pensions, unlikely retirement) of a colleague. "At that

40 Skopp, "Sprosse," 400.   41 Romberg, *Staat und höhere Schule,* p. 489.
42 Ibid., p. 497.   43 Ibid., p. 513.   44 Ibid., p. 521.
45 Wilhelm Lexis, *Die Besoldungsverhältnisse der Lehrer an den höheren Unterrichtsanstalten Preussens* (Jena, 1898), pp. 15–17.

time, the 'dear colleagues' accompanied the esteemed Departed to his last resting place with one weeping and one laughing eye, since there was now a possibility of promotion."[46]

4. THE ENGINEERING PROFESSION

The successful effort of engineers to organize themselves on a national footing in 1856 in the VDI contrasts, on first glance, with the failure of most other efforts before then. There are several reasons for such success. At the same time, one must be careful to place this "milestone" in professionalization in the correct historical context.

The relative lack of governmental opposition to the VDI has several obvious roots. Long-standing governmental policies had attempted to foster technology and industrialization, and any help from the private sector was welcome. The engineers who founded the VDI were primarily mechanical engineers and hence largely involved in private enterprise. Unlike doctors, lawyers, clergymen, and teachers, they had little direct connection with the state. Thus, their attempts to affiliate nationally did not engender the appearance of subverting state authority over regulated professions. Technology knew no political frontiers. The VDI was avowedly apolitical and interested chiefly in the advancement of technology and its benefits to society.

Second, even highly conservative German governments were not opposed to economic and technological progress. This had been the theme of the Crystal Palace Exhibition of 1851, the first great world's fair of the industrial age. German exhibitors participated in it, but the generally low quality of their products aroused considerable official concern about German technical backwardness. More exchange of technical information among German engineers could thus do no harm from the viewpoint of the bureaucracy.

The VDI, it should be added, initially embraced chiefly small manufacturers and industrial or mechanical engineers who up to then had found no institutional home. There already existed in several German states and regions associations of other kinds of engineers, such as the oldest, the Berlin *Architekten- und Ingenieurverein*, and others in four other cities.[47] These were however rather exclusive in membership, representing chiefly the technical and architectural cadres of the civil service. The VDI was much more open, and even nonengineers interested in furthering the intellectual and scientific bases of technology could join.

---

46 Mellmann, *Philologenverband*, p. 6.
47 Lars U. Scholl, "Der Ingenieur in Ausbildung, Beruf und Gesellschaft, 1856–1881," in Karl-Heinz Ludwig, ed., *Technik, Ingenieure und Gesellschaft. Geschichte des Vereins Deutscher Ingenieure, 1856–1981* (Düsseldorf, 1981), p. 49.

Still, the VDI stood on a higher plane of interest in "scientific" technology and education than the majority of "engineers" (*Ingenieure und Techniker*) at the time. "Engineer" was still a term with primarily military overtones, and the VDI founders wanted to underline the existence of "civil engineering."[48] Indeed, they were largely graduates of the Berlin Royal Industrial Institute (*Königliches Gewerbeinstitut*), which was reorganized in the 1820s under the influence of C. P. W. Beuth to give a more scientifically based education to Prussian industrial personnel. Reorganized again in 1850, it came more and more to resemble a technical college of a high order. The VDI was always interested in raising the level of technical education and the exchange of technical and scientific information. Its founding statement pointed to the need for "an intense cooperation of the intellectual forces of German technology for mutual stimulation and continuing education in the interests of all Germany's industry."[49]

Another point was the inclusion of all German engineers in one organization, an aim never quite achieved. But it was not quite a "professional organization" striving to represent the interests of all engineers. On the contrary, its self-understanding at the outset was closer to that of the *Versammlung Deutscher Naturforscher and Aerzte*, only on the basis of "applied science".[50]

If the founders of the VDI did not initially view it as an organization needing to fight for improvement in the lot of engineers, this may have been because of a naive faith in the need of a technologically expanding society for their services, as seemed then to be the case in industrially advanced England.[51] The original high-minded concern for raising and spreading technical knowledge also inclined the founders of the VDI to shun connections with other engineering organizations that had more self-interested goals, such as the *Verein für Eisenhüttenwesen*. This "Association for Ironworking" was originally accepted into the VDI in 1861 not like the regional associations that made up the infrastructure but as an associated specialist group. But the *Verein Deutscher Eisenhütterleute* (Association of German Ironfounders, or VDEh, as the subgroup later named itself) seceded from the VDI because both groups believed the VDI did and should not promote the economic interests of the iron and steel industry by taking positions on tariffs and similar "political" issues.[52]

The VDI did grow steadily from 1856 until 1871, and it came to be the largest organization of German engineers. With only 172 members at the beginning, it counted over 1,900 by the later date. At first, however, this growth was largely restricted to areas of industrial concentration, such as the Rhineland, Silesia, and Saxony. The wars of the mid-1860s also set back growth somewhat.[53]

---

48 Hans Schimank, *Der Ingenieur. Entwicklungsweg eines Berufes bis Ende des 19. Jahrhunderts* (Cologne, 1961), p. 36.
49 *VDI–Zeitschrift*, 1 (1857): 4.
50 Gerd Hortleder, *Das Gesellschaftsbild des Ingenieurs* (Frankfurt, 1970), p. 20.
51 Scholl, "Ingenieur in Ausbildung," p. 18.   52 Ibid., pp. 21–2.   53 Ibid., p. 25.

Growth brought with it changes in the occupational and social origin of the members. Some 65 percent were originally engineers, about 22 percent teachers, and only 9 percent and 4 percent respectively, were craftsmen and entrepreneurs. These proportions changed quickly, however, in the first years: by 1865 they were 52 percent engineers, 28 percent entrepreneurs, 13 percent technical directors of enterprises, and only 3 percent and 2 percent respectively, teachers and craftsmen.[54] During most of its first quarter century, the VDI's membership followed this general pattern, with engineers predominating but with entrepreneurs prominent.[55]

Factory owners and managers were much more prominent in some of the *Bezirksvereine* (regional associations) at the VDI's base. For example, they constituted 43 percent of the members in the Pfalz/Saarbrücken region and even 58 percent in Magdeburg.[56] The latter regional association was originally founded by local mill owners with the idea of pooling the common interests of competitors, in this case something as mundane as the standardization of nuts and bolts in machine manufacturing.[57]

The leadership of the national VDI, on the other hand, was dominated by teachers and engineers, not by industrialists.[58]

Considering its origins and early boards of directors, it is not surprising that the VDI spent a considerable amount of energy from the beginning on questions of reform in technical education. Even though the lower and secondary technical schools of Germany were already widely admired abroad, the VDI believed a good beginning must be expanded vertically, horizontally, qualitatively, and quantitatively. In the view of Franz Grashof, one of the most active VDI officers of this period, the importance of technical schooling "lay in the fact that Germany must substitute better training of her engineers for the material advantages of better situated industrial countries."[59]

In the mid-1860s, for example, the VDI set up a commission to prepare suggestions for German governments on the optimal reforms in technical education. In fact, the main point was the upgrading of "polytechnical schools" into technical colleges on a par with universities. The majority of this board consisted of engineering teachers (some of whom were also practitioners), but it spoke to the issue of better qualifications for German engineering graduates as well as the more diffuse issue of raising their social status by equating their studies with those at a university.[60] The "principles" formulated by this

54 Wolfgang Jonas, *Die Geschichte des Vereins deutscher Ingenieure bis 1880* (Habilitationsschrift, Wirtschaftswissenschaftliche Fakultät, Humboldt University of Berlin, 1962), p. 100.
55 Scholl, "Ingenieur in Ausbildung," p. 26.
56 Jonas, *Geschichte des VDI*, p. 104; Hortleder, *Gesellschaftsbild*, p. 23.
57 *VDI–Zeitschrift*, 2 (1858): 280.
58 Jonas, *Geschichte des VDI*, p. 102; Hortleder, *Gesellschaftsbild*, p. 27.
59 Scholl, "Ingenieur in Ausbildung," p. 31; Franz Grashof's reform proposals were reprinted in the *VDI–Zeitschrift*, 8 (1864): 591ff. and 9 (1865): 703ff.
60 Scholl, "Ingenieur in Ausbildung," p. 33.

commission, based on Grashof's ideas, were adopted unanimously and without discussion at the 1865 meeting of the VDI and were passed on to German governments, schools, and industries.

It is perhaps significant for the "professionalizing project" that the VDI attacked the educational problem closest to its members' hearts – the "academization" of the highest level of training – while relatively neglecting the reform of the "lower" technical education system, because its graduates were considered to be "mere" skilled operatives. Indeed, the lack of broader scientific (and general) education in the *Gewerbeschulen* and *Werkmeisterschulen* (trade and foreman schools) disturbed the VDI, which seemed lukewarm to them. When Prussia abolished its *Gewerbeschulen* and turned them into *Oberrealschulen* (higher realistic schools) in the 1870s, it did so largely without the input of the VDI, which had let this aspect of educational reform slumber. In areas of higher educational reform, however, the VDI was very active – and heeded by governments.[61]

One obvious reason for the concern of the engineers in private practice to raise the level of technical higher education was to open careers in the civil service: "The academically trained engineer, if he became a government official, did not want to be treated in rank or respect as an inferior to graduates of mining or forestry academies . . . ."[62] But it would be after the unification of Germany before such concern about *Standesfragen* (professional questions) became fully articulate.

Thus the VDI, in its beginnings, became one of the largest and most dynamic of the early German national professional organizations because it did not threaten the established professional order (despite its avowed nationalism), and because its early self-understanding was specifically not that of an *Interessenvertretung des Standes,* a lobby for the promotion of the special economic and status interests of engineers as such. It would tend more toward that as it grew and developed in the last quarter of the century, replicating a common pattern with German professional organizations.

5. CONCLUSION

Simple statements about the professionalizing process in Central Europe during the quarter century or so before 1870 are most difficult to make: the persistence of particularism and tradition, disparate policies of nearly forty governments large and small, rapidly growing regional variations in social and economic change, and the differential impact of *Wissenschaft* on various occupations all militate against generalization.

From the perspective of embryo national professional organizations, it was, generally, a time of frustrated hope, as we have seen. The national idea was still associated mostly with liberal, nationalist, and even democratic forces and thus

61 Ibid., pp. 35–6.   62 Schimank, *Ingenieur,* p. 39.

viewed as dangerous by conservative governments. Even strictly local professional organizations, ones that did not overtly burst the confines of the German states' jealously guarded sovereignty, were more tolerated than welcomed by state bureaucracies that persisted in thinking of learned professional groups as objects of rather than partners in regulation. Organizations that did survive, such as the *Verein Deutscher Ingenieure* and the *Juristentag,* were cautious in the extreme about appearing to promote *Standesinteressen,* the "selfish interests" of specific occupational groups. Instead, they attempted to reinforce already extant goals even of conservative governments, such as expanding technical progress in industry and (in the case of the DJT) harmonizing legal codes, including commercial law.

From the perspective of overall change, however, this period was far from sterile. Many German states did make significant reforms in the conditions involving professions. The differences in training, certification, status, and remuneration of many professions, for example, physicians, lawyers, and even schoolteachers, which had been such a barrier to unification of single professional groups, became palpably diminished. The second-rank category of *Wundarzt,* for example, began to disappear; more and more primary schoolteachers attended rigorous training seminars; and the profession of *Gymnasium* teacher came to rest in fact on a relatively homogeneous training in philology and auxiliary fields within the philosophical faculties at universities.

These steps toward a more uniform professional socialization, while yet far from complete, helped create a frame of reference for professionals across Germany before a German state even existed. The lack of such a common reference ground before had been a major impediment to the organization of individual professions.

Even the attempts to organize professional groups, whether they failed in the face of governmental opposition or not, encountered in this period a great deal of indifference or confusion on the part of their potential members. As meetings held in 1848 showed, during a time of minimal governmental constraint, only a minority of professionals participated, and even then they disagreed vociferously with each other. As voluminous as the literature on medical reform was, for example, most of it appeared as randomly published brochures and pamphlets; there was as yet no organized publishing system to serve as a universal forum for such discussions. In a period of slow communications, before the railroad and telegraph had begun to cover Germany, even the leaders of national professional organizations had often been strangers to each other until meeting face to face for the first time at regional and national conferences.

This inexperience and uncertainly in how to go about something so radically new may be illustrated by an anecdote from the first meeting of the Congress of German Attorneys in 1846. Some eighty-five lawyers sat listening to an opening speech by the president of the conference, the Leipzig attorney P. Römisch, who suggested the need for greater exchange and, to that end, a

national journal. His speech was greeted by confused silence. In order to bring
to life his colleagues (most of them unused to public debate because of the
written nature of court procedure up to then), another organizer of the conference, Wilhelm Heckscher (later foreign minister of the 1848 Frankfurt government), took the floor. He moved the group vote on "whether anything practical
can be achieved by such conferences." In the end, the shocked delegates did
begin to debate, although they never voted on the motion of the "devil's
advocate."[63]

The process of professionalization includes, in the language of sociology, re-
thinking and redefining roles. In this sense, the (largely undocumented) activities of leaders of several professions in Germany down to 1870 were evidently
most effective. Exactly a quarter century after Heckscher's desperate ploy, when
the Association of German Attorneys was founded, its delegates would not sit in
confused silence. In the interim, issues had been defined, even though open
national forums had not been readily available to debate them.

63 Weissler, *Rechtsanwaltschaft*, p. 518.

PART III

Unified professions in a unified Germany?

5

The organization of the "free" professions:
medicine, law, engineering, and chemistry

The unification of the German Empire in 1871 not only opened a new era in European history; it created radically new conditions for the German professions as well. Under these conditions the professions were able to organize and find their own voices as never before. The contemporaneous rapid transformation of Germany into an industrialized, urbanized country with a rapidly growing population (and an even more rapidly growing cadre of professionals) brought ineluctable forces of change to bear on the professions, too, in the decades following the *Reichsgründung*. Quantitative changes, such as the growth of employment possibilities for professionals, were often accompanied by qualitative changes, such as heightened competition within the professions, new types of professional working conditions, and nagging concern about the status of professionals in the rapidly shifting structure of German society.

It should be recalled at the outset that the German Empire created in 1871 was hardly a monolithic new nation-state, but initially an extension of the North German Confederation of 1867 to include the three South German states of Bavaria, Württemberg and Baden. It was not entirely German, because large ethnic minorities lived within its frontiers – notably French in the west, Danes in the north, and Poles in the east. It was an empire in that it had a hereditary emperor in the House of Hohenzollern. But it also remained a confederation of kings and other princes, with three ancient urban republics. Prussia dominated the Confederation, politically, demographically, and economically; but the other states retained considerable autonomous rights, in some cases (e.g. Bavaria) more than most countries could reconcile with national sovereignty.

The empire changed over its lifetime. Central government grew and took on more and more duties. But under the very complex national constitution, competencies remained split between central government and the various states. This tension was particularly apparent in matters concerning the professions.

A few examples may suffice to demonstrate the resultant confusion. The central government (Reich) was held to be responsible for common commercial matters such as coinage, weights, and measures, external tariffs, and the regulation of some trades. For reasons requiring further explanation below, this competence was extended to the medical profession in part; but the several states retained many other important rights over their doctors. For another set of complex reasons, the Reich regulated the framework of the legal profession. But it would not touch similar frameworks for teachers at all levels, clergymen, engineers, chemists, architects, or military officers. Decisions of this kind were not made on clear-cut constitutional grounds, but rather on the basis of ad hoc arrangements in many cases.

It should also be recalled that the German Empire developed socially and economically at vastly different rates in its various regions. The rural regions in eastern parts of the Kingdom of Prussia and Mecklenburg changed little; Prussia's newer Rhenish territories became an industrial powerhouse. The Junker class retained much of its power and conservative influence in Prussia, while a Bavarian nobleman quietly led his state's Social Democratic Party (SPD). The urban working class emerged as a potent oppositional force, alternately wooed and excoriated by government. Catholics and Jews, the religious minorities, similarly experienced outbursts of official or unofficial defamation that alternated or coexisted with accommodation. Historians of Germany have tried for at least a century to describe this complex and contradictory Reich, but none has been able to convince the others.

Whatever were the attitudes of the "outsiders" in the new German Reich – ethnic minorities, Catholics, Jews, socialists, particularists, radical liberals, and pacifists – German professional organizations appear to have accepted the new state with feelings of hope and even gratitude. In this they did not differ from the larger German *Bildungsbürgertum,* for whose liberal and national sentiments many professionals had provided leadership in past decades, as we have seen. By the turn of the century, however, one can detect a clear dissatisfaction with what the Reich had done for the professionals, coupled with an abiding hope that things would change for the better. As citizens, professionals undoubtedly remained deeply loyal to the German Empire. But as members of professional organizations, or even as separate practitioners, they displayed many signs of feeling they had not been accorded the place in German society that they considered appropriate to their skills and contributions.

The first years of the German Empire witnessed a hectic pace of economic activity and speculation which has given its sobriquet to the period generally – the *Gründerjahre,* or "founding years." For the German professions, however, the whole era of the German Empire may be called the *Gründerjahre.* Virtually all of the main groups of German professions organized or reorganized themselves in this period. The main professions were particularly active in the two decades following 1871.

If one can make a not completely irrelevant parallel, the German professions faintly followed at a two-decade remove the larger trends in German economic organization. As the German economic *Gründer* coalesced into larger combines and interest groups, the German professions broke down into more and more specialized and sectoral groups. Similarly, by the eve of World War I, well after the commanding heights of the German economy had come to be dominated by cartels, the professions began to cooperate in modest ways.

As we saw in Chapter 4, one of the main impediments to national professional organizations before 1871 lay in the suspicion and hostility of German governments toward them. Once the "German Question" was (temporarily) solved in 1871, there could be no further serious objection to such organizations. What had previously been perceived as a threat to the sovereignty of the various German states now could be cloaked in the mantle of patriotic duty. This is not to say that the Reich government gave any kind of direct stimulus to new national organizations; but it did protect the right to create them. And many governmental actions indirectly provoked such creations. The *Reichsgewerbeordnung* (Reich Commercial Law) of 1869, for example, redefined the framework of the medical profession and thus led to the creation of the *Deutscher Aerztevereinsverband* (German Medical Association, or DAeV) in 1873. A few years later, the Reich *Rechtsanwaltsordnung,* or Attorneys' Law, did the same for the German bar, which had already organized itself into a voluntary *Deutscher Anwaltsverein,* or Association of German Attorneys, in 1871, only weeks after national unification.

These two associations joined the VDI as national representative organizations of the "free" (service-for-fee) professions, although that term was not much used at the time. Like engineers from the outset, physicians and lawyers had been "disestablished" by the legislation mentioned above. Matters stood somewhat differently with those professionals who were still largely dependent upon public employment, for example, teachers and clergymen, civil servants, and many engineers and architects. These groups were understandably slower to organize, or as in the case of teachers, to assert themselves boldly.

Higher civil servants of all types were still a favored elite in the German Empire and had little reason to complain of their status. This was even truer of military officers. Both groups were furthermore carefully selected for their loyalty to state and corps. Indeed, the principal reason for mentioning the military establishment at all in this chapter has less to do with any desire on its part to organize and lobby for itself than because of its ability to touch on the life of German professionals through the institution of the *Einjährig-Freiwilligen,* or civilian reserve officers.

Despite the Prussian and German army reforms of the early nineteenth century, the principle of the "educated officer" had been successfully undermined by the aristocratic officer corps, at least until 1890. Bavaria was the only state to require an *Abitur* of its officer candidates, and the ability of regimental commanders to pick officers on whatever criteria they liked vitiated the use of academic or theoretical knowledge as a base of professional identity until World War I.[1] Only then did "the transition in the officer corps from an aristocratic-agrarian to a bourgeois-industrial mentality take place."[2]

The German clergy was also unlikely to express its discontents and aspirations through professional organizations: Protestant clergy were a pillar of the state and still highly privileged, while Catholic clergy were driven by the *Kulturkampf* of the 1870s toward an even closer dependence on the church hierarchy.

Only teachers among the larger public-employee professions forged their own independent organizations. Even these were beset by factionalism and uncertainties. The structure of the German educational system came to be replicated in the organizations of German teachers. The dream of 1848, a single organization of all teachers, collapsed in face of the reality of widely variegated social recruitment, status, income, educational requirements, and self-understanding of the various levels from *Volksschule* (elementary school) to university. These fissures were further complicated by religious and sex differences.

Another characteristic feature of the learned professions and their organizations in the last third of the nineteenth century was the perceptible trend toward clear lobbying functions. As noted in the previous chapter, justification by learnedness (*Wissenschaftlichkeit*) had usually formed the central public raison d'etre of early professional organizations. The exchange of ideas indeed continued to play a necessary and vital role in all such organizations. But pressing for *Standesinteressen* in ways related to economic improvement, status, and privileges became the central function of professional organizations. To the degree that some organizations resisted an aggressive pursuit of the *Hebung des Standes* (elevation of the profession), they often found themselves confronted with rival organizations willing to focus more exclusively on issues of economic self-interest, such as the *Hartmann-Bund* among doctors and various associations of industrial engineers.

One of the measures of the success of German professions and their organizations was the degree to which they were able to raise the levels of their autonomy; another was the degree to which they were able to make themselves more exclusive by raising standards of education and certification. These two matters will be dealt with extensively in the following chapters. To prefigure those later treatments, it is certainly possible to discern a general pattern of rising educational and certification standards in the last third of the nineteenth century.

The question of autonomy is more complicated. The rapid growth of public and private enterprises, coupled with a trend toward large organizations in in-

1 Manfred Messerschmidt, "Das preussisch-deutsche Offizierskorps 1850–1890," in Hans H. Hoffmann, ed., *Das deutsche Offizierskorps 1888–1918* (Boppard, 1980), pp. 36–7.
2 Wilhelm Deist, "Zur Geschichte des preussischen Offizierskorps 1888–1918," in Hoffmann, *Offizierskorps*, p. 40.

dustry and health insurance, for example, meant that more "free" professionals were in fact dependent on contractual labor arrangements. Proportionately more engineers and chemists worked in state, municipal, or private enterprise as employees in 1900 than in 1870, for example. Likewise, many physicians made most of their living in 1900 as contract doctors working in effect for the sickness-insurance funds or *Krankenkassen*. Yet, other groups sought a closer tie to the state as a means of insuring greater autonomy, as in the case of school-teachers. Many of these were convinced that becoming state officials would protect them from the petty infringements on their autonomy typified by municipal school systems or some other kind of local patronage.

The case of schoolteachers also clearly illustrates a trend toward demanding well-defined career ladders. But this tendency was also implicit in many of the reforms concerning education and certification among other professions, and this theme will be treated in the appropriate chapter.

Another central test of the success of the professions in "elevating" themselves concerns income levels and more general marks of social status. The answers vary of course from one profession to another. More importantly, generalizations are rendered difficult by the paucity of trustworthy documentation concerning incomes and the shifting structure of the professions themselves. It is, for example, meaningless to suggest that engineers or chemists as a group appear to have enjoyed higher incomes in 1880 than in 1900. The earlier groups included many entrepreneurs and managerial personnel in industry, whereas the growth of the profession embraced far larger numbers of salaried employees by the end of the century. The former group could and did exploit personal skills and inventiveness to economic advantage, whereas the latter found it difficult to achieve significant rewards from their own inventions. To cite another example, the growth of insured health care from the early 1880s onward undoubtedly helped create a sort of physicians' proletariat and may well have produced an overall reduction of doctors' incomes; but the triumphs of modern medicine and a general increase in prosperity equally obviously increased incomes among many private practitioners and a new breed of medical specialists.

A final characteristic of modern professions emerged more clearly among certain groups in this period: an articulated sense of altruism and the regulation of professional behavior. To be sure, this was unnecessary for the public professionals, with their oaths of office and bureaucratic controls. Two of the "free" professions, however, did obtain mechanisms for enforcing ethical behavior with the participation of their own members. The medical and legal professions, both "free" after the 1870s, obtained a system of "chambers" (*Kammern*) to deal with intraprofessional disputes and charges. These were public bodies maintained by mandatory contributions from all licensed doctors and lawyers. Mandated by governments, they were nevertheless run largely by local practitioners. The correlation between personnel in these bodies and the "voluntary" legal and medical associations was generally high. Unlike the voluntary professional associations, however, they had the legal power to assess penalties for unethical professional behavior.

Virtually all German professional groups expressed high degrees of altruism. Some of them backed up these declarations of public-mindedness with attempts to intervene positively for the public good. The German Medical Association repeatedly sought to influence public-health measures, and the VDI set up very influential committees to improve the safety of engineered products and systems. In a country with such a strongly profiled system of state concern for the public welfare, however, the room for displays of altruism was always somewhat limited.

Because of the differing environmental conditions of professional activity between the so-called "free" and state-controlled academic occupations, as well as for chapter brevity, the first group will be treated in this chapter and the second in Chapter 6.

1. MEDICINE AND DENTISTRY

The denouement of two decades of discussion of the medical profession in Germany came in 1869 with the passage by the North German Reichstag of the *Reichsgewerbeordnung*. This was generally an outgrowth of a long-standing desire, predating the unification of Germany, to create a single basis for commerce among the German states. Its significance for the professions is that it embraced the practice of medicine, including dental medicine.

Because there was no national medical association in 1869, any consultations with members of the profession had to be with existing local medical societies. In this respect none was more influential (and physically well placed to lobby the new Reichstag) than the Berlin Medical Society. This body was at the time dominated by a liberal spirit, as was the Reichstag itself; a majority of both groups approved several reforms that had far-reaching effects on the practice of medicine in Germany.

The petition of the Berlin Medical Society to the Reichstag called for four essential reforms eliminating many types of regulation from the practice of medicine: (1) an end to sanctions against "quackery" (*Kurpfuscherei*), (2) an end to the legal obligation of doctors to offer their services to all who needed them, irrespective of conditions or ability to pay, (3) the right of doctors to practice where they chose, and (4) abolition of fixed fee schedules for medical services. The Reich commercial law of 1869 granted the first three requests, but not the last.[3] Even at the time, many physicians disagreed with this legislation. They feared the competition of unlicensed medical personnel in particular. But the distinguished members of the Berlin Medical Society, many of whom were

3 Graf, *Vereinswesen*, pp. 20, 38.

prominent professors, evidently underestimated the threat to licensed practitioners in less sophisticated locales, trusted the people to choose qualified physicians over quacks, had a typically advanced faith in scientific medicine, and finally argued that existing laws against quackery were ineffective.[4]

Historians of the German medical profession have often expressed puzzlement at what appears to be behavior contrary to the drive toward monopoly over medical services by a leading segment of the profession in 1869. Clearly all the points demanded by the Berlin Medical Society fit into the category of greater professional autonomy, and the real gains in this area no doubt offset the merely normative loss of proscribing quackery. Conditions would furthermore be quite different under a system of expanding medical insurance, but this was not even on the horizon in 1869. For the time being, one could argue that quackery would go on with or without laws against it, that different classes of people would resort to doctors and quacks, and that the proven superiority of school medicine would sooner or later drive quacks to the wall.

It is noteworthy that the German dental profession was even more skeptical of the provisions of *Kurierfreiheit,* or "curative freedom," for unlicensed personnel. The head of the Central Association of German Dentists complained that the legislation of 1869 did nothing for the dental profession.[5] To be sure, the title *Zahnarzt* (dental physician) was now protected, as was the general title *Arzt* (physician). Only those who had attended a *Gymnasium* or first-class *Real-schule* in Prussia, for example, had further taken two years of medical study at a university, and had a certificate of practical training could call themselves a *Zahnarzt* after 1869 – a considerable step up on the status ladder.[6] To be sure, even a university-trained Zahnarzt was not yet a doctor (this academic title was not yet available). But the Reich commercial code of 1869 also opened the gates to those who had no such training and could call themselves *Dentist* or even, very close to illegality, *Zahnart.,* supposedly an abbreviation for "dental artist."[7]

The generally lower educational qualifications of university-trained dentists (compared to normal physicians) and the still relatively underdeveloped stature of dental medicine generally caused the organized German dentists to resent the *Gewerbeordnung* even more than some of their physician brethren from the start. On top of this uncertainty came the rise of the shadowy group of "American dentists," particularly after about 1880. These were Germans who obtained degrees from American dental schools, many of them quite bogus mail-order diplomas available for cash payments.[8]

The natural reaction among physicians and dentists was to organize voluntary associations. The German Medical Association was founded in consequence of a meeting of deputies from existing regional associations during a meeting of the Congress of German Natural Scientists and Physicians in 1872. The association

4 Huerkamp, "Aerzte und Professionalisierung," pp. 364–5.
5 Reinhard Seefeld, *Die Geschichte des Vereinsbundes Deutscher Zahnärzte* (Munich, 1937), p. 10.
6 Ibid., p. 11.   7 Ibid.   8 Ibid.

was formalized in 1873. German dentists had in the Central Association (ZVDZAe), founded in 1859, a kind of organization already; but it was by nature more a scientific society than an effective lobbying group. Dissatisfaction with its effectiveness, particularly under the impact of medical insurance, produced agitation to create a new organization more like the German Medical Association. This was completed after some years of meetings in 1891, when the *Vereinsbund Deutscher Zahnärzte* (Association of German Dentists, or VBDZAe) was born. The older Central Association continued to exist, as we shall see below, and eventually renamed itself to stress its essentially scientific character.

Much of the effort of both the German national medical and dental associations went into matters of educational reform and relations with the sickness insurance funds founded or consolidated in 1883. These aspects of their activities will be treated in the next two chapters. These struggles were of course connected with others to be discussed here. The rise of health-insurance funds had a growing impact on the nature of medicine in Germany, from at least two points of view: first, the medical insurance system contained numerous potential surfaces for friction over the economic and discretionary relations between physicians and patients and in effect tended to create a whole new class of physicians; and, second, it exacerbated the problem of unlicensed health-care providers, whom the medical societies sought to shut out of the insurance scheme. Increased educational qualifications for licensed physicians and dentists were, among other things, a means of underscoring the differences between those trained in school medicine and the "quacks."

For the purposes of this chapter, however, let us concentrate on the organizational and other efforts of the medical and dental professions to the end of the nineteenth century.

One predictable result of the opening of the medical and dental professions from 1869 on was a rapid increase in the number of practitioners. Despite some slight variations in statistics and estimates, it is safe to say that the growth of the medical profession vastly outstripped the growth of the general population after 1880. The number of physicians per million population remained relatively constant until the mid-eighties: for example, it fluctuated between about 300 and 350 in Prussia between 1847 and 1887.[9] By most statistical accounts, the number of physicians increased to at least 400 per million by 1892 and 500 by 1900.[10] Many doctors complained of a flood of medical students and licensed young physicians, who made competition worse and could barely sustain themselves. One authority writing after the turn of the century posited a relation of physicians to population of 300:1 million as "normal."[11]

9 Huerkamp, "Aerzte und Professionalisierung," p. 371; Bernhard Puppe, *Die Bestrebungen der deutschen Aerzte zu gemeinsamer Wahrnehmung ihrer wirtschaftlichen Interessen* (Wiesbaden, 1911), p. 5.
10 Theodor Plaut, *Der Gewerkschaftskampf der deutschen Aerzte* (Karlsruhe, 1913), p. 67.
11 Puppe, *Bestrebungen*, p. 5.

On the other hand, one must not lose sight of many developments in medicine that made a higher number of doctors supportable: in addition to the rapidly increasing cure rates deriving from modern school medicine, doctors' services were made more attractive by health insurance. With the advent of medical specialization and large hospitals and clinics in the last third of the nineteenth century, including the possibility of longer and more complex cures, demand for doctors certainly increased somewhat. [12] Much of this concentration took place in urban areas – university towns, wealthy trade centers, industrial areas, and even a few retirement centers, such as the "Pensionopolis" of Wiesbaden, where there were 2,200 doctors per million. [13] In 1898, cities over 100,000 population averaged nearly 1,100 physicians in a million; small towns of 5,000 or less had to get by with 240 per million. [14] In the countryside of East Elbia, by contrast, many rural areas virtually did without a resident doctor.

The growth of prosperous urban practices was aided only within limits by the increasing number of patients covered by mandatory medical insurance, however. As late as 1907, the number of doctors per million in some of the more densely populated industrial areas of the Ruhr was only about double that of small towns (e.g. 420:1 million in Essen, 330 in Duisburg). [15] This had much to do with the way medical insurance was set up in these predominantly proletarian areas, as will be discussed in a subsequent chapter. Thus, although insurance undoubtedly spurred the production of doctors, it was not a limitless bonanza (and was certainly not meant to be).

To some degree, the growth of medical personnel was a function of the overall growth of university enrollments in general and in medical faculties in particular. University enrollments in the territories of the later German Reich had remained remarkably steady, despite population growth, between the mid-1830s and mid-1860s – between about twelve and thirteen thousand. By 1870 they had crossed the fourteen thousand mark; by 1900, they had reached thirty-four thousand. This growth was, however, uneven. The philosophical faculties grew the fastest between the mid-1860s and the mid-1880s. The legal faculties began to grow rapidly in the mid-1870s. But medical enrollments began to burgeon only in the mid-1880s. [16]

These shifting professional choices by German students undoubtedly reflected to some degree contemporary perceptions of career chances in the various traditional fields. [17] Thus, as such public-employment fields as administration, courts, and teaching did not grow fast enough to absorb students, a

---

12 Plaut, *Gewerkschaftskampf*, pp. 68–9.   13 Ibid.
14 Friedrich Prinzing, *Handbuch der medizinischen Statistik*, 2d ed. (Jena, 1931), p. 636.
15 Ibid.; Plaut, *Gewerkschaftskampf*, pp. 70–1.
16 Charles E. McClelland, *State, Society and University in Germany, 1700–1914* (Cambridge, 1980), pp. 239–40.
17 Huerkamp, "Aerzte und Professionalisierung," p. 372.

field such as medicine became more attractive, despite its reputation for requiring time-consuming and difficult study.

The German Medical Association was from its founding in 1873 probably representative of a majority of German *approbierte* physicians. It was a federation of local medical societies, of which there were about 130 in that year. In 1874, 111 of these were members. Certainly by 1883, when official figures became available, some 52 percent of German physicians were represented by the DAeV. By 1890, some 11,000 out of the Reich's 18,500 doctors belonged to medical societies affiliated with the DAeV, or close to 60 percent. The most spectacular growth occurred in the decade beginning in 1900, however, when the German Medical Association grew to include 410 medical societies, representing nearly 25,000 physicians, or some 77 percent of all licensed practitioners. This growth undoubtedly owed much to the rising sense of solidarity in the medical profession in the face of ever-expanding insurance coverage of the German people and resentment of the insurance funds' perceived interference in medical practice, which will be discussed more fully in a later chapter.[18]

From its beginnings as an avowedly scientific society, the DAeV quickly grew into a lobbying organization. Its annual *Aerztetag* (Physicians' Congress) and its *Aerztliches Vereinsblatt*, which eventually became a weekly organ, became loci for the discussion of matters of interest to the medical profession. The annual meetings made resolutions and sent them to the popularly elected Reichstag and more especially the upper house of the national parliament, the *Bundesrat*. Although the organization was sometimes successful in lobbying for certain changes and reforms, particularly in medical education (about which more later), it was not particularly successful in convincing governments to alleviate the economic condition of the medical profession.[19] The loose structure of the organization and the fact that many doctors dissented from its majority resolutions on certain subjects probably weakened its effectiveness down to the years immediately after 1900.

The most important resolutions of the DAeV down to 1900 addressed matters of public health (such as legislation on inoculations, epidemics, pharmacopia, etc.); doctors' roles in giving expert testimony and certificates of illness; relations with private insurance companies; and a number of other matters not centrally concerned with the status of the profession. Two central areas of concern, which impinged on the economic well-being and autonomy of the profession, in the first case, and the size and quality of the corpus of doctors, on the other, will be treated separately later: mandatory health insurance and educational reform.

Otherwise, one of the central concerns of the DAeV was with the autonomous functioning of the medical profession. One tack it took was to encourage the

18 Plaut, *Gewerkschaftskampf*, p. 28; Graf, *Vereinswesen*, p. 25.
19 Plaut, *Gewerkschaftskampf*, pp. 30–1.

development of mandatory self-disciplinary bodies of physicians, the so-called *Aerztekammern*, or chambers of physicians. As we have seen in the previous chapter, some German states already had set up *Aerztekammern* before 1870, notably Baden, Brunswick, Bavaria, and Saxony. The DAeV wanted a national law to regulate the relationship between the profession and all German states, a so-called *Reichsärzteordnung*, or Reich Physicians' Law. It first called on Bismarck to arrange such a law at its second *Aerztetag* in 1874.[20]

Bismarck replied in 1875 that he did not regard the Reich as the proper level for such legal regulation or what would today be called in German legal parlance a federal "framework law." Although disappointed with this response, the DAeV never completely accepted it internally, and yet went ahead with suggestions for a state-by-state regulation through *Aerztekammern* at their fifth annual meeting in 1878.[21] Significantly, the DAeV recommended that official representations of regional doctors be elected by members of regional medical societies, rather than from all licensed physicians.[22] This was already the case in some states, for example, in Saxony, and would have reinforced connections between the "voluntary" medical societies and the "official" chambers of physicians.

As it came to pass, Prussia organized a system of chambers in 1887, as a nonvoluntary organization parallel to medical societies, with officials being elected by all licensed physicians. This pattern was ultimately accepted by most of the German states as they created or modified their own system of *Aerztekammern*. A few states, to be sure, did not adopt a system at all until the 1920s, and then left membership voluntary (e.g. Hesse, Württemberg, and Thüringen).[23] In actual fact, it appears that there was a high degree of personnel overlap between the voluntary local medical societies and the elected officials of the chambers. Since the medical societies picked the delegates to the *Aerztetage*, this meant in effect a close working relationship among local and national medical associations and the chambers of physicians.

Why was it necessary to have this seeming duplication of effort? Why could not the voluntary medical associations have been assigned the function of disciplinary bodies? Although this solution was adopted in some German states, and although most medical societies had either behavior codes or honor councils or both by the end of the century,[24] the advantage of having separate, official chambers of physicians lay in their obligatory nature. No physician in an *Aerztekammer* could escape judgment and punishment for infractions of medical ethics by simply resigning. Even though the maximum penalty assessable by the chambers was a fine of several thousand marks, and not exclusion from the practice of medicine, this was more than medical societies could impose: their most severe remedy lay in throwing offending members out of the association.

20 Graf, *Vereinswesen*, p. 36.   21 Ibid., pp. 36–7.   22 Ibid.
23 Finkenrath, *Organisation*, p. 50.   24 Graf, *Vereinswesen*, p. 54.

Usually all licensed physicians in private practice were required to belong and even to pay a hefty annual fee for the maintenance of the chamber (up to 1 percent of their taxable income). In most cases, military and state-employed doctors were exempt, because they had their own forms of disciplinary hierarchy. In return, physicians generally had a chance to elect the officers of the *Kammern* in a democratic fashion. When *Aerztekammern* were first instituted, and even as late as 1900, as we have seen, one could not have predicted that the inclusiveness of German medical societies under the umbrella of the DAeV would reach the heights it did. Thus chambers of physicians may have seemed at the time to be the only way to guarantee 100 percent accountability of doctors to their own peers in medical ethics cases.

To the extent that the *Aerztekammern* were in place and functioning by 1900, they seem to have achieved the goals envisioned for them by the DAeV. These were, to be sure, not primarily the protection of the public from incompetent or venal doctors, but more the prevention of unfair competition. The DAeV and individual regional medical societies struggled since the 1870s to come up with a universally acceptable code of medical ethics. In 1873, for example, the Munich medical society adopted a modified translation of the recently enacted code of the American Medical Association. Slightly different versions were adopted by individual medical societies thereafter.[25] By the seventeenth Aerztetag in 1890, the following six-point code was adopted almost unanimously as a common framework: (1) No public "praise" of a doctor's work will be allowed either by him or others; (2) Misuse of the terms specialist, clinic and polyclinic are to be rejected; (3) Offering free treatment, concluding contracts with insurance funds on the basis of knockdown prices, and other forms of advantages offered to third persons to increase one's practice are impermissible; (4) Prescribing or recommending patent medicines (*Geheimmittel,* or "nostrums") is impermissible; (5) Any attempt by one doctor to interfere in the treatment of a patient by another (without a consultation agreement) is dishonorable; (6) No doctor should make public statements damaging to a colleague's reputation.[26]

The second and fourth points may need some further explanation. Many physicians were describing themselves as "specialists" without corresponding training, or their premises as "clinic," a term the DAeV wanted to restrict to university clinics. Attesting to the efficacy of a patent medicine in advertising could bring handsome fees to doctors, even though the product was of little or no value.

These types of transgressions against the "honor of the profession" were the bread and butter of the honor councils and courts of the *Aerztekammern.* As we shall see elsewhere, however, conflicts of this sort became even sharper in the wake of boycott attempts against insurance companies after 1900.

25 Ibid., p. 52.   26 Ibid., p. 53.

For, indeed, the professionalizing project for German medicine could not be complete unless it could influence economic rewards for medical services. This was never possible as long as medical services were offered at less than private practice rates by doctors in civilian and military office, or by private doctors willing to underbid their colleagues, or by doctors working on flat-rate contracts with insurers, particularly the mandatory *Krankenkassen.* Charges were regulated on the upper limits by the so-called *Medizinaltaxen* or medical fee scales, a part of government regulation that had not been eliminated in the wake of liberalizing the medical profession.

At first, the DAeV did not press for eliminating fee scales. In its second annual meeting in 1874, it argued that a recent action along those lines in Baden had been unwise; that no national scale could be adopted (given widely differing costs of living); and that fee schedules were mostly in need of realignment with a rising cost of living.[27] But this attitude did not last long. By 1882, the DAeV at its annual meeting adopted by an overwhelming majority its "Basic Characteristics for a German Physicians' Law," which, with minor modifications, would remain a standing set of demands for decades. The right of doctors and patients to set fees by mutual agreement was one of the demands highest on the list.[28]

Most other points dealt with examinations, titles, and withdrawal of the right to practice only via penal process (not by administrative action); the right to move and settle freely one's practice; the right to refuse to treat patients; doctors' obligations regarding epidemics, death certificates, and similar public-health matters; and the matter of *Aerztekammern* and honorary courts dealt with already.[29]

Suffice it to say here that the DAeV made no headway with its demand to eliminate statutory fee schedules. Nor would this have become such a matter of worry had it not been for the double squeeze, beginning precisely in the 1880s, between mandatory health insurance and rapidly rising competition for patients. But we shall look at the economic impact of these in Chapter 8, and see what responses the medical professions offered.

One immediate way of restricting competition was to reintroduce the old prohibitions on quackery. Seeing that it was making little headway in its hope for an *Aerzteordnung,* the DAeV turned to this problem, which we may recall was raised by the *Gewerbeordnung* of 1869. The immediate cause of reopening this question had to do with the agreement by some of the burgeoning sickness funds to pay nonlicensed practitioners for treatment of the funds' clients.

The influential and liberal Berlin Medical Society had played a major role in swaying the government to remove restrictions on unlicensed practice in 1869, and as late as 1880 it debated the issue again and still, by a small majority, voted to meet the quacks head-on in an open market for medical treatment. By

27 Ibid., p. 30.   28 Ibid., p. 44.   29 Ibid., pp. 42–5.

1887 a similar debate resulted in a reversal of this vote, and the DAeV meeting of the same year approved by an 80 percent majority a statement calling for reimposition of prohibitions on medical practice by nonlicensed physicians. In the same declaration, they underscored that this prohibition should not be purchased by canceling three principles listed in the "Basic Characteristics" – freedom to move and settle, freedom to refuse treatment, and voluntary agreement on fees.[30]

In other words, the DAeV wanted to restore some of the features of pre-1869 protection of their market without returning to pre-1869 restrictions on their own practice. In this respect the DAeV was certainly exhibiting a preference for classical professionalizing strategies – guarantees of market monopolization coupled with their own autonomy from state interference in some of the most central areas of their working conditions. The DAeV voted 2:1 *against* the reintroduction of monopoly if it meant giving up doctors' freedoms, however.

There the matter stood unchanged throughout the rest of the empire and the Weimar Republic. The medical profession was poorly represented in the Reichstag and appears not to have convinced government ministries, either. No comprehensive *Aerzteordnung* was ever passed, although many of the demands of the DAeV were met piecemeal over the decades (e.g. chambers of physicians). Unlicensed medical practitioners continued to flourish legally, and mandatory fee schedules continued to exist. At the same time, medicine remained a "free profession" and did not revert to the semi-bureaucratic regulation of pre-1869. Had it not been for the continued expansion of the *Krankenkassen,* this might have remained an acceptable compromise for most German doctors.

But the reality was that German governments in the 1880s and afterward were much more concerned with the millions of presumably revolutionary-minded workers than the complaints of the thousands of doctors. Medical, accident, and old-age insurance formed the centerpiece of Bismarck's counterattack on the socialist opposition. Just as it set Germany apart from other capitalist industrial nations for decades, this social legislation had a distinct impact on the professionalizing project of German medicine.

The impact on the economic well-being of medical practitioners is difficult to gauge. Certainly the combination of more doctors per capita with constant expansion of the medical insurance system had the effect of shrinking the private sector and making competition keener. Subjective evidence indicates there was at least a perceived decline in physicians' incomes toward the end of the nineteenth century. Complaints mounted in medical publications about "proletarianization" of incomes. Such complaints had appeared in the early and mid-century only rarely. Objective data are somewhat inconclusive. But because the

30 Ibid., p. 47.

entire question of incomes in the medical profession cannot be separated from the problem of insurance funds, this question will be explored more fully in the appropriate chapter.

2. LAWYERS

The political unification of Germany led to even more far-reaching changes in the practice of law than in that of medicine. The existence of the national parliament, administrative system, and supreme courts and such enterprises as the codification of German law – most significantly the *Bürgerliches Gesetzbuch* (BGB), or civil law code, introduced only in 1900 – necessarily entailed a considerable amount of standardization and redefinition of lawyers' roles.

So much had already been clear to the *Juristentag* in the 1860s, as we saw in Chapter 4. In broadest outline, the judicial and legal reforms carried out by the Reich in the 1870s corresponded to many recommendations of that body. In the mid-1870s, the Reichstag debated and finally passed a number of fundamental laws affecting the organization and procedure of justice – the Civil and Criminal Procedure Laws (ZPO and StPO) and the Court Organization Law (GVG). Lawyers were originally supposed to be regulated by the latter, but in the end a separate law was passed in 1878 – the *Reichsanwaltsordnung* (RAO) – to lay the groundwork for a unified profession in Germany. With that, German attorneys became the first and, for a long time, the only learned profession to be anchored and defined in a national law specific to themselves.

This law did not, to be sure, nullify the existing modes of the member states concerning such matters as training and admission to the bar. These continued to vary slightly in various parts of Germany and will be discussed in the chapter on education.

But it did, in effect, set a capstone on the autonomy of the "free" profession of attorney. The RAO generalized the system of *Rechtsanwaltskammern* (Attorneys' Chambers) already in existence in some German states. These *Kammern* meant a transfer of disciplinary control from the courts to bodies elected by the lawyers themselves and comprising all members of the bar. Analogous to the medical chambers mentioned above, these constituted an independent form of self-government for the attorneys. To be sure, charges of unethical behavior could be brought by the State's Attorney, and the appeal procedure involved judges appointed from the official judiciary, so that self-administration by the lawyers had its limits.[31] Nevertheless, the creation of an *Anwaltskammer* for every *Oberlandesgericht* (land supreme court) constituted the "conclusion of the

31 Hannes Siegrist, "Gebremste Professionalisierung – Das Beispiel der Schweizer Rechtsanwaltschaft im Vergleich zu Frankreich und Deutschland im 19. und frühen 20. Jahrhundert," in Conze and Kocka, *Bildbungsbürgertum*, p. 312.

creation of the German attorneys' profession."[32] (The terminology of German courts can be confusing. Generally a *Landesgericht* corresponded to a district court, the second instance for appeals from courts of first instance, such as the *Amtsgericht*. In more important cases, the *Landesgericht* could also be a court of first instance. The district courts were subordinated to a supreme court for most of the German states, and these in turn were subjected to a new national supreme court, situated in Leipzig, after the founding of the Reich.)

A further Reich law of 1879, the *Rechtsanwaltsgebührenordnung* (RAGebO, or Attorneys' Fee Regulation) set fees for various kinds of legal operations. This in itself was not a new phenomenon in Germany, because only a few states, like Hamburg, left fees entirely up to the client-lawyer relationship. But the creation of a unified fee schedule for the country as a whole was a first. The attorneys did not oppose it in principle, though some (e.g. the Bavarian Attorneys' Association) protested that fees being contemplated for the national schedule were in some cases too low.[33] Only with the passage of many years, as the fee schedule remained unaltered but inflation and competition mounted, did German attorneys begin to chafe under the particulars of a normative fee schedule. They generally accepted it in principle, seeing no threat to their autonomy in it, but cried out for its adjustment to realities from time to time. (It is still the basis of West German attorneys' fees today.) The impact of this fee schedule on the economic well-being of the profession is discussed below.

Undoubtedly far more important to attorneys than legal regulation of their fees was the universal adoption of *Anwaltszwang* (mandatory representation), whereby every party in court had to be represented by a lawyer. This was in effect necessary with the universal introduction of oral proceedings and the elimination of any distinction between barrister and solicitor, as was generally the case after 1878. But it also gave the legal profession a powerful lever with which to pressure out untrained legal "counsel," the legal equivalent of quacks.

As mentioned above, the German attorneys were the very first professional group to organize nationally after the completion of German unity in 1871. The *Deutscher Anwaltverein* was founded in that year after a meeting called by two regional lawyers' associations founded a decade before – those of Bavaria and Prussia. Any German attorney could join, and about a third of the roughly 4,500 lawyers did so in the first two years of the DAV's existence.[34]

Unlike the German Medical Association, the DAV was a professional body made up of individual members, rather than regional professional societies. Both the convokers of 1871, the Prussian and later the Bavarian Attorneys'

---

32 Fritz Ostler, "Der deutsche Rechtsanwalt. Das Werden des Standes seit der Reichsgründung," *Schriftenreihe der Juristischen Studiengesellschaft Karlsruhe,* 56/57 (1963): 3. (Hereafter abbreviated "Werden" to avoid confusion with a book of the same main title by the same author.)

33 Ibid., p. 34.

34 Ibid., p. 13; Fritz Ostler, *Der deutsche Rechtsanwalt 1871–1971* (Essen, 1971), pp. 60, 88. (Hereafter abbreviated *Rechtsanwalt.*)

Association, dissolved as if to underscore the merging of their membership in the DAV. But in many places, local associations continued to exist, and in some cases regional lawyers' associations were assigned the functions of the legal disciplinary chambers. Thus the DAV appears in the period under consideration to have been more influenced by and representative of the attorneys at the national *Reichsgericht* (supreme court) or the higher regional courts (such as *Oberlandesgericht*) than of those practicing at the lowest and most local level, the *Amtsgericht*. The strong position of the elected board of directors, usually with supreme court attorneys greatly overrepresented, sometimes led to frictions with the rank-and-file membership, especially after 1900.[35]

The DAV by the turn of the twentieth century embraced about two-thirds of Germany's attorneys.[36] But it did not comprise a majority of all legally trained persons. The structure of the German legal profession, as we have noted above, sundered the lawyers from the judges and legally trained civil servants. When these latter groups finally decided to break with tradition and join voluntary professional organizations, they joined their own, rather than the DAV. The division of even the lawyers' professional identity into mandatory *Kammern* and voluntary DAV could not have lent the German attorneys the kind of strength shown by, for example, the American Bar Association.

On the other hand, the relationship among *Kammern*, DAV, and the *Juristentag* was characterized more by a spirit of cooperation than bitter rivalry. Although each overlapped to some degree the areas of competence of the others, each had a primary function. And there was a considerable overlap in leadership.

The *Deutscher Juristentag*, for example, continued to be exclusively a group devoted to the shaping of German law, as opposed to the professional interests of its delegates. It had only the loosest of organizations, met annually to debate and recommend on problems in jurisprudence, and had a distinctly scholarly air. Of the sixteen presidential elections of the *Juristentag* between 1871 and 1900, law professors won the post eleven times.[37] The Standing Deputation, or board of directors, usually contained a large number of law teachers, 40 percent in 1900, for example.[38]

The leadership of the *Juristentag* appears to have been drawn heavily from judges and justice administration in addition to the academic world. Still, attorneys figured sometimes in the leadership, and Carl Dorn, one of the founders of the *Juristentag* in the 1860s, was also a co-founder and the first chairman of the DAV. The periodical of the DAV, *Juristische Wochenschrift*, also served as a forum for learned discussions of the law, rather than an outright

35 Ostler, *Rechtsanwalt*, p. 91.
36 Estimates based on statistics in ibid., p. 60 and Wilhelm Kulemann, *Die Berufsvereine*, 2d ed. (Jena, 1908–13), vol. 1, p. 167.
37 Caemmerer, *Rechtsleben*, pp. 45–7.
38 *Verhandlungen des 25. Deutschen Juristentages* (1900), vol. 3, p. xiii.

mouthpiece for the economic interests of the barristers. Thus it provided a national legal journal for the periods between meetings of the *Juristentag* as well as an organ for the publication of decisions of the *Kammern*.[39]

Finally, the cooperation between the national, voluntary DAV and the regional *Kammern* was mostly cordial, with a high degree of overlap in the leadership level of both. As the *Kammern* became established in the decade after the *Rechtsanwaltsordnung*, a certain division of labor developed between them and the DAV, with the latter emerging more and more clearly as the representative of *Standesinteressen*, the former as the representative of disciplinary self-government in the profession.

This harmonious and relatively trouble-free picture of the German attorneys as a professional group down to 1900 was in part connected to low levels of competition. Despite a rapidly growing population, the legal profession did not at first grow at a comparable rate. Indeed, the number of lawyers in Germany appears to have sunk somewhat in the 1870s (from about 4,500 in 1872 to 4,000 in 1880). The number had recovered to 4,500 in 1885, risen to 5,200 in 1890, 5,600 in 1895, and leapt to 6,800 in 1900.[40] Population growth had not been quite as rapid, but the ratio of one attorney to 11,000 Germans in 1880 had risen to only one to 8,500 in 1895.[41]

The economic rewards of the bar during the three decades after the *Reichsgründung* are difficult to establish with any degree of statistical certainty. Most accounts agree that legal practice at first allowed for comfortable prospects. In 1884, for example, the *Juristische Wochenschrift* reported an estimate of average annual income for German lawyers of 3,500 marks, a little less than the salary of an *Oberamtsrichter* (senior local magistrate).[42] Nevertheless, the economic security of the bar appears to have been eroded gradually by a number of variables – the increase in attorneys per capita, modest though it remained; inflation in the cost of living and professional expenses; and a tendency toward longer duration of trials. None of these variables was compensated by the legal fee schedules, which remained fixed constants.[43]

By the 1890s, increased competition, especially in urban areas, plus rising costs and man-hours per case, led to increased discussion of remedies for what contemporaries believed was a deteriorating economic position of lawyers. The latter compared their position in particular to the members of the bench, whose incomes had better kept pace with inflation. Two basic changes appeared possible: raise the fees allowed by the *Gebührenordnung* or restrict the number of practicing attorneys. The former solution was called for by the DAV and some of the Attorneys' Chambers, but without favorable action from the side of government. The latter solution was proposed by some government officials, as in

39 Ostler, *Rechtsanwalt*, p. 90.   40 Ibid., p. 60; Ostler, "Werden," 13.
41 Ostler, *Rechtsanwalt*, p. 60.   42 Ibid., p.61.   43 Ibid.

the case of the Prussian Ministry of Justice in 1894. The ministry recommended new laws to introduce a *numerus clausus* or restricted number of lawyers admitted to practice, plus the introduction of a two-year practical training period between the state examination and admission to the bar.[44]

Such a course would have meant the end of the *freie Anwaltschaft*, one of the major achievements of the Reich legislation of 1878. Although some German attorneys had always cast doubt on the wisdom of unrestricted access to the bar, the DAV and the chambers largely continued to support it even in the face of what they perceived to be a worsening economic climate. The meeting of the Association of German Attorneys in 1894 debated the possibility of higher training qualifications, at least, as a way of reducing what was reported to be a problem of a surplus of very young attorneys entering the market. But the annual meeting of the DAV overwhelmingly defeated even this suggestion and remained clearly on record in favor of the status quo.[45] In its rhetorical posture, the DAV and the majority of chambers cited the public good accruing from the *freie Advokatur*, even if economic hardships were sometimes (as undeniably in large centers like Berlin) an unavoidable consequence.

3. ENGINEERS

The unification of Germany in 1871 had less sweeping direct consequences for the engineering profession than for law and medicine. The indirect consequences, including the rapid if uneven industrial development of the new country in the remaining decades of the nineteenth century, did not prove exactly propitious for the further consolidation of professional organization. The shift from small to large scale industrial production as well as the differentiation of engineering specialties resulted in fundamental reorientations among German engineers.

Two areas of effort by engineers stand out in this period as reflections of the professionalizing project and its difficulties. First, the organizational drive begun by the *Verein Deutscher Ingenieure* (VDI) in the 1850s began to falter after national unification. Torn between the high-minded ideology of engineering as a politically and socially neutral beneficence for Germany and the reality of economic and political positions taken up by representatives of industry, the VDI consciously opted for the former stance and lost a possible chance to be the overall representative of German engineers. Second, the engineering community as a whole was rather successful in raising its status through the route of educational reforms. This second area of endeavor, however, will be discussed in another chapter.

The position of engineers in the workplace changed considerably after 1871. Whereas many members of the VDI were engineer-entrepreneurs in that year,

44 Ibid., p. 62.   45 Ibid., pp. 63–4.

by 1900 most German engineers were employees in increasingly large enterprises or were employed in the civil service, including, for example, the state railways. The role of the engineer as entrepreneur declined, and even the role of the engineer as "right hand man" to technically untrained entrepreneurs yielded to a more complex organizational hierarchy. Increasingly, the decision-makers in large-scale private enterprises became businessmen; and in the public sector, as engineers complained with greater frequency, the decision-makers were trained in law.

The economic interests of private industry began to loom larger from the 1870s onwards. The economic slump after 1873 galvanized representatives especially of heavy industry to organize as the *Central-Verband Deutscher Industrieller* (CVDI) in 1876. One of the first priorities of this organization was to reverse the free-trade stance of the German government in order to protect German industry from foreign competition. Its goals were realized in the abandonment of the free-trade stance in 1879. In many other ways, too, German industry asserted its economic interests vis-à-vis the government.

Such a version of *Interessenpolitik* (interest politics) conflicted with the political neutrality that the VDI had adopted since its inception. The very political innocuousness of the VDI had been one of the conditions, no doubt, of its existence in the conservative 1850s. And, as we have seen with other national professional organizations, a recognition that one of their chief functions lay in representing the material and status interests of their membership took some time. The VDI had less time at its disposal than others; it was overtaken by the rapid development of the economic self-interest of German capitalism.

A good example of the results of such a dilemma can be seen in the story of the *Verein Deutscher Eisenhüttenleute* (VDEh). Originally founded as the *Technischer Verein für Eisenhüttenwesen* (Technical Association for Ironworking), it joined the VDI in 1860. Its founding statutes made it clear, however, that the TVEh was actually less interested in the dispassionate study of technology than the economic benefits of it. Some 80 percent of its members (principally from the Rhine-Ruhr and Upper Silesian industrial areas) were entrepreneurs or company directors.[46]

As the interests of German iron and steel consolidated and began the kind of collective lobbying for economic advantage that was to become characteristic for the rest of the century, the *Technischer Verein* saw fewer and fewer advantages in belonging to an association that eschewed political and economic stances. More to the relief than the chagrin of the VDI, the *Technischer Verein* withdrew from it in 1880 and set itself up as the independent VDEh.[47]

The sundering of ties between the VDI and the VDEh was not the only indication of a split in interests between a majority "neutral" professional organization and minority "pressure-group" one. The tendency of engineers to or-

46 Scholl, "Ingenieur in Ausbildung," p. 52.   47 Ibid., p. 53.

ganize by specialty produced a number of new professional associations before 1900. Two major ones were the *Verein Deutscher Maschineningenieure* (Association of German Machine Engineers, or VDMI) and *Verein Deutscher Elektrotechniker* (Association of German Electrotechnicians, or VDET) founded in 1881 and 1893 respectively. The former represented at first chiefly high-ranking functionaries of state and private railroads as well as suppliers of railroad equipment.[48] Another association embracing chiefly government officials was the *Verband Deutscher Architekten- und Ingenieurenvereine* (League of German Architect and Engineer Associations, or VDAIV) in 1871 to represent the local associations of such civil servants and civil and construction engineers, whose small numbers and social and educational background made them feel superior to the commonality of the VDI. Nevertheless, it was the VDI membership that rejected the VDAIV in 1871, because many VDI members would not have been able to meet the higher standards of admission sanctioned by the government architects and engineers' associations.[49]

The "elitist" tendencies exemplified by the VDAIV turned out, however, to have parallels in the VDI itself. It rewrote its statutes twice, and with each new version the voice of large industry and the academic world increased at the expense of "ordinary" engineers. In 1881 the position of the Board of Directors (*Vorstand*) of the VDI was greatly strengthened at the expense of the general meetings; only nine years later, a further change created an executive board and a single director of the VDI, further diluting the "democratic" voice of the general meetings.[50] The personal connection between the VDI Board and "the leadership elite of industry remained significant," representatives of teachers (especially professors) remained constant, but "employee-engineers, measured as a proportion of the general membership, were quite obviously underrepresented" on the executive board.[51] Entrepreneurs, factory directors and technical directors made up 19 percent of the executive board in 1883 but 29 percent in 1901; mere engineers sank from 16 to 5 percent at the same time.[52]

It was argued at the time that membership growth made VDI self-government through the annual general meetings unwieldy. It is true that the VDI was growing fast, reaching nearly 2,000 members in 1871 and over 4,000 a decade later.[53] By 1908, the VDI had nearly 22,000 members.[54] Yet, it had failed in its original purpose of being the main organization of German engineers. According to a recent rough estimate, Germany had between 120,000 and 180,000 engineers of all types around 1900, including 30,000 with higher-education diplomas and three to five times that number as graduates of other

48 Ibid., pp. 53–4; Hortleder, *Gesellschaftsbild*, p. 46.
49 Scholl, "Ingenieur in Ausbildung," p. 51.
50 Karl-Heinz Manegold, "Der VDI in der Phase der Hochindustrialisierung 1880 bis 1900," in Ludwig, *Technik, Ingenieure*, p. 136.
51 Ibid., p. 137.   52 Hortleder, *Gesellschaftsbild*, table 7, p. 51.
53 Scholl, "Ingenieur in Ausbildung," p. 25.   54 Kulemann, *Berufsvereine*, p. 180.

technical schools. Perhaps only one-quarter of the VDI membership consisted of technical college graduates.[55] The VDAIV had nearly 9,000 members the same year; the VDEh, 4,000; and the VDET, almost 4,000. All these were specialized engineering groups, some near to industry, others to government, but none willing to cleave to the VDI's self-proclaimed role as the "socially neutral" representative of all engineers. The unwillingness of the VDI to fight for economic interests made it a less attractive organization than its rivals; its initial reluctance to become exclusive by imposing high membership qualifications made it distasteful to some.

Finally, its unwillingness to function as an economic interest group for its members gave rise to new types of rivals after the turn of the twentieth century, such as BUTIB, to be discussed in Chapter 8. Even though it tried to avoid the appearance of being close to one or another German industrial interest, however, contemporaries, rightly or wrongly, began to refer to it by the turn of the twentieth century as an organization of the machine industry or a representative of German light industry.[56]

Unfortunately no reliable and broadly founded data are available on the incomes of engineers down to 1900, perhaps because so many of them at the outset were self-employed (thus obviating more easily collected salary information). But because the long-range trend was toward rising percentages of employee-engineers, and the entry-level salaries of their positions appears to have been comparable to that of chemists by about 1900, available evidence does not indicate increasing prosperity correlating with increasing career opportunities.

4. CHEMISTS

The emergence of a modern chemical profession in Germany coincided with the dramatic growth of the domestic chemical industry under the empire. Germany, still a backward country in this area in 1870, had become the world leader by World War I. Much of this growth – in both industry and the profession – took place in the subfield of organic chemistry. Unlike older industries based on inorganic elements, the new "dyestuffs" enterprises relied on discoveries of academic research such as chemical synthesis. As a recent study put the matter:

In the coal and iron industries as in textiles and generally in older, established branches the predominant view was that there were no further significant problems for science to solve for industrial purposes; therefore close cooperation with university researchers was hardly necessary and certainly not indispensable. The traditional path of trial and error within the factory under the aegis of experienced practitioners was regarded as more

55 Karl-Heinz Lugwig, *Technik und Ingenieure im Dritten Reich* (Düsseldorf, 1974), pp. 18–19. (Hereafter abbreviated *Dritten Reich* to avoid confusion with a similar title by the same author.)
56 Ibid., p. 23.

rewarding. But this view was not shared by the 'young' industries, i.e. the optical, electrotechnical and especially the organic-chemical industries.[57]

The simple fact that scientific discovery constantly multiplied the number of known organic chemical compounds from a mere 500 in 1800 to 3,000 in 1860, 15,000 in 1880 and 150,000 in 1910 may serve as an indicator of the increasingly complex knowledge required of chemists.[58] The chemists working in the new plants had increasingly to receive an advanced scientific education in order to apply the new discoveries to industrial production.

As we shall see in Chapter 6, the German educational system was not specifically designed to produce the kind of chemists industry wanted. Thus much of the professional activity of chemists revolved around questions of education and qualification. For our purposes here it is merely important to note that the relationship between industry and the academic world was a particularly important one for the chemical profession.

Academic chemistry obtained an organizational forum in the German Chemical Society (DCG), as we have seen, in 1867. The DCG owed its founding in large part to the work of Prof. A. W. Hofmann of the University of Berlin, who had returned from England in 1861 impressed with the activities of the Chemical Society in London. From the beginning, the DCG stressed the commonality of interests between academic and applied chemistry or, as Hofmann put it in his opening address to the new society, between "speculative and applied chemistry." The DCG, he stated, would "seal anew the alliance between science and industry."[59]

The DCG could not, however, serve as a national professional organization for German chemists: it was founded originally as a Berlin organization, although it did gain members from outside, and its original membership comprised largely academic chemists.[60] Industrial chemists participated only sparingly in its activities.[61] Other local chemical societies sprang up around Germany, many of them in university towns, in succeeding years. But a clearly professional organization for the entire country would have to wait two decades more. Meanwhile, the *Berichte* of the DCG served as a major forum for new scientific discoveries, principally in inorganic chemistry.

The German chemical industry also organized in the 1870s, along with many other industries. The *Verein zur Wahrung der Interessen der Chemischen Industrie Deutschlands* (Association for the Protection of the Chemical Industry of Ger-

57 Lothar Burchardt, "Die Zusammenarbeit zwischen chemischer Industrie, Hochschulchemie und chemischen Verbänden im Wilhelminischen Deutschland," *Technikgeschichte*, 46 (1979):196–7.
58 Otto Krätz, "Der Chemiker in den Gründerjahren," in Eberhard Schmauderer, ed., *Der Chemiker im Wandel der Zeiten* (Weinheim, 1973), pp. 269–70.
59 "Constituierende Versammlung," in *Berichte der Deutschen Chemischen Gesellschaft zu Berlin*, 1 (1867), p. 3.
60 Ibid., 13–15.
61 Bertold L. P. Rassow, *Geschichte des Vereins Deutscher Chemiker in den ersten 25 Jahren seines Bestehens* (Leipzig, 1912), p. 3.

many, or VWIC) arose, however, chiefly as a lobbying organization in questions of patents and customs tariffs. Somewhat parallel to the view of the *Centralverband Deutscher Industrieller* by engineers, the VWIC was viewed by chemists as an industrial lobby rather than as a possible representative of their professional interests.[62] After a decade of existence, the VWIC had only 240 members, but these included virtually all chemical factory owners in Germany.[63]

In the same year as factory owners founded the VWIC, 1877, a small number of specialized working chemists banded together as the *Verein Analytischer Chemiker* (Association of Analytical Chemists), the first national professional organization for working chemists. Its narrow limitation to analytical chemists prevented it from attracting many members until it was renamed *Deutsche Gesellschaft für Angewandte Chemie,* or German Society for Applied Chemistry, in 1887 (and ultimately the *Verein Deutscher Chemiker,* or Association of German Chemists, VDC, a decade later). Having outgrown the chemical section of the Congress of German Scientists and Physicians, and confronted with continued difficulties in their industry, the rapidly multiplying numbers of "employed" (as opposed to factory-owning) chemists flocked to the VDC after 1877. In its aims the organization owed much to the example of the VDI. The main force behind the new organization, Ferdinand Fischer, had been inspired by the German engineering association, of which he had been an active member.

The refusal of the new society to affiliate with the VWIC aroused suspicion among chemical factory owners that the former might be a sort of chemists' union.[64] Certainly many of its members had cause to be dissatisfied with working conditions. But despite the climate of capitalist fear of unions and strikes in the late 1880s, the industrialists had no need to worry about the new chemical society.[65]

As reflected in the boards of directors, the VDC was firmly dominated by professors and factory owners, unlikely leaders for a labor union. Professors alone constituted one-third to one half of the directors down to 1900.[66] From 1897 on, the board regularly included Carl Duisberg of the Bayer chemical empire. So complete was the control of the chemical establishment in the VDC that it required a revolt of the rank and file after 1900 to force the inclusion of younger chemists on the board.

There were some other, small specialized chemical associations, such as the German Electrochemical Society (since 1902 the Bunsen Society) and others dedicated to chemical problems of the leather, foodstuffs, and celluloid industries, but they need not detain us here. The VDC was the strongest and biggest professional organization of German chemists, reaching some 2,100 members by 1900 (and about 5,300 by World War I), some two-thirds of all German chemists.[67]

62 Ibid., p. 4.   63 Burchardt, "Zusammenarbeit," 194.   64 Rassow, *VDC,* p. 6.
65 Burchardt, "Zusammenarbeit," 195.   66 Rassow, *VDC,* pp. 56–9.
67 Ibid., p. 63; Burchardt, "Zusammenarbeit," 195.

Aside from wishing to "raise the status of the chemical profession," a concern that the VDC, like so many other new professional organizations, quickly came to recognize as principally realizable through educational reform, German chemists also worried about their economic standing. Despite the rapid growth and increasing prosperity of the chemical industry, chemists did not, in their view, benefit in proportion to their contributions. As the number of chemists grew, so did dissatisfaction with the economic rewards from chemistry.

As with German engineers, the proportion of chemists who were employees rather than entrepreneurs or leading directors of companies grew rapidly. In the early days of the chemical profession through the 1800s, the differentiation process among the three major member-groups of the VDC, owner/manager of a chemical works, practicing chemist, and academic theoretician, had not yet advanced far. Most factories and laboratories were small, with very few employees. Not infrequently, the three roles were combined: academic chemists frequently operated their own private laboratories and worked in them as practicing chemists as a sideline to teaching.[68] The economic rewards (as well as risks) of such entrepreneurial activity could be considerable.

Chemists employed by others did not bear such high risks – demand was apparently strong enough that job security was relatively high – but neither did they reap large rewards. Estimates around 1900 agree that an academically-trained chemist might earn 200 marks per month as a starting salary, 250 after a year, and as much as 350 after several years' experience. This compared with the salary of a *Gymnasium* teacher with a comparable number of years' experience.[69] Chemists often received bonuses, too.

Such mediocre salaries might have been offset by a better system of rewards for inventions made by individual chemists in their companies' laboratories, but the predominant system aroused continuous complaints. Most firms treated such inventions as their own property. Chemists who had a working knowledge of such new processes (even those who had invented them) often had to promise not to reveal such knowledge to any rival companies for which they might subsequently work: a so-called *Karenz* period of up to several years thus effectively hobbled chemists from marketing their knowledge outside their own firm. The VDC did not act on these mounting complaints until after the beginning of the twentieth century, however, and its action will be discussed later.

First, however, we should examine the efforts toward self-help of professions still dependent on public careers rather than the private market for their services.

68 Krätz, "Chemiker," pp. 276–8.
69 Hans-Werner Schütt, "Zum Berufsbild des Chemikers im wilhelminischen Zeitalter," in Schmauderer, *Chemiker im Wandel*, pp. 303–4.

6

~~~~~~

Organization of state-service professions: teachers and the clergy

1. TEACHERS: THE FIRST ORGANIZED BUREAUCRATIC PROFESSION

"The Prussian schoolteacher won the battle of Sadowa," as a widely quoted phrase went in 1866; later the French government shared a similar view regarding Sedan. As the highly centralized French education system underwent reforms in the 1870s prompted by France's defeat by Prussia, new winds also began to blow in the school corridors of Germany.

Perhaps the most significant immediate result of German unification for the school lay not in structural reform, however, but in the *Kulturkampf* that weakened the traditionally close cooperation between church and state in educational affairs. The "battle for modern civilization" (as the Prussian professor Rudolf Virchow dubbed it) was especially acute in Prussia, which constituted roughly two-thirds of the new German Reich. The various measures passed by the Reichstag and the Prussian Diet under Adalbert Falk as *Kultusminister* (Minister of Cults and Education) in the 1870s rallied many of the German teachers who, since Diesterweg and the 1848 Revolution, had favored secularizing schools.

In this atmosphere, attempts to found vigorous professional associations of teachers appeared to make sense again after decades of overt government hostility. German schoolteachers took advantage of the new liberal spirit in the Reich to found the *Deutscher Lehrerverein* (German Teachers Association, or DLV) in 1872.

As will be seen below, the DLV generated at first only a modest attraction for schoolteachers. First, in the spirit of the 1848 radicals who had founded the *Allgemeiner Deutscher Lehrerverein,* the leaders of the DLV tended to favor reforms that would secularize and democratize the school system. This program, plus the traditional gulf in social origins and training between teachers in elementary and higher schools led to the DLV being from the start chiefly an organization of *Volksschullehrer.* More conservative Protestant and Catholic schoolteachers also appear to have shunned the DLV; both founded their own "confessional" teachers' organizations around 1890. Teachers in higher schools also founded or reshaped their own associations. And female teachers, whose very existence appeared as a threat to many male pedagogues, went their own organizational way as well.

Second, many teachers in all levels at first saw little point in a national teachers' association because of the federalized structure of education in the new Germany. Thus, a good deal of organizational energy went into state and regional organizations. These, many teachers believed, would be better able to influence public educational policy in the individual German states, which were autonomous in the area.

The organizational history of teachers' professional groups in the thirty years after national unification is therefore one of rivalries accompanied by tedious negotiations and some eventual meshing of interests and structures. But at no time was there a national body comparable to that of lawyers and physicians.

The DLV, after a slow start following its foundation in 1871, nevertheless grew to become the largest German teachers' organization by World War I. From a mere 5,000 members in 1875, it grew to over 18,000 in 1880 and, after a period of turmoil in the early 1880s to about 44,000 in 1890 and nearly 83,000 by 1900.[1] By World War I, it had gained by some accounts the adherence of 90 percent of the male elementary schoolteachers in Germany.[2]

The DLV achieved such membership, however, only after allaying suspicions and rivalries from other organizations. The old teachers' organization from 1848, the ADLV, it may be recalled, had been successfully suppressed in the course of the postrevolutionary reactions, but an annual national teachers' congress, the *Allgemeine Deutsche Lehrerversammlung*, continued to cast the shadow of the ADLV's traditions. Those teachers who believed that state-level rather than national organizations were more likely to achieve their professional goals were also likely to regard the ADLV as an adequate symbol of national teacher solidarity. Such was the view of the *Preussischer Lehrerverein* (Prussian Teachers Association) after its foundation in 1872.

Thus, several years of negotiation had to follow before the Prussian association allowed its branches to join the DLV in 1879, but only after assurances that the state organization would remain competent in purely Prussian school matters. In a comparable way, the ADLV and the delegates' congress *(Deutscher Lehrertag)* of the DLV agreed to meet in alternative years after 1877, so as to complement each other's work.[3] Not until 1910 did the last independent regional teachers' association join the DLV.[4]

The *Kulturkampf* had also stimulated the growth of regional Catholic teachers' associations; a national one, the *Katholischer Lehrerverband des Deutschen Reiches*

1 Carl L. A. Pretzel, *Geschichte des Deutschen Lehrervereins in den ersten 50 Jahren seines Bestehens* (Leipzig, 1921), p. 112.
2 Rainer Bölling, *Volksschullehrer und Politik. Der Deutsche Lehrerverein 1918–1933.* [*Kritische Studien zur Geschichtswissenschaft*, 32] (Göttingen, 1978), p. 33.
3 Ibid., p. 35.   4 Gahlings, *Volksschullehrer*, p. 65.

(Catholic Teachers League of the German Reich, or KLVDR), was established in 1889. Eyed suspiciously by the DLV and the Prussian government alike, the KLVDR was principally successful in organizing Catholic elementary teachers who did not belong to other teachers' organizations. Although it was the second largest teachers' organization by 1910 (with nearly 19,000 members), the KLVDR was not even able to persuade all regional Catholic teachers' groups to join because of its supposed subservience to the Catholic Center Party.[5]

Conservative Protestants also founded an association for teachers devoted to the "confessional" or denominationally segregated elementary school in 1890. This *Verband Deutscher Evangelischer Lehrer- und Lehrerinnen-Vereine* (League of German Protestant Teachers Associations, or VDELV) never achieved considerable size or influence, perhaps because it forbade its members to join the DLV, which it perceived to be its main rival.[6]

Finally, female teachers generally encountered either exclusionary policies or undisguised hostility from their male counterparts in these years and so founded their own organizations. Male and female schoolteachers tended to come from different worlds: the latter usually came from higher social circles than the former, frequently taught in private girls' schools patronized by wealthy urban parents, were usually obliged (until after World War I) to remain celibate, and were trained in a more uniform way, enabling them to teach in both elementary and higher girls' schools.[7] The number of female teachers grew rapidly after the founding of the German Empire, reaching over 22,000 in 1901, or about one-seventh of all German teachers. In 1861 there had been only about 1,800 in all of Prussia.[8]

The *Allgemeiner Deutscher Lehrerinnenverein* (General German Female Teachers Association, or ADLnV), founded in 1890, was less divided along elementary/higher school lines than comparable male organizations, although it also had to compete with small Catholic and Protestant female teachers' organizations. Shortly after the turn of the twentieth century (1906), the ADLnV had some 18,000 members, compared to half that many for the Catholic teachers' association *Verein Katholischer Deutscher Lehrerinnen* (VKDLn) and one-twentieth as many for the Protestant *Verein Christlicher Lehrerinnen* (VCLn).[9]

Teachers in *Realschulen* also perceived the need to organize nationally in the 1870s, creating the *Allgemeiner Deutscher Realschulmännerverein* (General German Realistic Schoolmen Association, or ADRV) in mid-decade, although it re-

5 Ibid., pp.66–7; Bölling, *Volksschullehrer und Politik*, pp. 36–7.
6 Gahlings, *Volksschullehrer*, p. 66.
7 Ibid., p. 67; Bölling, *Volksschullehrer und Politik*, p.16; Jürgen Zinnecker, *Sozialgeschichte der Mädchenbildung* (Weinheim/Basel, 1973), passim; James C. Albisetti, *Schooling German Girls and Women: Secondary and Higher Education in the Nineteenth Century* (Princeton, 1988), esp. chap. 7.
8 Ernst Cloer, "Sozialgeschichtliche Aspekte der Solidarisierung der preussischen Volksschullehrerschaft im Krieg und in der Weimarer Republik," in Manfred Heinemann, ed., *Der Lehrer und seine Organisation* (Stuttgart, 1977), p. 72.
9 Gahlings, *Volksschullehrer*, p. 70.

mained relatively small and devoted particularly to the protection of the hybrid school form that lay between the classical *Gymnasium* and the lower, purely technical school and came to be called the *Realgymnasium*. Splintering off from the older *Schulmännerverein* (VDS), the ADRV represented teachers with higher training than DLV members, but thanks to the partly "modern" and technical orientation of their upper schools, they were often snubbed by the classical schoolteachers. Although quite effective in drawing public attention to the equal value of their school type by 1900, the ADRV does not appear to have been an unalloyed professional representational group, and many of its members were not even teachers (only about one-third were in 1877).[10]

Gymnasium teachers were virtually the only ones not to organize nationally in the first three decades of the new Reich. Instead, they established new state-level organizations or built on ones already extant. The *Versammlung Deutscher Philologen und Schulmänner* of 1837 remained the only national forum. Generally their aims included those already articulated as early as 1848, equality with other university-trained state employees, usually judges, in points of rank and salary. Another objective, broadly shared with the DLV, which the academically-trained "philologists" did not however make common cause, was the institution of a career ladder.

The history of the entire German school system under the new Reich is very complex, and perhaps for this reason a satisfactory definitive history of it does not yet exist. Still, the first thirty years of the new Reich did witness some limited movement toward greater homogenization. Pressures in this direction came from the predominance of the Prussian educational model; from the orientation of many schoolteachers' groups on bureaucratic organizational models; and from the leadership provided by a concerned Kaiser Wilhelm II in organizing the Reich school conferences of 1890 and 1900.

Still, German teachers did not enjoy the advantages, say, of their colleagues in medicine and law in having either an increasingly agreed-upon canon of professional standards – derived from scientific medicine or a national lawyers' code, respectively. Teacher's autonomy was constantly undercut by the demands of parents, church authorities (who still after 1870 had supervisory rights over religious and other instruction), and civic and state officials. Teaching was still not a full-time profession as late as 1900: *Volksschullehrer*, at least, were often expected to carry out menial tasks in rural churches, and even *Gymnasium* teachers often had to take on outside work (tutoring, writing, etc.) to augment their salaries. Rivalries based on differing class origins, educational background, religious creed, humanistic versus practical pedagogical objectives, and even sex – all in part reflecting the complexity of the pupil population – undercut teacher solidarity.

10 Otto Schmeding, *Die Entstehung des realistischen höheren Schulwesens in Preussen bis zum Jahre 1933* (Cologne, 1956), p. 83.

The desire for further bureaucratization of schoolteaching as a profession reflected the welter of differing historical and actual situations in which schoolteachers found themselves. At the beginning of the German Reich, elementary schoolteachers in the various states did not enter anything like a unified system, even on the state level. Obligations, working conditions, and salaries varied widely from village to village and town to town. There was little prospect for advancement, that is, no career ladder, for elementary schoolteachers anywhere. Even obtaining a position, no matter how poorly paid, sometimes required what we would today call "kickbacks" from aspiring teachers to older ones who wanted to retire but had no pensions on which to do so. The slender opportunities for advancement consisted in taking further examinations after some years of teaching, with the hope of advancing to the only slightly better-paid positions of school director (principal) or teacher at training seminars for other schoolteachers. Collecting school fees in the elementary schools was often up to the teachers, with fluctuating success and sometimes loss of income to the unlucky.

The way to eliminate local erraticism, guarantee a modicum of equity, and raise the status of elementary schoolteachers therefore appeared to lie in pressing for a regularization of the bureaucratic status. Because most higher schoolteachers had achieved this goal, at least nominally, through their university education, elementary schoolteachers also pressed for raising educational standards for their own group, a topic to be discussed in the next chapter.

The problem, a very complex one, lay in the definition of bureaucratic status of state employees. In Prussia, for example, "real" civil servants, from prime minister to railway crossing-guard, came to be defined as "immediate to the state" in that they were not subject to any other chain of command than the one from state to employee. Schoolteachers were usually still regarded as "mediate" or indirect employees. If the state decreed public education but left its implementation to the local community, for example, then the status and income of the teachers was dependent on the community, even though the school was in a way the outcome of state legislation.

The problem was further complicated by the way in which the higher school system, especially as initiated by Prussia, functioned: most classical *Gymnasien* and some other higher schools were carried on the state budget. But other higher schools, including even some *Gymnasien,* were not state-sponsored, but rather locally and sometimes privately sponsored (like girls' schools). Thus, some higher schoolteachers were state officials, others were not.

The lack of uniform career ladders in German schools, the differences from school to school and locality to locality, were further complicated by the absence of a career ladder even within the same school. Two of the reasons for renewed organizational activity among Prussian upper schoolteachers in the 1870s, for example, had nothing to do with the alleged victory of the Prussian schoolteacher over the French, but rather the double defeat of the former by the Prussian Diet. First, the Diet refused once again to elevate the state *Gymnasium* teachers to the same rank as the "equally trained" judges. Second, although it raised the salaries of all officials, including schoolteachers, in 1872, it continued to discriminate between school directors and other teachers, and failed to create a career ladder. The only way for most *Gymnasium* teachers to advance in income or stature was to become a school principal; any other form of achievement remained unrewarded. And achieving the status and income of a school head remained notoriously a question of sufficient longevity coupled with correct political attitudes.

Thus, both the DLV and the various organizations of higher schoolteachers fought consistently for the creation of a career ladder and reward system in the schools comparable to that of the regular civil service.

These struggles went forward on very different levels. Elementary schoolteachers, lacking the educational background of high-school teachers, fought to achieve the sort of bureaucratic regularity of minor officialdom. This meant not only a regular career ladder in their view, but also the kind of freedom from local interference enjoyed by even lowly officials: who could imagine local parents or clergy telling a state railway-crossing guard or a policeman how to do his job? For teachers in *Realschulen,* it meant achieving equality with the classical higher schools. And for the teachers in the latter, it meant formal and pay-scale equality with the university law graduates employed by the state – the judges.

All teachers and their organizations complained about the material rewards of their profession. Elementary schoolteachers, who had compared themselves to the less successful local peasants in the 1848 era, began to make comparisons to the manual and industrial laborers of Germany. Although the *Volksschullehrer* rarely came from the working class, but rather mostly from the lower end of the middle class (over 80 percent in Brandenburg, over 70 percent in Baden,)[11] they had had to undergo several years of study to achieve the possibility of becoming a teacher. They typically graduated from the *Volksschule,* studied on their own two or three years longer, took an entrance examination for a state normal school (seminar), and spent several more years, usually two or three, to attain the credentials to enter the schoolteaching profession. For all this effort, they complained, they were often rewarded with less than their untrained confreres who had gone right out to work at age fourteen.

Such complaints are supported by statistical information. In Prussia in 1864, nearly 30 percent of all schoolteachers were paid less than 150 thaler per year, and another 56 percent received between that and 300 thaler. (The thaler was the equivalent of about one dollar.) Some 57 percent of Prussian schoolteachers earned less than the average wages of unskilled coalminers in state mines at the same time.[12] By 1897, at the end of the period under discussion, the first

11 Bölling, *Volksschullehrer und Politik,* p. 22.   12 Cloer, "Sozialgeschichtliche Askpekte," p. 63.

Prussian Teachers Pay Law established a minimum pay scale between 900 and 1,800 marks, or about $225 to 450 per year (somewhat less for female teachers). Considering extra pay for administrative and other functions, the average elementary schoolteacher salary in Prussia by 1901 lay around 1,400 marks in the countryside and 1,800 in cities. This meant a considerable improvement during the three intervening decades, at least in comparison to industrial and artisanal wages, which by some measures were only half as much.[13]

Still, teachers' salaries, though much improved by 1900, were still inadequate for a comfortable standard of living. A survey of *Volksschullehrer* in Württemberg, whose salaries also improved rapidly in the 1890s, indicates the minimum outlay for a family of three was still more than income from school salary. The difference, often significant amounts, had to be made up from outside work.[14]

Teachers in higher schools had comparable complaints, although their salaries were always significantly higher. After the financial and personal sacrifices of *Gymnasium* and an equivalent number of semesters of study at universities, they were paid less and had less chance of advancement than judges. Figures for Prussia may give some idea of the financial position of higher schoolteachers. Under the 1863 budget plan, the average salary of a full-time, regular teacher ranged between 950 and 750 thalers, depending on the size of the city.[15] This was several times the salary of an elementary teacher, but not as much as junior judges on the Prussian bench. These salaries were raised in 1872 (the range averaged 1,200 thalers in Berlin, and 1,050 elsewhere). On the heels of Kaiser Wilhelm's school conference, they were raised again in 1892 (range: 2,100 to 4,500 marks). A step-scale for raises based on years of service and pensions were also added.[16] These figures are, however, somewhat misleading, because they refer only to regularly contracted teachers; they do not take into account the actual salaries earned by probationary teachers who were technically not yet *regular* employees and were paid far less. In Prussia in 1902, the majority of regularly contracted schoolteachers had had to put in between two and ten years in such "assistant" positions, and 35 percent had had to wait between four and ten years.[17] Continuing dissatisfaction with such conditions eventually, in 1903, led to national organization of higher schoolteachers in what came to be called the Philologists' Association.

Like other organized groups of professionals or professionalizing occupations, German schoolteachers ended the nineteenth century with a sense of frustration, yet they had achieved here and there some significant successes with their efforts. The full fruits of these efforts would not come until after 1900. And,

13 Bölling, *Volksschullehrer und Politik*, p. 24.
14 Friedrich, *Volksschule in Württemberg*, pp. 397–8.   15 Lexis, *Besoldungsverhältnisse*, pp. 15–16.
16 Ibid., p. 49.
17 Hartmut Titze, "Die soziale und geistige Umbildung des preussischen Oberlehrerstandes von 1870 bis 1914," *Zeitschrift für Pädagogik Beiheft* 14 (1977): 125.

unlike other professions, German teachers still had no organization approaching uniformity.

Yet, in their various organizations schoolteachers pressed hard, loudly, and with some success for at least a measure of social recognition of their demands. Both Bismarck and William II publicly recognized the importance of schoolteachers, undermining to some extent the traditional public mistrust and indifference to them. The DLV made implicit alliances with liberal political groups that undoubtedly helped shake the foundations of the purely clerical school. Conservatives even accused the DLV of harboring secret sympathies for social democracy, but this hardly seems documentable. And, although at the beginning of our period German governments had eyed teachers' organizations with great suspicion, seeing in them a form of organized rebellion, by the end of the century a measure of acceptance and even heedfulness had replaced earlier hostility. The German Emperor himself intervened repeatedly after 1890 in school reform issues and for the improvement of conditions for teachers. In return, William II expected "loyalty to duty and understanding dedication" on the part of his teachers, especially the inculcation of nationalistic and socially conservative values. [18]

2. THE CLERICAL PROFESSION

Although a sort of bureaucracy itself, the "evangelical" pastorate was buffeted by the winds of secularism as industrializing and urbanizing forces eroded its traditional authority. In one case, that of Hesse, the immediate cause of the founding of a pastors' association was government "interference," specifically a warning against clergy becoming involved in anti-Semitic movements. Doctrinal and other disputes among the various Protestant state churches and among individual clergymen had long acted as a hindrance to a national organization.

But by 1892 such a structure was erected in the *Verband Deutscher Evangelischer Pfarrervereine,* or VDEP, the Association of German Evangelical Pastors. In addition to pressing for the unification of various Protestant state churches and for the perpetuation of the religiously denominated elementary school, the association clearly intended to lobby for the *Standesinteressen* of the pastorate, particularly in matters of salary and benefits. For example, the VDEP (unsuccessfully) petitioned the Prussian government and diet for increases beyond those laid down in the 1898 Pastors' Compensation Law: a minimum range of 2,700 to 6,000 marks was deemed essential by the pastors to prevent "proletarization" of their profession. [19] Clearly, in compensation matters the pastors looked to the *Oberlehrer* (senior teachers) of the upper schools as their reference group; but they also appear to have been influenced by the physicians and

18 "Allerhöchster Erlass vom 26. November 1900," in Wilhelm Lexis, ed. *Die Reform des höheren Schulwesens in Preussen* (Halle, 1902), p. x.
19 Kulemann, *Berufsvereine,* pp. 11–13.

lawyers' "chambers" in requesting a reform of disciplinary procedures (e.g. the introduction of disciplinary courts) to enhance their autonomy vis-à-vis church and state authorities.[20]

The Protestant Pastors' Association achieved few of its demands prior to World War I. But after initial suspicion and even hostility by higher church authorities, the regular meetings of the association gradually achieved a certain benevolent toleration from these quarters. The VDEP had, by the eve of the war, organized over 11,000 pastors and included most of the local associations in Germany.[21]

3. CONCLUSION

The period from the *Reichsgründung* to the turn of the twentieth century included the greatest organizational and structural changes among professions in any period of German history. The general pattern followed by most organizations went from initial altruistic and knowledge-based justifications to a more open advocacy of the material and legal privileges of each profession, new and old. This advocacy role was perhaps strongest among the "new" professions, such as engineering and chemistry, but it was certainly not restricted to them.

The three decades after 1870 also witnessed an important loosening of bureaucratic control over many professions. The upper bureaucracy itself, still based (and as many critics began complaining, archaically) on university legal studies, enjoyed sufficient privileges, status and income that it did not yet require the self-promotion that a professional organization could have hypothetically provided. Nor did military officers, with their own socially exclusive and professionally revered standing in postunification Germany, perceive the need to organize. But as we have just seen, one traditional profession, the Protestant clergy, did feel threatened enough by the rush of modernity to found a rather weak professional organization.

As we shall see, the organizing drive of German professional groups did not stop: after 1900 even such traditional professional pillars of the existing order as university professors and civil servants banded together nationally to press for their own interests.

Before turning to this next period, however, we must look in Chapter 7 at the ways in which existing professional groups in the first three decades after the founding of the Reich approached the problems of professional education, certification or "credentialing," and the status, privileges and autonomy conferred traditionally through the higher educational system in Germany.

20 Ibid, pp. 13–15.   21 Ibid., p. 16.

7

Professional credentials in the new Reich

In the preceding chapter, frequent references were made to education, certification, examinations, and other forms of credentialing that preoccupied most of the new professional organizations in the German Reich. These issues are rarely far from the central concerns of any professional organization; but they were particularly burning ones in the Wilhelminian era. Nor did they cease to be important after the turn of the century, and we shall have to return to them in subsequent chapters. But the beginning of the twentieth century did mark a certain cesura in some ways, bringing to a climax a number of separate or intertwined debates that had been swirling for decades in the hot currents of Imperial German rhetoric. This chapter focuses upon this highly charged area of professional concern and activity separately from the others discussed in Chapters 5 and 6.

In treating the disparate policies and desiderata of the German professions together and topically here, I hope to show certain patterns that they shared in their strategies for changes in educational structures, examinations, and related aspects of the complex system of credentials based on expert knowledge that is the heart of modern professional self-justification. Thus, the chapter will deal with a series of topics, ranging from preprofessional education (e.g. the debate between "humanists" and "realists" about higher schools) to the admission of women to professions.[1] Within each topic, the positions of each major professional group will be discussed.

The professional groups were not the only members of German society interested in education and certification issues in the last three decades of the nineteenth century. It would be a distortion to think of them as prime movers behind change (or opposition to it), but by the same token, their influence has usually been unduly ignored or underrated by historians of educational change.

---

1 For an excellent recent general study of school reform, see James C. Albisetti, *Secondary School Reform in Imperial Germany* (Princeton, 1983).

Suffice it to recall that the last third of the nineteenth century witnessed a number of significant socioeconomic changes that called for response by the educational system. The rise of industry and technology forced several re-valuations of what one might call collectively "technical education." To cite two examples, by about 1900, the "realistic" higher schools were declared equal to the traditional classical *Gymnasium,* and Germany's technical colleges had won the right to award doctorates and consider themselves equal to the ancient uni-versities. The expansion of the student population of both types of higher edu-cational institutions, which grew about twice as fast as the general one under the German Empire, produced other problems. The public-school system also grew and differentiated, with multiple consequences for the learned professions, and not only for teaching. Thus educational reform or refinements in existing systems were much a part of the background, moving constantly, irrespective of the specific wishes of professional organizations.

There were patterns in the professional groups' discussions and demands for changes in education and certification, but that does not mean they wanted the same identical changes; indeed, sometimes, they disagreed with one another (or even within the same group) on details. These tactical disagreements often proved to have a strategic common theme – what would reflect best on the prestige of the profession. Thus, physicians and engineers might disagree about the usefulness of Greek as a part of preprofessional training, but they both argued for maintaining high standards in higher schools generally.

One question that must be posed concerns the effectiveness of emerging pro-fessional groups in imposing their views on the educational and certifying sys-tem. The degree to which the states' bureaucracies or even the professoriate in the institutions of professional training cooperated with or resisted professional group wishes may be viewed as a significant index of the level of control over the professions by organizations representing their members.

Let us first address a more fundamental question, however: why were educa-tional qualifications, examinations, and certifications so important to German professional groups at this time?

One part of the answer may be given as "tradition." By the 1870s, the vir-tual state monopoly over the higher education system had become sufficiently entrenched as to be called "traditional." If there was any lingering doubt about this, the *Kulturkampf* against the German Catholic Church in the 1870s re-affirmed important aspects of secular state sovereignty over education. With very few exceptions, German professional groups accepted this tradition in general principle. The simple fact that there would be no question in Germany of private, proprietary, clerical/denominational, municipal, or other types of higher educational institutions offering preparation for professional careers shaped the agendas of professional organizations in important ways.

In other words, accepting this tradition, German professionals had to deal with the state bureaucracies when they wished changes in the education or certification of professionals. Normally this meant the state educational administration, although other ministries played roles as well (trade for technical education, war for special student military status, finance, frequently, for feasibility, and so on). But other players entered the game, as well, making it far less simple than before the founding of the Reich. For example, both the national and state parliaments now played a more significant role in professional legislation, and interested parties outside the political arena such as industrialists sometimes became involved. Given a general tendency toward convergence of the professional standards and practices of the twenty-six member states of the German Empire, the wishes of Prussia and the smaller states had also to be reconciled in negotiations.

Another part of the tradition now cemented was acceptance of the civil service as the general model for professionalization in Germany, if only loosely. By this I refer to the British and American experiences of the same time: there a modern civil service was just in the course of being established, and the medical profession served rather as the leading model for others. The German tradition rather paralleled that of the civil service: mandatory completion of a classical education, with examination and certificate (*Abitur*); followed by a mandatory number of years of higher education, further examinations, and certification by a state board; followed by further years of service in poorly remunerated trainee positions. Not all professions matched this model, but most aspired to it, with suitable modifications.

As with other aspects of rank in civil services, questions of educational qualifications became more acute among the professions or even divisions within them. On the basis of comparable years of university training, for example, higher school teachers began to claim with increasing volume their right to be placed on the same footing as judges. The civil service itself was not immune to complaints about status based on insufficient recognition of educational qualifications. As one might expect the beneficiaries of the system – senior state counselors and men of similar rank – did not tend to complain, but the less fortunate judiciary (and private attorneys, who had the same basic training) did. Outside the legal profession, other groups made increasing reference to it when claiming disadvantaged treatment despite equivalent education.

Nor was the education of civil servants, or legal education in general held up as a model – quite the contrary. The training of lawyers came in for some of the harshest criticism of the century during the 1870s and 1880s.

But in terms of a standardized professional education and examination system, that of civil service took precedence in terms of its age, and doubtless its traditional social prestige. One small but significant sign of the latter was the continued desirability of civil service honorary titles among nonbureaucratic professionals, for example, *Medinzinalrat, Hofrat* (medical counselor, court counselor). Much as isolated scientists and professional leaders might poke fun at the practice or refuse such "honors" on the grounds that their standing in their profession was enough, they could not stem the tide.

The seeming inconsistency between the civil service as a general model for other professions and sharp, unquestionably deserved criticism of inadequate educational preparation for that career points up the importance of the process of *Verwissenschaftlichung*, or "scientificization." This process constitutes a second major reason for the importance of educational and certificational change to German professional groups. As noted earlier in this book, the process was a continuous one, placing ever higher demands of knowledge – quantitatively, qualitatively, and in terms of specialization – on future practitioners. This process took a quantum leap after 1860, however, chiefly, but not exclusively, in the medical, natural, and engineering sciences.

This was the classic period of breakdown in the traditional "faculty" organization of universities, to be replaced by the system of seminars, institutes, and laboratories that sprang up in such profusion after 1860. The nature of training for the professions was also necessarily affected by this process, among other things by the appearance of specialization. That development occurred as a result of special dynamics in science and university growth, reflected, for example, in the creation of new subdisciplines in such fields as natural science and medicine. Resulting trends toward specialization within professional practice were not always welcomed by the representative professional groups, however, as we shall see. The latter might press for the academicization of the profession (with the goal of all its members passing through a university-level training) only to be alarmed at the later implications (overspecialized and therefore inadequate "general" training for the upcoming professionals).

That dilemma points to a third reason why education and certification were highly important in this period. Higher education represented not only desirable training (*Ausbildung*) but also the social cachet of personality formation (*Bildung*). University attendance and the preconditions for it (including study of the classics and eligibility for the coveted special status as military reserve officer) traditionally bestowed social status unconnected to professional skills or training. Although one can only cautiously and remotely compare the social "ranks" of the Anglo-American "gentleman" and the German *gebildeter Mensch* ("cultivated" man), the "right kind of school" played a role in both systems of status allocation. Consequently, changing the curriculum or privileges of the different higher school types, placing universities and technical colleges on a footing of equality, or similar reforms, no matter how innocuous or sensible they seemed on the surface, indirectly threatened to undermine or augment the social prestige of one profession or another, and sometimes even different segments of the same profession.

Finally, the factor of increased competition for professional careers lent new urgency to concern with the educational and qualificational system. The growth of student bodies, greatly disproportionate to population increase, led to mounting fears of overcrowding in the learned professions. Although there had been occasional complaints about oversupplies of "learned men" before 1870, the causes after 1870 were different. In place of a relatively steady state in both supply and demand in the early nineteenth century, with smaller or larger imbalances, from the 1870s on both supply and demand increased overall, with mounting surpluses on the side of supply. Whereas "unfair competition" for professionals' offerings of service had previously come from "unqualified" practitioners ("quacks" or "corner scribes"), it now came increasingly from other "qualified" practitioners. Thus, the temptation to manipulate educational and examination "filters" to reduce competition became more seductive than before.

And if potential ruinous competition from young male graduates was not enough, the prospect of female competitors began to surface by the end of the century as a result of agitation by the German women movement. Actual competition did not become significant until after World War I, and women were only admitted in small numbers to professional programs beginning at the turn of the century. But German professional groups were quick to sense danger from this quarter and to take positions about it.

Let us now turn to the various main topics of reform discussion concerning education and certification for the professions.

1. PREPROFESSIONAL EDUCATION

A full (usually nine-year) *Gymnasium* education (following preparatory elementary education) and the passing of a "maturity examination," or *Abitur*, at its conclusion as the precondition to university entrance had become an established tradition in the German states in the early nineteenth century. This form of college preparation undoubtedly made much sense at a time when a curriculum encompassing classics, ancient languages, history, and a little mathematics and natural science related well to what was studied at universities. Obviously, theologians and future schoolteachers had to know the classical languages and literatures, and much of the older medical literature was still in Latin and even Greek. Much of law was still based on Latin texts, as well.

In the decades around mid-century, and in response to the needs of commerce and industry, "realistic" (as opposed to humanistic) schools began to proliferate as well, or to replace the older Latin, town, or civic schools. They stressed modern rather than classical languages and spent far more time on mathematics, science, and auxiliary subjects. Although these schools came in many varieties and were often municipal creations (sometimes as continuations of older grammar schools), one might for our purposes distinguish between the two types most common in the late nineteenth century, the *Oberrealschule* and the *Realgymnasium* (also called for a time in Prussia *Realschule I. Ordnung*). The *Realschule* changed shape and function every few decades in Prussia at least; by the 1880s it had become a six-year school and thus not directly a preparatory institution for higher studies. The *Realgymnasium* was a sort of hybrid between the *Gymnasium* and the *Oberrealschule*, offering Latin but not Greek, more modern languages than the *Gymnasium*, but somewhat less math and science than the *Oberrealschule*. Some *Oberrealschulen* also offered Latin. Graduates of all three school types could sit for the *Abitur*, but they could not all qualify for university doctoral programs or state examinations, making the *Abitur* after any school but the *Gymnasium* somewhat devalued.[2]

Thus, some exceptions were made to the general rule that both *Gymnasium* attendance and the *Abitur* were needed to study at the university; chemistry, dentistry and pharmacy students could attend university courses, for example, without being fully matriculated students. Particularly in the fields relating to natural science, complaints about the inadequacies of *Gymnasium* graduates' preparation multiplied among the professoriate. Some argued that graduates of the realistic schools were really much better prepared in what mattered for the study of science or medicine in the modern world.

An example of the kind of debate that could result may be drawn from the experience of the medical profession. As early as 1878, the *Allgemeiner Deutscher Realschulmännerverein* decided to press for the right for First-class *Realschule* graduates to study medicine at universities. This strategy was the opening wedge for the eventual entitlement of such graduates to study in any university faculty. At the time, a new examination order for physicians was being prepared by the German authorities. The *Verein* petitioned the Reichstag in this sense. An expert advisory commission, while granting some of the teachers' points, objected that opening only the medical faculties to *Realschule* graduates would disadvantage the doctors, who would no longer be considered *Gelehrte* (scholars) among their colleagues.[3]

Variations on this argument would be used in medical circles for another quarter-century, although not all physicians were hostile to the *Realschulen*. A poll taken among member associations of the German Medical Association, at the request of the Prussian Education Minister Falk, produced an overwhelming negative response to admission of *Realschule* graduates; but nearly two-thirds of them also stressed the need for better scientific instruction in the *Gymnasium*.[4] Thus it was not science curriculum as such, but the "inferior" *Realschule* that the medical associations rejected.[5]

---

2 For a thorough description and suggestive interpretation of the different school types and changes, see Detlef K. Müller, *Sozialstruktur und Schulsystem. Aspekte zum Strukturwandel des Schulwesens im 19. Jahrhundert* (Göttingen, 1977), pp. 37–45 and passim. And for a comparative, international symposium on the reshaping of schools to provide new "qualifications" for adult life, see Detlef K. Müller, Fritz Ringer and Brian Simon, eds., *The Rise of the Modern Educational System. Structural Change and Social Reproduction 1870–1920* (Cambridge, 1987).

3 Schmeding, *Schulwesens*, p. 91.   4 Ibid., p. 94.

5 For an illuminating sample of arguments from contemporary physicians for and against the classical requirements, see Wenig, *Ausbildung*, pp. 123–5. Wenig sees the medical profession about equally divided on the issue and dismisses it as unconnected to professional status. The strongly one-sided, proclassical stands of the Medical Association indicate, however, that at least the medical elites were very worried.

By 1883 the Prussian ministry finally reformed school curriculum, cutting back Latin hours at *Gymnasien* in favor of science and mathematics and increasing Latin hours in the First-class *Realschulen,* which were now renamed *Realgymnasien.* But the graduates of the latter still had no right to study medicine.[6]

The leaders of the *Realschulmännerverein* continued to press for the admission of their pupils to medical study; for example, in 1889 they again petitioned the Reichstag and even organized some support among deputies.[7] But despite William II's personal advice to the school reform conference of 1890 ("We want to educate young national Germans, not young Greeks and Romans!"), it took a further conference in 1900 before major changes in the rights of non-*Gymnasium* students would be instituted. And when this happened, the declaration of equality among the three nine-year school types meant that the arguments concerning admission of Greek-less "barbarians" merely into the medical faculties had been rendered moot. But more of this important change later.

The question of keeping nonhumanists out of an increasingly scientific discipline (medicine) tells us something about both the teaching and the medical professions in Germany at this time. The *Realschulmänner* were fighting the *Gymnasium* teachers for equal recognition and treatment, and one way to do so was to demonstrate the equal qualification of their pupils to study at least medicine at university without the full panoply of classical learning. The German Medical Association and most of its members were at least skeptical about abandoning the classics as a precondition for their profession, not because they regarded scientific preparation at the *Gymnasium* as adequate, but because they regarded the various realistic schools as socially inferior. Most importantly, the physicians were horrified at the thought that their profession might be the first and only among the university-linked ones to be opened to non-*Gymnasium* graduates, thus degrading it relative to the others.

The tone of an editorial appeal in the official journal of the DAeV in 1901 may give some flavor of the physicians' renewed concern:

Can something be done against this rape? The doctors declared almost unanimously in 1879 for keeping humanistic pre-education and have lately demanded . . . that in no case should a sundering from the other learned professional types take place. Thus have the German Physicians . . . unanimously spoken, and now we are to get a new slap in the face with a regulation to damage and demean us, which we must fight and resist![8]

The Prussian government soon issued instructions, however, to allow non-*Gymnasium* graduates to attend law and philosophical faculties if any stated deficiencies in Latin were shown to have been remedied by the late stages of professional preparation. With this "equalization," the medical profession gave up its fight over Greek, Latin, and the *Gymnasium.*

It was not only the "old" professions such as medicine that looked nervously at school reform. Such "new" ones as dentistry, chemistry, and engineering

6 Schmeding, *Schulwesens,* p. 107.   7 Ibid., p. 135.   8 *Aerztliches Vereinsblatt* 28 (1901): 144.

did as well. The trend, if not always achieved in practice, was to press for a uniformly high (if not qualitatively identical) schooling for entrance into these new professions so as to make such requirements equal to those of the "old" academic professions and, of course, to reduce opportunities for those who had previously slipped in with lesser schooling levels.

Educational issues virtually dominated the German Dental Association (VBDZAe) from its first meeting on.[9] As a part of school reform proposals, a study commission considered recommending a change in the regulations concerning admission to dental practice nation-wide that would have reduced the schooling requirements to completing the six-year *Realschule.* After energetic protests by the VBDZAe in 1893, this proposal was dropped.[10]

The association naturally feared that such an "alignment" with requirements for surveyors and veterinarians would fling the profession back into a purely artisanal occupation (as there were still plenty of "dental technicians" competing with "academic" dentists). As the editor of the *Vereinsbund*'s journal argued, however, the idea of serving the public by lowering school requirements for dentists and thereby producing more was passé: enough academic dentists were being trained already, and standards should if anything be raised. Another significant argument betrayed the constant comparisons made between the dental and "normal" physicians: "The public is better served if the dentist has a collegial relationship with the doctor and if they can understand each other in a difficult case than if the [educational] gap between them is too great for mutual understanding. Such a gap can occur if the preeducation of dentists is further reduced."[11]

The organized academic dentists were able to celebrate a small victory in preventing erosion of the schooling gains they already had. But they failed to reach their higher goal – the requirement that candidates for academic study of dentistry must also finish the final year of higher schools and obtain the *Abitur* – until 1909.[12]

A slightly different aspect of the school-reform problem faced the chemical profession. Increasingly the German chemical industry complained about poor preparation and above all narrow specialization in young graduates, which meant they were not adaptable to rapidly changing situations in industry. Part of the fault was found in the fact that academic study in chemistry did not require the *Abitur* – perhaps as much as half of the graduate chemists in the mid-1890s lacked it.[13] The *Verein Deutscher Chemiker* finally pressed the German authorities for the *Abitur* requirement along with its request for a state exami-

9 Seefeld, *Zahnärzte,* p. 13.   10 Ibid., p. 21.
11 Julius Parreidt, "Rückwärts?," *Deutsche Monatsschrift für Zahnheilkunde* 11 (1893): 159.
12 Seefeld, *Zahnärzte,* p. 22.
13 Lothar Burchardt, "Wissenschaft und Wirtschaftswachstum: Industrielle Einflussnahmen auf die Wissenschaftspolitik im Wilhelminischen Deutschland," in Ulrich Engelhardt et al., eds., *Soziale Bewegung und politische Verfassung. Festschrift für Werner Conze* (Stuttgart, 1976), pp. 775–6.

nation for chemists (about which more below). In the struggle, however, for improving tertiary examinations for chemists, the demand for the *Abitur* was assigned a secondary place. Nevertheless, as a side-effect of the VDC's compromise with universities and technical colleges over the *Staatsexamen*, admission to the doctorate stage in chemistry at German universities was greatly tightened up. By 1909, as an indirect result, the percentage of non-*Abitur* holders studying chemistry had dropped to 14 percent, down from 60 percent in 1898.[14]

The educational reform ideas of the *Verein Deutscher Ingenieure* closely paralleled those of the chemists. From its earliest days, already in the 1860s, the VDI had vigorously promoted polytechnical education and linked the status of the profession with successful reforms in this area. Franz Grashof, a leading VDI spokesman in the 1860s and 1870s, early argued for the requirement of the *Abitur* for attendance at technical colleges as a part of the VDI's long-range goal of full equality between the latter and universities. The radical implications of such a change were pointed out by other engineers (in the mid-1870s, five-sixths of all living German engineers had been trained in middle-level trade schools), but Grashof insisted such engineers were in effect superfluous.[15]

From 1886 onward, the VDI's officially resolved policy favored more school curriculum that would strengthen the claim of future engineers to be *gebildet* and the equalization of "realistic" and "humanistic" school types.[16]

To be sure, the engineering profession was much more divided about other school issues, e.g. whether a new system of terminal mid-level trades schools (*technische Mittelschulen*) ought to be set up now that the *Oberrealschule* and *Realgymnasium* had grown into preparatory institutions. Recognizing that not all engineers required higher education, the VDI nevertheless argued about the precise level at which "lower" engineers should leave school; significantly, the VDI resolved in 1889 that at least the level of achievement required for eligibility as a reserve officer candidate must be built into such hypothetical new trade schools, otherwise engineers would be further segregated into different social classes.[17] The VDI had considerable success influencing the setting up of such schools in following decades, but that story cannot detain us here.[18]

As mentioned earlier in this work, the status of *Einjährig-Freiwilliger* assumed a particular touchstone symbolism in the Wilhelminian Reich, although its origins stretch back to the military reforms of Napoleonic times. The elevated prestige of the military in the wake of national unification wars and Wilhelminian imperialism made reserve officers fashionable, even as recruiting reserve officers from the middle classes became more necessary because the armed forces' growth outstripped the traditional aristocratic supply. Few obviously

14 Rassow, *VDC*, p. 76.   15 *VDI–Zeitschrift* 20 (1876): 639.
16 Manegold, "VDI," p. 141.   17 Ibid., p. 157.
18 For a lucid and provocative treatment, see Cornelis W. R. Gispen, *New Profession, Old Order: Engineers and German Society, 1815–1914* (Cambridge, 1989), esp. chap. 7–12.

took advantage of the right built into the *Abitur* to enter the professional officer's career without taking the usual ensign's exam.

Far more attractive was the right accorded to successful completers of the
eighth year of higher schooling to be "one-year volunteers," that is, avoid military conscription and its long term of service by "volunteering" for special
training, at the end of which the cadet was eligible for regimental selection as a
"Royal Reserve Officer," a highly prized social title. No matter how much more
rationally schooling and preeducation for the professions could have been imagined, any system that did not include this level with its built-in rights tended
to be rejected by professional groups.

2. TERTIARY EDUCATION, EXAMINATION, AND CERTIFICATION

On the level of tertiary education, one concern for many professional groups
was the structure of curriculum. Although they almost never presumed to interfere with personnel matters (e.g. appointments to chairs or institutes), they
did sometimes press for the expansion of fields or the creation or upgrading of
teaching positions.

One clear example of such pressure can be found in the case of the chemical
profession. In two periods, the late 1880s and again a decade later, the *Verein
Deutscher Chemiker* asked the Prussian education ministry to make curricular
changes, particularly at technical colleges. In the first instance, in 1888, the
Verein complained that chemists emerging from the colleges were receiving
training "remote from practice," that is, too theoretical for them to be able to
make practical applications when entering industry. In particular the VDC
wanted more chairs and laboratories in dyestuff and textile technology.[19] A decade later, and in the context of the debate over state examinations for chemists
(to be discussed fully below), the VDC complained that German chemistry
students were being trained too narrowly and allowed to specialize too early.

The reactions of the Prussian education ministry were open-minded, but
chemistry professors at both technical colleges and traditional universities re-
sponded to this professional interference more negatively. Surprisingly, technical
college professors were even more reluctant to introduce special chairs or courses
to respond to the needs of industry because of the implied infringement on
academic freedom, a privilege they very much wished to see expanded in their
struggle for equality with the old universities.

By the very end of the nineteenth century, the chemical profession (which as
we have seen had the closest ties of any to the leaders of the corresponding
industry in Germany) had reached a compromise with the educational community and government. As Lothar Burchardt has summarized the end of these
conflicts: "After the controversy over technical colleges had been settled through

19 Burchardt, "Wissenschaft," p. 782.

granting them the right to award doctorates and the deficiencies in education complained of on the industrial side had been eliminated, the two main obstacles to cooperation between industry and higher education no longer existed."[20]

Other professional groups appear to have worked more quietly and piecemeal to affect changes in curriculum and teaching chairs or institutes, a process that was easy to carry out given the informal dual citizenship of professors as leading members of most professional organizations. Unlike the chemists, they usually did not mount large campaigns to affect such changes and were usually content to leave university professors and ministries to decide what direction to take in the rapid expansion of their institutions and teaching offerings.

An example of this type of discussion may be found in the German Medical Association, whose congresses and learned journal were the sites of discussions about the nature of medical education. Just as chemists often complained about inadequate practical preparation in their field, physicians sometimes denounced young doctors who were clumsy and badly trained in such areas as surgical technique. Discussions of medical training raised little interest in the quarter-century or so between the collapse of the 1840s "medical reform" movement and the mid-1870s; but the rapid advance of medical science gave new urgency to reforms in this area from then on.

The leadership of the DAeV of course supported the teaching of scientific, theoretical medicine (whatever older general practitioners in the provinces might think), but much of scientific medicine came to be based on observation. Clinical and other "practical" experience thus became more and more important in medical education. This problem could be handled in several ways, including the British, hospital-based mode, a more theoretically oriented lecture mode with reference to a patient present in the hall, or a combination of the two involving clinic work, the compromise that most German physicians accepted. Clinical experience could in turn be improved by more clinic *Praktica* (practical exercises) at the university, a period of internship (*Famulatur*) under a practicing physician, or a "practical year" in a qualifying hospital (in effect a residency). Much good was expected by various commentators from one or more of the three approaches, but the DAeV moved only slowly toward adopting a preference. In the end it urged more practical courses, more work in specializations, and the "practical year," all of which had the effect of greatly lengthening medical training.[21] But these issues will be treated below.

Coming much further behind on the professionalization spectrum, German dentists also pressed for changes in curriculum and institutes, namely for the creation of the latter at universities: after a quarter-century of efforts, they were rewarded by the creation of dental institutes in Berlin and Leipzig beginning in 1884.[22] By the end of the century dental institutes had been established at the

20 Ibid., p. 785.   21 Wenig, *Ausbildung*, p. 129.
22 Lafrenz, *Zahnärtzlichen Unterrichts*, pp. 10–11.

universities of Breslau, Kiel, Erlangen, Strasbourg, Marburg, Bonn, Jena, Königsberg, Greifswald, Würzburg, Heidelberg, and Munich.

Much more vital to the interests of the professions than what curriculum was offered to its trainees was how well they mastered the fundamentals. Thus examination and certification formed the core of discussions about education and its reform among most of the German professional groups.

The general trend among all German professional groups in the last third of the nineteenth century was to press for higher and more difficult standards in examinations and certification procedures. In some disciplines, driven for example by rapid growth in knowledge, such as medicine, engineering, and chemistry, a clear case could be made for the objective merits of raising standards.

But even in such fields other motivations stood behind calls for more stringent standards, including fear of rising competition and its consequences for already established practitioners as well as young beginners. As the great Viennese medical professor Billroth candidly wrote: "If you want me to be consistent and add that better scientific education requires significant financial resources, therefore attainable only by the prosperous class of people, and that therefore I am advocating not only an aristocracy of the mind but also one of money, then I have to admit that."[23]

The medical profession was the first in Germany to have uniform nation-wide standards for examination and certification, an anomaly in the general pattern of the federal states' right to regulate the professions in their area. This anomaly flows from the *Reichsgewerbeordnung* passed by the North German Reichstag in 1869 and later extended to the new member states in 1871.

This legislation, with revisions in 1883 and 1901, remained the basis for medical examination and certification in Germany through the end of the period considered in this work (as is basically the same system used in West Germany today). It normalized the minimum number of semesters of study before the state examination at eight, with an intermediary examination in preclinical areas of knowledge (*tentamen physicum*) after four semesters. This examination was much more narrowly limited to scientific subjects than the older philosophical examination based on broader humanistic knowledge had been. The content of the state examination changed considerably between 1869 and 1901 to incorporate more specialized subjects.

The requirement of a doctoral dissertation (and even a title of doctor) was abolished, although most students continued to do one and obtain the M.D. degree as well. But in principle, with the successful passage of the *Staatsexamen* (state examination) in medicine, the candidate was *approbiert*, that is, licensed to practice. (Hence the distinction in German between *Arzt* and "doctor" thenceforward.) Now the voluntary nature of the medical doctoral title in effect also

23 Theodor Billroth, *Ueber das Lehren und Lernen der medicinischen Wissenschaften an den Universitäten der deutschen Nation* (Vienna, 1876), p. 64.

allowed medical faculties to raise standards for obtaining it – they no longer "needed to be debased out of pity" for the duller medical students.[24] Local medical faculties continued to administer the preclinical examinations, however, and were appointed by the ministry to administer the state examination, opening them to charges of keeping standards low to attract more students.[25]

In 1878 the DAeV, in its annual *Aerztetag*, addressed the problems of the examination system, then under review by a national commission. As years of drafts and consultations dragged on, the Medical Association's membership gradually came to call for a longer term of study, usually ten semesters. The revised national examination regulations of 1883 took a step toward accommodating the medical profession by mandating nine semesters of study. By the mid-1880s, however, student enrollments in medicine began to expand rapidly.[26] The connection between the growth of competition ("overcrowding") and increasingly vocal calls for making medical credentials harder to get was rather open in the debates of the German Medical Association since then.[27] In 1889, out of four motions concerning medical examinations, the only one to be accepted almost unanimously by the Seventeenth German Medical Congress was a recommendation for ten semesters of study.[28] By 1891, the congress passed a resolution for ten semesters of study and for a one-year "practical year" after the state examination but before the final medical license (Approbation). In a similar context, it is remarkable that another suggestion for cutting down the stream of new doctors – issuing an official warning against medical study – was defeated (but by only one vote) at the 1892 congress.[29] By 1901, when the medical examination regulations were once again revised, they contained virtually the identical demands of the DAeV – a considerable index of the influence of this organization, considering that the 1901 reform commission consisted primarily of jurists and only one physician![30]

If German physicians achieved many of their objectives in certification by the beginning of the twentieth century, German dentists were still largely dissatisfied. At its 1894 meeting, the German Dental Association resolved in favor of an extension of medical training and examination procedures so as to require a preclinical examination (comparable to that of physicians) after five semesters and a state examination for certification only after the seventh semester.[31] In 1900 the dentists asked for the creation of a German doctorate in dentistry, perhaps even a Ph.D. in a dental specialty, with the reasoning that dentists had

24 Wenig, *Ausbildung*, p. 118.
25 Adolf Hartmann, "Die neue Prüfungsordnung für Aerzte," *Aerztliches Vereinsblatt* 5 (1878); 95–6.
26 See the debates of the Fourteenth German Medical Congress, *Aerztliches Vereinsblatt* 13 (1886).
27 See, for example, "Verhandlungen des XIX. deutschen Aerztetages," *Aerztliches Vereinsblatt* 18 (1891): 293.
28 "Verhandlungen des XVII. deutschen Aerztetages," *Aerztliches Vereinsblatt* 16 (1889): 401–20.
29 "Verhandlungen des XX. deutschen Aerztetages," *Aerztliches Vereinsblatt* 19 (1892): 470.
30 Wenig, *Ausbildung*, p. 141.   31 *Deutsche Monatsschrift für Zahnheilkunde*, 12 (1894): 40–1.

to study about as long as humanists but could not earn a doctoral title. The background of this bizarre reasoning was American: for decades American proprietary dental schools, some of them quite shady, had been "selling" D.D.S. degrees with little or no actual study, sometimes even by mail order. The German Dental Association understandably wished to create a mechanism of German dentists to acquire a "legitimate" doctorate, in part to be able to compete for public favor with Germany's "American mail-order" dentists. In neither request were the dentists successful by the turn of the century.[32]

If reforms in examination and certification were at least partly linked to advances in science with physicians and dentists, the legal community faced no such unarguable innovations to which it would have to adapt. Nevertheless, the functions carried out by legally trained personnel became more diversified and specialized as German society modernized. By the end of the nineteenth century, the legal community was divided into roughly equal-sized quarters: one on the bench, one in the bar, one in the higher civil administration, and a final one (still growing) working in the private sector. All still received the same basic legal education, however, and for the time being only questions of the quality of that education, not its curricular structure or content, tended to be discussed. The German Bar Association appeared largely content with the examination and certification system in the last thirty years of the last century.[33] Problems and considerable discussion did arise with an area outside the concerns of the bar itself, on the level of legally trained civil servants. On several occasions the *Deutscher Juristentag* debated and resolved upon these issues, all without achieving results satisfactory to reformers before the turn of the century.

Complaints about both university and on-the-job legal training, examinations, and other aspects of what one might call the system of certification were loud and repeated from the 1860s through the 1890s. In the year of the Austro-Prussian war, Eugen Richter complained of the superficiality of knowledge of the law among civil service candidates.[34] Over three decades later, describing preparation for a legal career in Tübingen, an anonymous pamphleteer repeated many of the old complaints. Cutting classes, copying other students' lecture notes, signing up for (but not necessarily attending) all the courses offered by professors who will later sit on examining boards, discovering by guesswork or even more scurrilous ways the questions on the examination, currying favor with professors by inviting them to dinner, and the wasted months of the military "volunteer year" were the main complaints. The author clearly described the "important" achievements of the successful candidate in cataloging what he

---

32 Seefeld, *Zahnärzte*, p. 45.
33 The educational and qualificational requirements of the Reichsanwaltsordnung of 1878 were the only part of the proposed ordinance to which the DAV did *not* take exception. See Ostler, *Rechtsanwalt*, p. 12.
34 Eugen Richter, "Die Vorbildung der höheren Verwaltungsbeamten in Preussen," *Preussische Jahrbücher*, 17 (1866):1–19.

wanted to see abolished: "Whether the candidate belongs to this or that fraternity, how many duels he has fought, whether he flirts with a professor's daughter or niece and calls upon him at the beginning and end of the semester."[35] In the thirty years between these very similar denunciations, other leading lights of jurisprudence had also weighed in with reform proposals.

The central problem lay in the way both civil servants and officers of the courts were trained and examined. The opposing models at the beginning of the nineteenth century were offered by Prussia and Württemberg, which we might call juridical and cameralistic, respectively. In the latter, candidates for the civil service were given courses in cameralistics or what later came to be called state or administrative sciences (e.g. economics, finance); in the former, university courses strongly emphasized civil and criminal law.[36] As the nineteenth century progressed, more and more German states moved toward the Prussian model, even as the mounting complexity of administrative tasks might have suggested a move in the other direction.

The Prussian bureaucratic tradition of the time held that all future *Verwaltungsbeamte* (administrative officials) should have the same university training (three years) as court officers (judges and attorneys), then all should pass a first examination. Then followed a period of unpaid training and, for would-be Prussian administrators, a second examination that was widely decried as farcical and was finally abolished in 1869. Next came the "great state examination" after several years of unpaid work in the courts (and for upper civil servants, subsequently in government bureaus), where practical on-the-job training was meant to supplement the "theoretical" training at the university. After 1879 Prussian candidates for the upper civil service had to serve four years; judges and lawyers could get by with a couple of years training attached to a court as a *Referendar*. And although the German Bar Association requested that a two-year training period in a lawyer's office be made mandatory for future lawyers, this was not incorporated into the *Rechtsanwaltsordnung* in 1878.[37] As for candidates for the upper civil service, only after four (or more) years of practical training were they tested in theoretical knowledge about administrative science (although the examination was supposed to test practical knowledge), much too long after university to remember much about it.

Because the first exam that all jurists took was as easy as the various regional courts wanted to make it (and that was easy enough), Prussian (and many other German) candidates for high government office had come to rely on cram schools to get them through examinations. If they could (and perhaps needed to) rely on cramming factories, why waste time studying while at the university? By 1869, Prussia reformed its examination procedures, partly under successful pressure from the *Juristentag:* the old first and second exams were

35 "Ein Jurist", *Die juristische Vorbildung in Württemberg* (Stuttgart, 1895), p. 12.
36 Wilhelm Bleek, *Von der Kameralausbildung zum Juristenprivileg* (Berlin, 1972), pp. 262 ff.
37 Ostler, *Rechtsanwalt*, p. 16.

combined and university professors were admitted to the examining boards, before then staffed only by bureaucrats, a step that supposedly guaranteed that questions about university subjects would at least be asked.[38]

Thus, as early as 1863 the Jurists' Congress called for a longer course of university study (four years) to allow for more real study of administrative science, and the reduction of the number of exams to two and the creation of examining boards composed of professors and practicing lawyers with limited terms.[39] In 1878 it changed its mind about four years of study (instead of the usual three) but debated the creation of another, "intermediary" examination obviously intended to make the students work.[40] As skeptics had pointed out, forcing students to stay at the university longer might simply force them to waste even more time on drinking and dueling!

Understandably, the *Juristentag*, dominated by legal professors, showed a continuing interest in making university education count for more in the preparation of civil servants, and it did score some significant successes with its repeated resolutions.[41] But as long as the normal four-year unpaid "practical" training period before the final state examination and therewith certification as a life-tenure *Verwaltungsbeamter* remained, academic training would continue to be, at least for the minority of law students who went into the higher civil administration, a mere antechamber to a career. As Wilhelm Bleek concludes:

Legal study transmitted technical capacities; qualification for comprehending and dealing with the problems of an industrial welfare state was left to 'natural giftedness' and 'correct views' such as were formed in the student fraternities, military service and the time of practical training (*Referendarzeit*). De-liberalization and feudalization of a large part of the Prussian bureaucracy were therewith only a part of the comprehensive political and social degeneration of the German citizenry into a bourgeoisie.[42]

Today such descriptions reflect the harsh judgment of some of the leading legal theorists of the late nineteenth century. The words of the Berlin professor Rudolf Gneist, one of the grand old men of German legal education in the 1880s, put it ruefully: only a third of law students studied hard, another third scraped by with mass lectures, class-cutting, and skipping material they thought unlikely to appear on an examination. The bottom third rarely attended lectures and experienced the university as a social rather than an intellectual experience. Of the third group,

about half pass and half fail. . . . From this third type of law student comes the main stock of those practitioners who so much despise 'gray theory' and who know professors

38 Otto Gierke, "Die juristische Studienordnung," *Schmollers Jahrbuch*, 1 (1877): 2.
39 *Verhandlungen des Deutschen Juristentages*, 4/2 (1863): 123, 154.
40 *Verhandlungen des Deutschen Juristentages*, 14/2 (1878): 202, 279.
41 An excellent summary of the various suggestions put forward in the legal press and at the *Juristentag* in the 1870s and 1880s can be found in Levin Goldschmidt, *Rechtsstudium und Prüfungsordnung* (Stuttgart, 1887).
42 Bleek, *Kameralausbildung*, p. 190.

only from their weak sides or peculiar habits. The professors reciprocate the feeling, and there you have the basis of our juridical exchange of ideas.[43]

Gneist went on to blame the legal examinations, which he said "anybody" can pass.[44]

Despite some minor changes (e.g. in Prussia in 1906), the basic system for training and certifying all lawyers, judges, and civil servants in Germany went largely unchanged until after World War I. As had been the case since the seventeenth-century compromises between enlightened despotism and aristocracy in Germany, the civil service remained staffed by elites, albeit ones stamped superficially with higher learning in the field of law. Only after World War I did debate about law training erupt again, at which point even the administrative elites organized themselves professionally to defend their privileges against the Weimar Republic's reformers.

Thus, the German legal profession, broadly speaking, could not be unified by a completely common educational and certification system; lawyers and judges went one way, higher civil servants another. Ironically, although the civil service acted as a model for many aspects of professionalization in Germany (e.g. careers ladders, single occupational activity), it did not lead the way in the imperial era in raising educational and certification norms, quite the contrary. The political, social, and economic filters through which its members had to pass, while quite effective in creating a narrow elite, could not give away to completely knowledge-based criteria for selection without democratizing, at least by tendency, the entire German system of government.

None of the other "old" professions, for example the clergy or military officers, articulated educational reform plans (nor had national organizations through which to do them) during the late nineteenth century. It was especially among the new or newly professionalizing groups – schoolteachers, engineers, and chemists, in particular – that one found considerable eagerness to revamp existing educational requirements and professional credentialing. All sought to increase their prestige and standing through raising educational levels and certification procedures to the levels of the older professions. Such proposals and actual reforms proved difficult and divisive at times, however.

Among schoolteachers, for example, higher school teachers (*Gymnasiallehrer*) appeared relatively content with their educational qualifications and certification. At the other end of the teaching profession, elementary school teachers looked upon upgrading their own education and certification standards as vital to raising their stature as a group, and upgrading that many *Gymnasium* teachers considered a threat to their own standing. Similarly, attempts among chemists and engineers to "raise standards" ultimately tended to create, not a unified profession with a common high level of education, but "first" and "second" class tiers in the profession.

43 Rudolf von Gneist, *Aphorismen zur Reform des Rechtsstudiums in Preussen* (Berlin, 1887), p. 15.
44 *Ibid.*, pp. 17ff.

In the VDI, thanks to the persuasiveness of Franz Grashof, the "academicization" of engineering education became a major desideratum in the 1870s, with considerable success for VDI agitation: the creation of new *technische Hochschulen* (technical colleges), such as the amalgamation of the Berlin technical college out of the academies of architecture and commerce in 1879,[45] and the grant of university-style prerogatives to such colleges (academic freedom, a "rectoral" constitution, and above all the right to award the titles of *Diplomingenieur* (diploma engineer) and Dr. Ing.). Most of these demands were achieved by 1900.[46]

This promotion to equality with the old academic professions still not did solve the fundamental problem of the engineers' occupational identity and social role, however. Throughout the period down to 1900, they felt left out. In the 1880s, for example, VDI meetings discussed how many engineers occupied leading positions in the French state or parliament (and how few in Germany — never more than two engineers as Reichstag deputies before World War I).[47] Locked out of the higher civil service by the "jurists' monopoly" and increasingly forced to work as employees of others, the German engineers had every reason to hope to differentiate themselves from other "engineers" (e.g. mechanics) through the mechanism of higher degrees. Yet, at the same time the VDI attempted to carry on pretending that it was the organization for all German engineers, not just the academically trained ones — a posture that came more and more into conflict with the consequences of its perennial fight for "academicization" in the last third of the nineteenth century. We shall have to discuss those consequences in later chapters.

German chemists approached professionalization in ways comparable to those used by engineers, including the dimension of educational and credential reforms. Chemists were in a somewhat different position in that their field was less diversified than that of engineers and that academic degrees in chemistry (e.g. the doctorate) had long been available. Chemistry had been a subject at German universities long before it also settled into the technical colleges. Although there continued to be many nonacademically trained chemists, the chemical profession grew chiefly in those areas (organic chemistry) with the closest ties to academe. Hence, educational and credential reforms aimed at increasing the prestige and social exclusivity of the chemical profession appear to have been more easily achieved than with the engineers.

The German Chemists' Association, so renamed in the mid-1890s from the German Association for Applied Chemistry, drifted more and more firmly under the influence of the elites of German industry and academia. As one recent study argues, the VDC "by emphasizing social status and education as the cri-

---

45 A step based on a VDI memorandum: see Scholl, "Ingenieur in Ausbildung," p. 38.
46 For a typical expression of the "meaning in cultural history" of engineering degrees and equality of engineering colleges with universities, see "Rundschau," *VDI–Zeitschrift*, 44 (1900): 1,216–19.
47 Manegold, "VDI," p. 140.

teria for membership in the profession, . . . blurred the difference between the economic interests of employers and employees, and it obscured the purposes and effects on the profession of the industry's control structure."[48]

Splits in the chemical profession between "academic" and "nonacademic" practitioners became serious enough to provoke breakaway organizations after 1900, as was the case too with engineers. We shall treat these in Chapter 8.

But attempts to "raise the profession" by raising educational and examination standards were crowned principally by two events already in the 1890s: introducing the so-called *Verbandsexamen* and granting doctoral degrees by technical colleges. Both steps in effect made the study of chemistry both more respectable and by tendency (at this level at least) more exclusive.

Chemistry, like engineering, lacked a tradition of titles and degrees before the very end of the nineteenth century. One could at least obtain a doctorate in chemistry at a university, but not yet at the technical colleges where so many applied chemists studied. Doctorates at the university were furthermore of uneven quality, given the autonomous standards of the various university chemistry departments around Germany. (The problem was less acute at technical colleges, where prescribed course work and frequent examinations were more common; also, the diploma in engineering, a degree somewhat less illustrious than the universities' doctorates, involved an examination and a research thesis.)

By 1886 the VDC came to view the answer to the problem, in addition to granting technical colleges the right to award degrees, as a state examination for university chemists, in effect the equivalent of the first examinations all lawyers had to take at the end of their time at the university. In 1889 the VDC even adopted a version of the examination it would like to see instituted.[49]

Directors of the chemical institutes at universities opposed such a solution on the grounds that it would increase government control over their work. Led by Adolf von Baeyer of the University of Munich, they founded an ad-hoc committee, the *Verband der Laboratoriumsvorstände an deutschen Hochschulen* (League of Laboratory Heads at German Universities), and put forward the idea of a voluntary *Verbandsexamen*. This "League exam" was made available at all universities by informal agreement among the professors and addressed the problem of lacking or uneven certification of chemistry students' progress about halfway through their studies. Most significant, students could no longer apply for the doctorate (and hope for lax supervision) without passing, in effect, a predoctoral examination.[50]

The VDC accepted the countermoves of the professors and the defeat of its state examination proposal. It went on in subsequent years to cooperate

48 Jeffrey A. Johnson, "Academic, Proletarian, . . . Professional? Shaping Professionalization for German Industrial Chemists, 1887–1920," in Geoffrey Cocks and Konrad Jarausch, eds., *German Professions, 1800–1950* (New York, 1990), p. 124.
49 Burchardt, "Wissenschaft," p. 777; Schütt, "Berufsbild," p. 291.
50 Burchardt, "Wissenschaft," pp. 779–80; Schütt, "Berufsbild," p. 293.

smoothly with government and university authorities in developing a national *Chemische Reichsanstalt* (Imperial Chemical Institute). But the defeat of the VDC over the *Verbandsexamen* showed how difficult reform efforts against the wishes of professorial leaders in the profession were. Both groups working together could affect changes, but their professionalizing strategies and agendas did not always coincide.

As mentioned in earlier chapters, the differentiation into "academic" and "nonacademic" tiers of the profession that began to emerge only toward the end of the nineteenth century in the engineering and chemical fields had already been present for some time in the teaching profession. Since the school reforms and particularly the institutionalization of the *Gymnasium* in the early part of the century, teachers at that type of school were usually required to have studied at a university, passed a qualifying examination, and undergone a year or more of practical training. The Prussian system dating back to 1810 tested subjects – philological, mathematical and historical – that required study in a philosophical faculty rather than a theological one. The Prussian examination *pro facultate docendi*, modified in 1831, 1866, 1877, and 1898, became in the course of the nineteenth century the model for the North German states. Bavaria and Württemberg did not at first follow Prussia in sundering teacher training from theology, but by 1854 and 1865, respectively, those states had abolished the advantages previously accorded theology students and effectively made the career of *Gymnasium* teacher into a secular, philologically based one.[51]

The educational and certification requirements imposed from above the state from the time of the general Napoleonic-era reorganization of Germany can thus be said to have created the new academic profession of higher schoolteacher. Not only academic training, but continuing expectations that such teachers would remain active in *Wissenschaft*, in a way comparable to university professors, created a professional esprit and identity based on the disciplines of humanism. As we have seen earlier, teachers were sometimes unhappy with their working conditions, but the *Gymnasium*-level teachers rarely complained about the nature of their own education and certification. When they did finally organize a national body, the *Vereinsverband Akademisch Gebildeter Lehrer Deutschlands* (League of Associations of Academically Educated Teachers of Germany, or VALD) in 1903, its chief concerns were still more economic than educational. The League, it may be recalled, changed this unwieldy name in 1921 to *Deutscher Philologenverband* (German Philologists' Association, or DPV).

For the nonacademically trained majority of Germany's schoolteachers, of course, the establishment of higher educational and credentialing standards was an obvious strategy in their struggle for higher status. Already in 1848, as we have seen in Chapter 4, German schoolteachers demanded university-level training for their profession. This issue was discussed from time to time in the

51 Romberg, *Staat und höhere Schule*, pp. 473–510; Lexis, *Reform*, pp. 75–83.

last decades of the nineteenth century, but it did not become a realistic possibility until the twentieth.

What teachers' organizations were able to institute on their own was the idea of *Fortbildung*, or continuing professional education. Like physicians toward the end of the century, schoolteachers saw the advantages of keeping up with developments through postgraduate courses. Indeed, the effectiveness of such courses forced the Prussian education ministry to decree in 1880 that teachers' seminars ought to inaugurate such postgraduate courses to head off the potential for socialization of teachers through their own organizations rather than by "their natural authorities," such as the state-controlled seminars.[52]

As long as the only qualification for entering a teacher-training seminar was completing elementary school, however, teachers' organizations could hardly demand higher education for their members without in effect calling into question the purpose of public elementary schooling itself – to produce reliable citizens who could read, write, and reckon just enough to carry out orders.

3. CONCLUSION

The last third of the nineteenth century was obviously not the only time when educational and credentialing debates were carried out as a major item on the agenda of the emerging modern professions. But it may be said that most of the fundamental patterns for later periods took shape in this era. The original model in the minds of most professional leaders was clearly that of the preparation and certification of the legal community (not merely of the civil service). A full preparatory education capped by the *Abitur,* or certificate of maturity, led through higher educational institutions with an optimally "free" academic setting, then finally through state examinations (and in most cases some form of practical experience) before full entry into practice.

Such a statement would have met with considerably more challenges in 1870 than in 1900, by which time a broad measure of consensus existed about what constituted the desirable model for all the learned professions, or those that were striving to become so. No doubt one reason for this drift toward consensus about the structure of becoming professionals had to do with new dynamics in German society at large. The individual practitioner, of whatever type, found himself increasingly confronting large, powerful organizations, ranging from cartels to labor unions, which threatened to diminish his autonomy if he did not act in concert with his fellow professionals. We shall address this development in the next chapter.

52 Manfred Heinemann, "Der Lehrerverein als Sozialisationsagentur," in Heinemann, *Lehrer,* pp. 46–7.

PART IV

Breakthroughs and breakdowns: The professions enter the era of cartels and unions

8

~~~~~~

The "free" professions, 1900–1918

As argued in previous chapters, some German professional groups had achieved a number of innovations and changes by the turn of the twentieth century that satisfied at least part of their professionalizing programs. At the same time, none could be described as completely satisfied with the status quo. As we shall see in this chapter, the last two decades of the German Empire brought both widening conflict and some degree of resolution for professional groups.

A certain measure of discontent and instability emerged from the very dynamics of the economic, social, and cultural change in these important years. To mention one dynamic, specialization came increasingly to characterize much professional activity, not only in such science and technology-based occupations as engineering, chemistry, and medicine, but in law and teaching as well. The organizational consequences of specialization could be harmless to professionalization, as when gynecologists and physical chemists wished to found their own societies and journals; but it could also lead to fragmentation of the power and force of central professional organizations.

Another centrifugal force that emerged especially strongly before World War I might be called "labor unionism." The threat of socialist revolution and, perhaps even more concretely, of successful union agitation and strikes had haunted the sleep of the German authorities and property owners increasingly in the 1890s. By the turn of the century, bourgeois or not, some German professionals were beginning the turn to the union model of occupational organization and adapt it to professional use.

The spectacle of middle-class physicians going out on strike in Wilhelminian Germany, for example, is not one that fits easily with received notions about either doctors or Germany. But there were in fact several doctors' strikes in the first decade of the century, and they appear to have been modestly successful. Other professional groups also emulated at least some aspects of labor-union organization, principally by making blatant issue of pay and working conditions, unlike the more "scientific" and hesitant organizations of "academic" practitioners. Thus while groups like the VDC and the DAeV were indignantly

131

rejecting charges that they were like unions, new organizations that promised to "do something about" economic conditions sprang up like mushrooms. The Hartmann League and BUTIB, the first an economic combat association of physicians and the second a league of technical employees irrespective of background and training, were two examples.

Tendencies toward radicalization of course had real causes. Just as the labor movement in Germany was in a way the reflection of big business, so professional "unions" were responses to the cartelization of working conditions. The Hartmann League and the BUTIB owed much of their appeal to the belief that only an economic "combat organization" could stand up to the increasing power of sickness insurance boards or large chemical combines, for example. Analogously, civil servants began to organize for better salaries and working conditions, daring to confront a state bureaucracy that had grown so much as to become faceless and impersonal. Confrontation and pressure-group tactics, not persuasion and conciliation, entered the arena of professional life for the first time on a large scale in the last prewar years.

We shall have to examine the impact on professions of what some recent analyses regard as a process of "deprofessionalization" or as a conflict between unionization and professionalization as implicitly incompatible models of occupational organization[1]. One must of course note that one group's view of "deprofessionalization" corresponded to another group's view of "professionalization," and we must therefore be careful to view the entire picture of German professions, not merely the academic ones.

In the centrifuge affecting German professions, certain forces became more important than before. Sex and class distinctions, as well as increasingly complex educational backgrounds and certain aspects of a generational crisis introduced new and potentially disaggregating forces into the various professional groups at the very time their increasing consciousness of their economic self-interest implied a need for solidarity. The insistent if not very successful drive of feminists for equal access to the professions, a matter that was still usually laughed off by male professionals in the 1880s, had become a serious challenge (and as many males saw it, a threat) by 1900. Influxes of lower-middle-class students into higher education and technical training threatened further to dissolve the traditional connection between the broader *Bildungsbürgertum* and "free" academic professions, whether already extant (medicine, law) or merely aspired to (engineering, chemistry).

---

1 Cf Johnson, "Academic, Proletarian. . . . ?" and Cornelis W. R. Gispen, "Engineers in Wilhelmian Germany: Professionalization, Deprofessionalization, and the Development of Non-Academic Technical Education," in Cocks and Jarausch, *German Professions*, pp. 104–22. Gispen's title neatly suggests the paramenters of debate in the first decades of this century. "Deprofessionalization" has a somewhat different meaning when discussed in the context of the Great Depression and Hitler eras, as we shall see in subsequent chapters.

For younger practitioners in particular, becoming a professional after 1900 was not necessarily to have arrived in a safe haven. Although cries of overcrowding and pauperization could be found at most times in the nineteenth century, it really does appear that increased competition and decline in the standard of living were more than empty grumbles before 1914. If one includes the war years, with their 300 percent inflation and lack of compensatory increases in salaries, fees, or other income, there can be no doubt about a decline.

Caught in these cross-currents, German professional groups tended to push on with their long-standing programs, marking occasional successes, and to debate at least solutions to new problems, such as overcrowding. The older, established ones generally managed to accommodate themselves to the challenge of new organizations using strike or other "union" tactics, or even to meld with them. Some of the more radical "unionist" professional organizations, after scaring the authorities, ended up having little more success than the radical German teachers in 1848 and after. More characteristic of the period was a pattern of small concessions (and few losses of previously won privileges) to the mainline professional associations by government, educational establishments, insurance companies, and certain sectors of private enterprise.

Professional associations continued to grow and achieve higher degrees of inclusiveness, although new competitors were established to represent both subdivisions and specialties and new fields altogether. Part of the reason for this growth was the perception of success by the tireless efforts of the professional associations, which turned more and more to direct political lobbying in legislatures. Sympathies in the latter in turn brought pressure to bear on governments to listen with more respect to the demands of professional groups, or even to allow some to form that had theretofore been prohibited or persecuted. Prussia, as we shall see below, finally began to accept the idea of civil-servant organizations after 1900, partly in response to legislative pressures.[2] Ironically, it was the success of schoolteachers, in particular, in both raising their salaries and achieving recognition as full civil servants that spurred on other civil servants to organize. But the achievement of professional goals through bureaucratization – or, in a broader sense, through *joint market regulation* with an outside authority – was not only emerging as a German variant of professionalization before World War I: it became the dominant German model for the rest of the twentieth century, and a strong argument can be made that it showed the way for developments in professionalization for the whole twentieth-century world.

In any case the "liberal" idea of professional self-government and autonomy from the state and society, still to be found during and after the founding of the empire, had begun to give way to greater willingness to work with outside political and social entities for the achievement of professional goals through

2 Bernd Wunder, *Geschichte der Bürokratie in Deutschland* (Frankfurt, 1986), p. 98.

compromise. It is in the sense of these new behavior patterns that one can see professional developments as a successful adaptation to a new "social corporatism" in Germany rather than as a failure of "professionalizing goals" set by liberals a generation or two before. As one recent analysis argues:

Wilhelminian Germany . . . with her strong bureaucratic tradition and apparatus; her capitalism so amply provided with networks of firms, professional cartels, business associations, trade unions, summit associations, Chambers of Commerce and of Trade, Economic Councils, and so on; her coexistence of pluralism (for this sector, of course, also continued to exist), state corporatism (which failed eventually) and societal corporatism, which became the dominant feature of German economic and social life; this Wilhelminian Germany presents the appearance less of an 'ancien regime' than of the avant-garde of twentieth-century advanced capitalism.[3]

Other environmental influences can be registered on the German professions from the broader German and European historical context. The German Empire in 1912 was quite different from that of 1880 or even 1890. The relative decline of political liberalism and the mobilization of the bourgeoisie for the adventures of imperialism had a clear impact on thinking about the role of professions in the national enterprise and help explain the unquestioning cooperation of professional groups (even to their own disadvantage) in the gamble of World War I. The rise to electoral significance in the Reichstag of the Social Democrats (the largest party in the 1912 elections) as well as the eclipse of the "personal rule" of William II pointed to a shift in the balance of forces in the legislature. Even struggling with the unresolved problems of financing the "warfare and welfare" state that Prussia-Germany was increasingly becoming had implications for the professions. Particularly for those deriving in large part from the traditions of the *Bildungsbürgertum*, the economic growth and financial policies of the late empire led to palpable shifts in the distribution of income, with a rich entrepreneurial class rapidly bounding ahead and the growing "revolutionary" working class being tied to the existing order by a higher standard of living. The deprivations felt by professional practitioners may have been relative but were no less infuriating for that.

For, as noted above, this was an era when even the state bureaucracy, the alleged model for social respect as well as economic security, began to complain it was losing both. The successes achieved by some professions in shoring up the edifice of their "professionalizing projects" – including ever higher educational and certification requirements, career ladders and unification of professional standards, propagandistic if not legal progress against "quackery," self-government of ethics through chambers and honor courts, and even economic gains could be wiped out quickly by the triumph of either the freebooting high capitalism predicted by Marx or the proletarian revolution posed by Marx as its

3 Werner Abelshauser, "The First Post-Liberal Nation: Stages in the Development of Modern Corporatism in Germany," *European History Quarterly*, 14 (1984): pp. 295–6.

consequence. Conflicts and compromises with either capital or labor had to be faced, but the state, often regarded as standing "above party" in Wilhelminian bourgeois ideology, came to be viewed as an increasingly possible ally, rather than a stubborn and uncomprehending opponent of professional goals.

1. THE MEDICAL PROFESSION AND SICKNESS INSURANCE

The most prominent professional question concerning the medical profession in this period was one of control of practice by the burgeoning medical insurance system in the Reich. Such control touched upon matters of professional autonomy, income, models of market monopoly, education and certification, medical ethics – in short, virtually every aspect of medical professionalization. Conflicts between insurers and physicians as well as among physicians themselves threatened to split the medical profession irrevocably, and physicians' strikes and boycotts aroused considerable furor. In the end, however, a compromise was achieved that could serve as a model for the corporate redefinition of professions. Although not representing a sweeping triumph by the organized medical profession, this compromise of 1913 attested to the efficacy of the doctors' "union tactics."

Medical insurance funds (*Krankenkassen*) had a long history in Germany already before the 1883 introduction of mandatory coverage for certain classes of individuals everywhere in the Reich. At first the principal objective was to cover industrial laborers (farm laborers being presumed to have village kin to take care of them when ill, just as the middle and upper classes were presumed to have sufficient income to pay their private medical bills or join voluntary sickness funds). The German Medical Association raised no objections, viewing compulsory health insurance as a marginal issue as far as private practice was concerned and probably a good thing in terms of public hygiene: it would mean that urban workers would now be able to obtain professional medical care for the first time. Indeed, the association was not even consulted by the Reich government in laying plans for the insurance scheme.

German state-mandated health insurance departed from the principle of equivalence, that is, the law "set the premiums according to the income of the sickness-fund member and not according to health risk."[4] Decisions about how to spend the sickness funds were to be made by elected boards, in which covered members and employers had the same ratio of votes as their contributions to the fund (2:1). The boards of the thousands of local sickness funds tended over time to be taken over by socialists, who were ideologically unsympathetic to the financial claims of the medical profession. But even without this factor, the principle of limiting contracted medical care to the amount of premium

---

4 Peter Rosenberg, "The Origin and the Development of Compulsory Health Insurance in Germany," in Donald W. Light and Alexander Schuller, eds, *Political Values and Health Care: The German Experience* (Cambridge, Mass., 1986), p. 114.

available, rather than the inflationary principle of reimbursement for any and all individual medical services, placed a strict limit from the beginning on how much doctors could make from treating fund members.

The proportion of the population belonging to these funds grew constantly, both because the urban working class increased rapidly in size, and because the law was amended to extend coverage to ever wider groups.[5] The 1883 legislation (if one includes special funds for miners) about doubled the percentage of medically insured population of the Reich (to about 10 percent); by 1890, nearly 13 percent; by 1900, over 16 percent; over 20 percent for the first time in 1911; and 23 percent in 1914.[6] In addition, special funds for miners, civil servants, and others covered large groups of the population, so that as much as 50 percent was actually insured.[7]

The relationship between local physicians and sickness funds was complex; suffice it to say that in all cases a contract was worked out between the parties that placed all members of the fund under the care of one or more physicians in return for a stated payment to the physicians. Thus, the patient's freedom was greatly reduced (even if he did not want to seek medical help, the doctor alone now had the power to declare him unfit for work and therefore eligible for wage replacement), just as was the doctor's autonomy vis-à-vis the fund's board of directors. Some funds paid doctors on a per-patient or per-visit basis, but it appears the larger funds (and this was the growing trend) usually preferred to offer a flat contractual fee for the care of all covered members, irrespective of the frequency or severity of illness. Such fees rarely exceeded local minimal fee schedules for individual patients and very often lay considerably below them.

To compound the problem, sickness insurance funds were not obliged to contract only with licensed (*approbiert*) physicians, but might do so with medical students or what we would call paramedical personnel. With the expanding number of doctors available, the temptation, especially for young physicians just starting out, to underbid for contracts was strong. Although statistical compilations differ in detail, most agree that the number of physicians had at least doubled between 1876 and 1900 and increased almost another quarter by 1911. Although, as mentioned earlier, population growth and specialization justified some of this growth, the ratio of physicians per 10,000 population rose from a little over three in 1876 to around five in 1910.[8] Medical school enroll-

5 One of the best and most recent discussions of the origins of sickness insurance and the medical profession is to be found in Claudia Huerkamp, *Der Aufstieg der Aerzte im 19. Jahrhundert. Vom gelehrten Stand zum professionellen Experten: Das Beispiel Preussens* [*Kritische Studien zur Geschichtswissenschaft*, 68] (Göttingen, 1985), chap. 6.
6 Ibid., table 13, p. 198.   7 Ibid., p. 199.
8 Plaut, *Gewerkschaftskampf*, p. 67; Manfred Stürzbecher, "Die medizinische Versorgung und die Entstehung der Gesundheitsfürsorge zu Beginn des 20. Jahrhunderts," in Gunter Mann and Rolf Winau, eds., *Medizin, Naturwissenschaft, Technik und das zweite Kaiserreich.* [*Studien zur Medizingeschichte des 19. Jahrhunderts*, 8], (Göttingen, 1977), p. 251; Huerkamp, *Aufstieg*, p. 151.

ments in 1900 were about double what they had been in 1876, but they were in a temporary decline from a high point around 1890 that had come close to tripling 1876 enrollment and had 30 percent of all German students matriculating in medicine! The decline through the 1890s bottomed out about 1904; what followed was a doubling of enrollments by 1912, to an all-time high of 11,500 medical students in German universities, or nearly four times as many as in the 1870s. This prewar spurt undoubtedly had a connection with the 1900 school reforms, allowing non-*Gymnasium* graduates and later women to study medicine.[9] The great enrollment spurt of the 1880s coincided neatly with the introduction of sickness insurance, and thus the vast expansion of the medical market must always be kept in mind from then on as a major factor in the medical profession.

Whether there was an oversupply of physicians, and whether it was causing a decline in medical incomes, were then and are today disputed questions. The medical profession reacted quickly to increased enrollments in the 1880s with complaints about "overcrowding" in the profession, and the campaign to raise study and examination requirements and to introduce an intern year, all achieved in 1901, were undoubtedly motivated in part by a wish to throttle competition.[10] But by effectively raising the course of medical study (with internship) from a minimum four and one half to six years by 1901, the profession still did not stem the tide of new students. Had World War I not intervened to carry off so many physicians into the armed services or a more terminal fate, the "overcrowding" problem would probably have reached crisis proportions.

Yet, the question of how many physicians Germany "really needed" was not easy to answer. Some within the contemporary profession took a ratio of one doctor for every 3,000 inhabitants as "normal."[11] This ratio, acceptable to a spokesman of the medical profession in 1911, translates into a ratio of about 3.3 doctors per 10,000 population – almost exactly what it had been in 1876. By contrast, Weimar and Nazi Germany had seven or more per 10,000, while the Federal Republic crossed the fourteen threshold in 1959 and fourteen in 1970.[12]

Considering the expansion of the market for services by insurance as well as increasing specialization, one can share some of the skepticism of recent analysts about "overcrowding" of the German medical profession before 1918.[13] The long-range trends, however, left many future questions unanswered. As the number of physicians per capita increased, so did the coverage of national health insurance, causing the ratio of *private* patients to physicians to decrease.

Unable to produce more private patients, German doctors thus faced three choices concerning their market situation: (1) do nothing, (2) try to reduce the

9 Huerkamp, *Aufstieg*, pp. 62, 118.   10 Ibid., pp. 110–18.
11 Puppe, *Bestrebungen*, p. 4.   12 Stürzbecher, "Medizinische Versorgung," p. 251.
13 Heinz Goerke, "Grossstadtmedizin und Kassenarzt," in Mann and Winau, *Medizin, Naturwissenschaft*, pp. 116–17; Huerkamp, *Aufstieg*, p. 112 and passim.

number of doctors, or (3) try to change the sickness insurance system in their favor. Although choice (1) had long since been abandoned by most doctors, more radical medical opinion charged that this was exactly what the German Medical Association *was* doing: nothing.[14] As we have seen, the DAeV did successfully push measures to make becoming a doctor much more difficult, but without the numerical results expected by many after 1900. We shall see below what form reactions took. But the most immediate new initiative was choice (3), particularly as exemplified in the so-called Hartmann-League, or *Verband der Aerzte Deutschlands zur Wahrung ihrer Wirtschaftlichen Interessen* (Association of German Physicians for the Protection of their Economic Interests, or VAeWI, also known in preference to its longwinded full title as the *Leipziger Verband*), founded in 1900 by Dr. Hermann Hartmann of Leipzig.

Hartmann, echoing the frustrations of many members of the German Medical Association, published an impassioned plea in its journal, identifying the central issue as financial. "Until now we physicians have fought our battles by stressing our professional dignity and honor. Money, I tell you, money is the main thing!" Hartmann proposed a separate medical organization whose members would be willing to contribute to a strike fund to take on the *Krankenkassen* and force them to reward "our difficult, all-consuming and self-sacrificing work" with "a decent compensation – that is how we will best assure our professional honor and dignity."[15]

We shall consider the Hartmann League in greater detail below. What were the "money" and other working-condition-related issues mentioned by Hartmann and his avid following? As with the "overcrowding" issue (with which it is linked), the income issue cannot be discussed precisely before 1900 because of the weakness of the sources. We might accept some regional surveys around 1900, which indicate that an annual income of 5,000 marks was not far from the median (i.e. about half the doctors earned less, half earned more). Although a substantial minority might earn up to 10,000 marks per year, only a diminishing minority appears to have earned upwards of 20,000.[16] Beyond the question of statistical income lie matters of interpretation.

In her unusually careful and judicious history of the Prussian medical profession, Claudia Huerkamp, although admitting medical education was longer and more expensive and the exigencies of the career harsher than, say, of a teacher or judge, nevertheless does not share "the impression that the doctors were exactly starving or had grounds to fear proletarianization." By the same token, one can imagine the opposite conclusions that could have been drawn by the roughly 7 percent of Hamburg physicians Huerkamp cites as earning less than 2,000 marks – certainly a proletarian income and one that would have entitled them (ironically!) to sickness insurance if they had been factory workers.[17]

14 Plaut, *Gewerkschaftskampf*, p. 30. 15 *Aerztliches Vereinsblatt* 27 (1900): 381.
16 Plaut, *Gewerkschaftskampf*, pp. 50–5. 17 Huerkamp, *Aufstieg*, p. 213.

The proper comparative group is surely not factory workers, however, but rather other professions. As Huerkamp points out, Prussian judges around 1900 began at 3,000 marks and rose to 6,600 after twenty-four years of service, for an average of 5,000 marks yearly over thirty years. The figures for *Gymnasium* professors, as we know, lay a little lower, between 2,700 (beginning) and 6,000 (highest) with a lifetime average of 4,760 marks.[18] Providing the equivalent of a judge's or teacher's pensions, insurance, professional tools and office space cost of course a thousand or more marks a year.

A contemporary champion of doctor's rights wrote in 1911, however, that the salary of a *Gymnasium* professor (which had meanwhile been increased to that of a judge in 1909) ought to be the "minimum for existence" for physicians, or 6–7,000 marks per year in fees. He personally felt this necessary to attract the kind of middle- and upper-class people into medicine whose "feeling of responsibility" constituted a necessary requirement for the profession; and such people were used to "a better standard of living than workers."[19]

But the final point was not whether all doctors should have such incomes; it was that up to half of them did not. "Thus," as the same commentator wrote, "the fact . . . that about half of German physicians . . . were forced to live in a way that did not correspond to their status or their education . . . [produced] the preconditions for union-like organization."[20]

What other complaints about their working conditions did these new "unionists" articulate? One entire class of complaints derived from experience with the sickness funds and their patients. The funds, as noted above, contracted with one or more local physicians to treat all their patients, often for a flat per-capita annual fee. Doctors complained that insured patients would now appear with imaginary or trivial complaints, perhaps so as to obtain the free medicines the physicians could dispense and that patients would otherwise have to buy.[21] The multiplication of patients, and the reduction of medical care to "routine work" and "writing prescriptions," all without increased fees, remained a constant source of irritation among physicians.

Perhaps the sorest point of contention with the funds after fee schedules was the question of *freie Arztwahl*, the freedom of the patient to choose his doctor. In effect a completely free choice of physicians by the insured would have broken the contracting power of the funds, because it would have meant the end of single-doctor contracts for all fund members and the virtual opening of the market of insured patients to all local physicians. The *Aerztetag* had written this demand on its banners as early as 1891, but without much initial success.[22] Significantly, such a change would have benefited young physicians starting their careers; it was also a demand shared by many workers and socialists. The boards of the sickness funds, however, feared freedom to choose might lead to

18 Ibid., p. 212.   19 Plaut, *Gewerkschaftskampf*, p. 56.
20 Ibid.   21 Huerkamp, *Aufstieg*, p. 203.
22 *Aerztliches Vereinsblatt* 18 (1891): 254.

patients choosing those doctors most willing to prescribe medicine or certify inability to work and thereby raise medical costs astronomically.[23] And many doctors who benefited from relatively lucrative contracts (e.g. with railroad and miners' funds) opposed free choice of physicians.

The Hartmann League, however, continued the fight after 1900. Although originally concerned with the central issue of "proper" fees for doctors, it quickly added the demand for free choice to its program, a fact that no doubt won it many adherents. At first many physicians did not know what to make of such pseudosocialist rumblings as paraphrasing the Communist Manifesto. By 1903, however, nearly 10,000 doctors had joined the Hartmann League, a process done by direct personal membership (in contrast to the Medical Association's membership through local medical societies). Although claims of 98 percent membership among German doctors by the eve of World War I should probably be taken with a grain of salt, it would appear that nearly 24,000 doctors had joined and paid the rather high membership fees into the "strike fund" by 1911, a figure representing nearly 77 percent of all German privately practicing doctors.[24] This may be compared to the 77 percent membership in the German Medical Association in 1910, an organization that had also grown considerably since 1900 (when it claimed 61 percent of all German doctors). The Hartmann League and the German Medical Association fused in 1903, except that the League's strike fund remained intact. Indeed, the Hartmann League tried to credit its own propaganda for the sudden growth of the DAeV by 25 percent in one decade after only sluggish expansion in the two decades before.[25]

The success in raising membership and solidarity of German doctors to such unprecedented heights undoubtedly can be explained by the success of the "strike" tactics employed after 1900. There had been isolated refusals to work for sickness funds in the nineteenth century, but with unimpressive results: the solidarity of the profession was not sufficient to prevent recruitment of outside medical personnel or even local defections. After 1900, however, a series of tough new tactics by the Hartmann League led to several signal successes in "doctors' strikes," notably in Leipzig and Cologne in 1904. Leipzig was an excellent testing ground, having the largest single health insurance fund in Germany.

The Hartmann League's tactics included signed agreements by doctors not to work for a fund involved (even incipiently) in a contractual dispute; prosecution of doctors who broke such agreements (and even those who never signed them) before medical honor courts; massive propaganda, moral pressure on colleagues to honor "picket lines," and even financial settlements to doctors tempted to hire on as "strike breakers" with the funds. Social cutting and other unpleasant

23 Huerkamp, *Aufstieg*, pp. 224–7.   24 Ibid., p. 283; Plaut, *Gewerkschaftskampf*, p. 96.
25 Plaut, *Gewerkschaftskampf*, pp. 28–9.

harassment were also employed on recalcitrant physicians. The League even incorporated an efficient free placement service for doctors to eliminate the temptation of working as a "strikebreaker."

As long as a fair degree of solidarity could be maintained for a relatively short period (a month or a few weeks), the funds were placed in a difficult position: they were required by the Reich insurance law to provide medical service to their patients. The Leipzig doctor's strike was notable for the refusal of the physicians to treat any fund member, even as a private patient paying out of his own pocket, until the strike was settled. (Cases of life-threatening need were excepted.)

One after another of the strikes ended in the failure of the funds to round up enough doctors to carry on, so that contracts favorable to the Hartmann League's principles – concessions about free choice of doctors as well as higher fees – were the only alternative. So impressive were the physicians' "strike" tactics that the mere threat of one came to suffice. (These tactics involved announcing a "lockout," or *Sperre*, against a troublesome fund, which then often obtained an inadequate response trying to recruit enough physicians from outside to break the back of any strike.)[26]

As a series of regular and extraordinary meetings of the *Aerztetag* showed, the success of the strike movement had galvanized the medical profession and eradicated many of the divisive doubts of previous years. Even physicians who had been skeptical now saw that the limited free choice of physician and the demand for higher fees benefited most doctors, without causing any of the suffering among those well-served by the previous, fund-dominated system.

The average incomes of physicians appear to have increased dramatically as a result of the successful "union" actions against sickness funds, as well. According to some estimates, that average nearly doubled (from 6,000 to 10,000 marks) between 1900 and 1913.[27]

Yet, the medical profession, now well-organized through the melding of the old (DAeV) and new (Hartmann League) elements in the professionalization process, still encountered rough going when it came to influencing new legislation. The annual national medical conventions renewed in the decade or so before the war their old complaint against quackery and sought government action, but without success. As the Reich prepared a complete overhaul of the sickness and other social insurance laws (eventually to become the *Reichsversicherungsordnung*, or Reich Insurance Code, of 1911), the DAeV voted unanimously against a liberal increase in the annual salary ceiling for mandatory inclusion in sickness funds, which would have excluded anybody earning less than 3,000 (instead of the previous 2,000) marks from the private health-care market.

26 For an excellent account, see Huerkamp, *Aufstieg*, pp. 285–96; also Plaut, *Gewerkschaftskampf*, pp. 109–57; Puppe, *Bestrebungen*, pp. 73–132.
27 Karin Bergmann-Gorski, *Aerztliche Standes- und Berufspolitik in Deutschland von 1900 bis 1920* (Dissertation, Medizinische Fakultät, Free University of Berlin, 1966), p. 82.

The Reichstag did not consider the doctors' wishes. The new law neither granted an *Aerzteordnung* (Physicians Code), nor protection from quacks; but it did extend sickness insurance to almost all workers who earned less than 2,500 marks. Therewith, by some estimates, half the population of Germany now came under some kind of insurance coverage, and so did the vast majority of doctors for most of their practice. Shortly before the new code was scheduled to go into effect (New Year's Day, 1914), the DAeV held a special congress and voted almost unanimously to go on general strike against the new law.[28] This extraordinary show of solidarity provoked immediate negotiations between the medical organization and national representatives of the sickness funds, presided over by the Reich Interior Ministry. A strike was averted by the "Berlin Agreement" shortly before Christmas, 1913: the doctors in effect won the right to determine, together with the insurance industry, the national framework conditions for individual contracts between local physicians and funds. Through "union" tactics, the medical profession had in fact achieved a great victory for its members and created a new kind of cartel with the public insurance industry.

There were some less dramatic indicators of heightened professionalization of medicine in this period, as well. By 1914, job placement services, insurance, pension, and other self-help schemes were available for German doctors through the DAeV/Hartmann League or the medical chambers.[29] The chamber system had become fairly widespread in Germany by World War I.[30] More importantly, the chambers and the local and national medical associations worked harmoniously together in most questions and showed a considerable overlap of personnel.[31] As the successful prosecution of "strikebreaking" physicians showed, the "honor courts" set up for the medical profession were very effective in disciplining the profession not so much for mistreating patients as undermining the monopolistic drive of the "strikers."

As mentioned in the last chapter, the demands of the DAeV anent educational and certification reform, including a relatively close regulation of specialized studies, extension of minimum study to ten semesters, plus an obligatory "practical year," were largely met by the national Examination Code of 1901. This not only satisfied the medical profession; it had the reciprocal effect of considerably unifying it through a common, highly regimented, and long-lasting medical education and examination system. As a result, the DAeV did not find it necessary to call for a closure on the number of physicians being trained and certified.

The dental profession continued to lag somewhat behind the main branches of medicine; but its development nevertheless shows many parallels and, by 1914, the achievement of a number of important "professionalizing" demands.

28 Huerkamp, *Aufstieg*, p. 302.   29 Plaut, *Gewerkschaftskampf*, pp. 114–28.

30 For a list of such chambers, their dates of incorporation or of increased authority, and their powers, see Finkenrath, *Organisation*, pp. 50–5.

31 Goerke, "Grossstadtmedizin," p. 116.

As with normal physicians, dentists wished for a national dental code setting them up as a privileged profession (and of course excluding nonlicensed practitioners) or, failing that, at least the same kind of honor courts and chambers achieved in most states by their medical colleagues. They did not attain the first goal, partly because of the lower educational standards of the profession. But Dental Chambers were instituted in some German states, e.g. Baden (1907) and Prussia (1912), in which a similar pattern of overlap between personnel with the German Dental Association (VBDZAe) occurred.[32] In 1909, however, the Examination Code for dentists was revised to require higher school graduation (*Abitur*), longer university study (seven semesters), an intermediary examination, and required courses in certain medical specialties. Thanks to these provisions, dental students could now be matriculated in regular medical faculties and their studies regarded as a form of medical specialty.[33]

As with the physicians, the dental profession at first split over tactics vis-à-vis the sickness funds, with a *Wirtschaftlicher Verband Deutscher Zahnärzte* (Economic League of German Dentists) splitting off from the older *Vereinsbund*; but the two reconciled in 1910 to fight the provisions of the impending Reich Insurance Code.[34] Nevertheless, they were unable to shut out dental technicians from payment under the Insurance Code and thereby secure a monopoly for university-educated dentists only. This status insecurity could be pursued into World War I, when dentists complained that they did not usually get to wear uniforms (although in military hospitals where they were engaged for the duration they were treated and paid as officers) or that they were not treated with sufficient deference to set them apart from lesser trained military dentists or civilian dental technicians![35]

Apothecaries need only be mentioned here in passing, as they were even less further along the path of academicization than dentists. Theirs was still more of an apprenticeship trade than an academic profession, although the apothecary *Prüfungsordnung* of 1904 advanced educational requirements to just below the *Abitur* and from three to four semesters of nonmatriculated study in university courses, in addition to the apprenticeship and several years of on the job training. Nor did the *Deutscher Apothekerverein* (German Apothecaries Association or DApV) develop before World War I into an active promoter of professionalization; it was more a national society of pharmacy owners.[36]

2. THE CHEMICAL PROFESSION

Another profession caught between cartels and union activity in the first two decades of the twentieth century was that of the chemists. As with medicine,

32 Seefeld, *Zahnärzte*, pp. 56, 73.   33 Lafrenz, *Zahnärztlichen Unterrichts*, pp. 14–15.
34 Seefeld, *Zahnärzte*, p. 70.   35 Ibid., pp. 79–80.
36 Alfred Adlung and Georg Urdang, *Grundriss der Geschichte der deutschen Pharmazie* (Berlin, 1935), pp. 142–5, 242–4.

the chemical profession underwent significant structural changes in the market for its services: the chemical industry grew vastly, but the number of chemists employed in small concerns declined as big industry became the rule. Between 1895 and 1912, for example, the largest firms (4–6 percent of all companies) increased their share of all employed chemists from 41 percent to nearly 60 percent.[37] In 1912, of the roughly 8,000 German chemists, 40–45 percent are estimated to have worked in industry.[38] Thus, although there were more positions for chemists in absolute terms, an increasing proportion of them were dependent on the offerings of large combines. Much as the medical profession saw its market reshaped by the sickness funds, so did the chemical profession with the arrival of the *Grossbetrieb*, the "big factory" style of production and management. The decline in autonomy, income, and respect was a widespread consequence, at least an anticipated one; and the responses included attempts to form union-like organizations.

But the parallels with medicine more or less end there. The chemists were never able to organize on a scale comparable to physicians, were never able to carry off effective strike actions, and were dealing with entities—those comprising the chemical industry—that were in a better position, for many reasons, than the funds to resist such pressures as the organized profession could bring.

As we saw in Chapter 7, the German chemical profession, as organized in the VDC, but increasingly led by industrialists and professors, had taken successful steps to regularize and raise educational qualifications for chemists. The "raising of the chemical estate" did not, however, translate directly into other signs of heightened status, for example, income, autonomy, or the recognition of the scientist's independent contributions in matters of patents.

Indeed, one excellent recent study has suggested that the development of the VDC around 1900 followed more the model of a *Berufskonstruktion* than of professionalization.[39] This word refers to H. A. Hesse's observation that some professions do not develop from within but may be "constructed" from without, for example, by the chemical industry itself, to suit its own needs, in this case with a considerable assist from the educational authorities (chemistry professors).[40] Certainly the interaction in the development of the *Verbandsexamen*, analyzed in Chapter 7, fits this model. The presence of such captains of industry as Carl Duisberg in prominent leadership positions of the VDC also suggests a "guided" form of professionalization that was little more than a cover for industry's molding of a pliable and well-trained technical labor force. Yet, so rapidly changing was the chemical industry that Duisberg had himself begun as

37 Based on Johnson, "Academic, Proletarian, . . . ?" p. 125.
38 Lothar Burchardt, "Professionalisierung oder Berufskonstruktion? Das Beispiel des Chemikers im wilhelminischen Deutschland," *Geschichte und Gesellschaft* 6 (1980): 331.
39 Ibid., 326–48.
40 See Hesse, *Berufe im Wandel*. Hesse's conceptualization suffers from the contemporary (Federal Republic) orientation of his work.

an academically trained chemist who had worked his way up the corporate ladder: thus he could plausibly claim to be an "insider" to the profession.[41]

Whether constructed from without or developed from within is ultimately a misleading way of analyzing the VDC. As we have already seen, it was the interaction between internal and external pressures that shaped most German professions; and the disentangling of what American legal thought (including contemporary "antitrust" legislation) would call "conflicts of interest" were not perceived as problematical by a society that increasingly tried to solve its conflicts by "corporate" mediationism. Indeed, one of the interesting aspects of the VDC is that it contained both "labor" and "management" in its membership.

The clearly emergent version of "professionalism" in the VDC under Duisberg's leadership by 1900 was one based on academic training and expertise.[42] The alternative organizational model of the time was much less elitist – indeed was self-consciously democratic – and looked to labor unions for inspiration. Both approaches had to face some discontentment from those occupied in chemistry. As we shall see below, the "elitist" approach seems to have been more successful than the "democratic" one in satisfying the respective membership desiderata, at least in the short run.

Central issues for both types of professional chemical groups were the working conditions and economic status of their members. As in most other professions around this time, reliable figures are difficult to find, and contemporaries themselves, lacking full statistical information, disagreed and fell into the anecdotal. Even recent studies by different authors in the same volume point to different conclusions.[43] Surveys undertaken by the VDC itself and published in the *Zeitschrift für Angewandte Chemie* indicated a starting salary range of 150 to 200 marks monthly, not vastly higher than nonacademic technicians. After five years or so, academic chemists in the published sample might earn a salary between 3,000 and 4,000 marks.[44]

As badly as these salaries compared to those of other academically trained professionals, they do not constitute a complete picture of the compensation available to chemists: bonuses, profit sharing as a reward for inventions, pen-

41 Johnson, "Academic, Proletarian, . . . ?" 124.
42 Ibid., 29. For a typical statement of the ideal of the "cultivated" chemist see Carl Duisberg, "Die Abnahme der allgemeinen Bildung bei den Chemiestudierenden," *Zeitschrift für die angewandte Chemie* 13 (1900): 131–3.
43 Heiner Ramstetter, "Der deutsche Chemiker in Krieg und Frieden," in Schmauderer, *Chemiker im Wandel*, p. 312, cites a beginning salary of 110 marks a month as not unusual for a university-trained chemist in 1914; "You don't become a chemist," the author remembered from his professional beginnings about that time, "you hire chemists!" H.-W. Schütt, in the same volume, claimed a beginning monthly average salary of 200 marks around 1908, rising to 250 monthly after a year and up to 350 "a few years later" (pp. 303–4).
44 According to the salary survey, the vast majority of beginners earned 150–300 marks monthly; if a trial period of several months was involved, about half the beginners earned 250–300 marks after finishing it. *Zeitschrift für angewandte Chemie* 21 (1908): 1,943. See also *Die Chemische Industrie* 31 (1908): 399–400.

sion plans, and other benefits were available in many chemical companies, particularly larger ones. On the other hand, as chemical research and invention became more routinized, employers appear gradually to have become more reluctant to share profits or hand out bonuses. The rapid increase in the numbers of chemists, at a time when the industry was undergoing a relative technological stall, increased the pressure of competition: the total number grew from 4,000 in 1897 to 9,000 in 1914.[45]

In addition to such limitations on chemists' incomes, there were problems with the so-called "competition clause" (Konkurrenzklausel), a normal part of every contract signed between chemist and company. In order to prevent chemists changing employment and taking company secrets with them (a practice that increased chemists' bargaining power in the "wild and wooly" early days of the industry), new employees were obligated not to take work in a competing company for a stated period of time or Karenz (often five years) after leaving the firm, sometimes with no compensation from the original employers, or anyway far less than their salary would have been. Breach of this promise could be (and was) prosecuted in court, often with high fines imposed on the employee.[46] If this were not enough inducement for restricting chemists' mobility, the bonus and benefit plans of most companies only became available to employees after lengthy terms of service.[47]

In the face of these barriers to the "raising of the chemical profession," a radical solution came, not from within the ranks of the chemists themselves (as with the Hartmann League) but from a group of disgruntled engineers. In 1904, several unemployed Berlin engineers founded the Bund der Technisch-industriellen Beamten (League of Technical and Industrial Officials, or BUTIB). Employers were specifically excluded from this league, which hoped to speak for technical employees in all branches of industry, irrespective of field or level of education.[48] No pretense was made to furthering scientific interests; the League demanded higher salaries, mechanisms for adjudicating disputes with employers, and radical changes in the rights of employees concerning patents and the competition clause.

Of the League's claimed 24,000 estimated members by 1914, perhaps 10 percent came from the field of chemistry.[49] Although hardly of proletarian background, yet certainly not as well-educated as the majority of the VDC members, the League membership adopted trade-union tactics (including the threat of strikes) and a frankly adversarial (if hardly socialist) stance toward industry.

BUTIB did not achieve any of its demands directly and need not detain us here. Suffice it to note that the possibility of its being attractive to VDC mem-

45 Burchardt, "Professionalisierung oder Berufskonstruktion?" 331.
46 Rassow, VDC, pp. 82–3.   47 Johnson, "Academic, Proletarian, . . . ?" 131.
48 Bund der technischen Angestellten und Beamte, 25 Jahre Technikergewerkschaft – 10 Jahre Butab (Berlin, 1929).
49 Johnson, "Academic, Proletarian, . . . ?" 129.

bers obviously forced the leadership of that organization, so heavily dominated by industrialists, into conciliatory actions vis-à-vis the masses of disgruntled member chemists. Their first concrete action was to appoint "a young gentleman with connections to wide circles of employed chemists" in order to "establish contact" with them.[50] This token proving insufficient, the VDC set up in 1907 a "social committee," not, however, to plan parties. It was designed to advise the association board of directors (and therewith presumably the industry) on ways of "harmonizing the conflicting interests of the members." Significantly, the social committee was made up of equal numbers of representatives of employers and employees.[51] It immediately began debating three issues: patents, the competition clause, and employee insurance.[52] Also in 1907, Carl Duisberg became the chairman of the VDC, determined to advance professional status for all chemists.[53]

The Social Committee's compromise suggestions for the competition clause and inventions were presented and accepted by the VDC general assembly in 1909. Henceforth, the VDC recommended that inventors be guaranteed an "appropriate" share in the profits and their own names in patents taken out by companies.[54] In 1908, stung by BUTIB's claim that starting salaries for chemists were falling below poverty levels, the VDC published a survey refuting this. By 1913, the VDC had drawn up a "standard contract" which, while far from representing a suggested collective contract, tried to set guidelines for individually signed contracts between employer and employee (including patent and competition-clause points). One historian points out that it "performed some of the functions of a uniform, professional code of ethics."[55] Although no minimum salary or other figures were included (so as not to abridge the "freedom of contract" that Duisberg insisted must be a part of professional ethics), certain improvements in the central questions exercising young chemists were implied.

The war interfered with the final outcome of legislation recommended to the Reichstag on such issues. But, for reasons perhaps beyond the control of Duisberg or any chemists, economic growth and declining numbers of graduated chemists (perhaps as a result of rising educational expectations in the profession) appear to have greatly improved the position of chemists vis-à-vis their employers by the eve of World War I. This was one of the factors that allowed the industry-dominated "professionalizing model" of Duisberg and his supporters in the VDC to triumph over the "labor union" option offered by BUTIB.

The VDC continued to be active in other areas of professionalization, as well, particularly in the area of education. As a means both of reducing competition on the chemical labor market and of upgrading the profession, the VDC decided to issue warnings against studying chemistry in 1907 — but the warnings

50 Rassow, *VDC*, p. 82.   51 Ibid., p. 44.   52 Ibid., p. 45.
53 Hans-Joachim Flechtner, *Carl Duisberg: Vom Chemiker zum Wirtschaftsführer* (Düsseldorf, 1959), p. 245.
54 Rassow, *VDC*, p. 83.   55 Johnson, "Academic, Proletarian, . . . ?" 136.

were directed only to would-be students who did not have the *Abitur*.[56] The reorganization of the VDC in 1907 also headed off incipient centrifugal forces within the organization by recognizing "specialty groups" within the association to meet the specialized needs of subgroups of chemists. Particularly in contrast to the engineering profession, to be discussed below, this move prevented specialization from becoming a force destructive to professionalization. The further academicization of chemistry corresponded entirely to the wishes of Duisberg and his supporters and incidentally was assumed, probably correctly, to be one of the best antidotes to BUTIB-style unionizing efforts. The argument that educated professionals would not join unions is thus a creation of the early twentieth century.

In other small ways the VDC attempted to influence educational policy, for example, by resolving in 1910 that more technical chemistry should be taught in universities, and not merely technical colleges.[57] Such resolutions did not find much echo, not because universities vigorously resisted, but because of lack of funds to expand such programs.

In conclusion, one can see that the chemical profession made significant strides toward elevating itself into an academic and increasingly respected, well-remunerated, and well-organized group under the leadership of the VDC by 1914. With well over half of all chemists in Germany joined to it by 1913,[58] with a reorganized and highly centralized constitution and the obvious influence of captains of chemical industry, the VDC was a force to be reckoned with. The professionalizing tendencies obtained, however, were achieved at the price of more democratic or union-oriented options. The corporate mode of professionalization, with the illusion of "freedom of contract" and of a vast gap in the workplace between academically trained chemists and all others, had won out over the confrontational tactics of disgruntled (mostly nonacademic) employees in BUTIB – but only by bending to some of the demands of the rank and file.

3. THE ENGINEERING PROFESSION

Many of the same forces working to reshape the chemical industry and profession affected the engineers, too. Indeed, at this particular time, perhaps no two professionalizing groups had more in common in terms of changing conditioning factors. But the outcome for the further professionalization of the engineers was on the whole much more ambiguous.

Organizationally the engineering profession continued to be rent by fissures. In addition to rival engineering associations already mentioned in earlier chapters, the VDI witnessed the establishment or evolution of several more. Although the VDI still had a very large membership (22,000 in 1908), it had been surpassed by the relatively young *Deutscher Technikerverband*, with 25,000

---

56 Rassow, *VDC*, p. 81.   57 Ibid., pp. 77–8.   58 Ibid., p. 63.

members, representing mostly construction technicians. The League of German Architectural and Engineering Societies (VDAIV), representing primarily civil engineers and government architects, had reached a membership level of 8,600. Private architects (still a small number in Germany) dissatisfied with it, instead of joining the VDI, created their own *Bund Deutscher Architekten*, or Federation of German Architects (BDA), in 1904. And BUTIB, mentioned above in connection with the chemists, was chiefly an organization of engineers and thus principally a threat to the VDI.[59]

Also unlike the VDC, the VDI was unable to please those engineers who pressed for professionalization through elite education. Indeed, the VDI's policies concerning education appear at times to have crossed each other. Manufacturing interests in the VDI in particular were behind a movement to expand secondary technical education, which after 1900 produced large quantities of low-wage but highly skilled nonacademic engineers. These employees were sometimes hired to do the same supervisory work as academic engineers, who received no special protection or consideration in industry, for all their degrees and diplomas.[60]

It is perhaps telling that one of the areas in which the VDI found it could cooperate with (and for the most part dominate) rival engineering professional associations was that of education. The VDI was the main force behind the DATSCH (*Deutscher Ausschuss für Technisches Schulwesen,* or German Committee for Technical Schools) founded in 1908. Eventually such old rivals as the Mining Engineers and Electrical Engineers Association (VDEh, VDET) and new ones such as VDDI and BUTIB joined this committee, a self-appointed "corporate" body designed to negotiate with the government in reconciling disputes about educational reform and particularly about nonacademic technical middle schools. DATSCH, reflecting the middle-of-the-road compromises of the VDI itself, however, refused to recognize any innate superiority of academic over nonacademic training for the engineering career, even as it tried to raise the standards a little for technical middle schooling.[61] Thus, for the engineering elite (if not the manufacturing elite), DATSCH and the VDI turned in at best a mixed performance in the period 1900–18. Leaders such as Alois Riedler, who had been instrumental in persuading governments to grant doctorates of engineering by 1900, now even denounced the VDI as an agent of educational backsliding.[62]

One is therefore hardly surprised to find engineers with diplomas and doctorates turning away from the VDI to other solutions in the first decade of the twentieth century. One recent study notes that some 20 percent of the BUTIB's membership were *Diplom-Ingenieure* and accounted for a disproportionate share

59 Kulemann, *Berufsvereine,* pp. 179–84.
60 For an excellent discussion of this and other dilemmas of the VDI, see Gispen, *New Profession, Old Order: Engineers and German Society,* chap. 8.
61 Ibid.   62 *VDI-Zeitschrift* 42 (1909): 702–7.

of the organization's leadership.[63] Another group set up a separate German Diploma-Engineers' Association (*Verband Deutscher Diplomingenieure,* or VDDI) in 1909 after failing to obtain a change of statutes of the VDI to exclude non-academic engineers from the Association. By trying to identify its members as the educated elite of the engineering profession, the VDDI's strategy aimed at procuring special treatment from employers, both industrial and public (where engineers were still, they claimed, treated as second-class citizens). The VDDI, with only 3,500 members (an estimated 13 percent of the *Diplomingenieure* graduated in the previous fifteen years), could hardly be called a great success.[64] But its very existence shows how little solidarity or agreement existed among engineers by 1914 on what their profession was or should do.

The VDI itself followed shifts in membership and internal governance comparable to those of the VDC. Between 1900 and 1910, the number of employed engineers (as opposed to entrepreneurs and directors of larger firms) increased from roughly 40 percent to over 60 percent in several of the larger locals of the VDI.[65] As with the VDC, the VDI changed its constitution in 1910 to hand over most decision-making authority from the national conventions to an elected permanent executive committee (*Vorstandsrat*) in which ordinary engineers sat only in token numbers.[66] This centralization of power was a trend for most professional groups in the period, as they grew ever larger in membership and thus also more unwieldy. But in this case the centralized power was not used to force forward the professional or economic interests of the membership. In the words of one of its historians, the VDI

did not separate itself from industry, but did not influence its policies, either; it served industry by raising its efficiency through increasing the professional qualifications of the membership and regulating essential technical questions. The era of an unequal partnership began; the VDI became a junior partner without rights.[67]

As with the VDC, the professionalization drive of the VDI had by tendency been taken over as a weapon in the struggle against unionizing tendencies in a larger industrial matrix. Unlike the sickness funds facing "unionizing" doctors, engineering "unions" faced a fairly well cartelized heavy industry already before World War I, and management could use the double weapon of influence in the "professional" engineering associations as well as blacklists against "unionizing" engineers. Furthermore, the industrialists in the VDI seem to have taken fewer steps to solve complaints about inventors' rights and the competition clause than was the case in the (much less heterogenous) chemical industry.[68]

63 Gispen, "Engineers in Wilhelmian Germany," [Manuscript version 1987], pp. 14–15. The extent to which dual membership in VDI and BUTIB overlapped cannot be established.
64 Ibid., p. 16. 65 Hortleder, *Gesellschaftsbild,* pp. 40, 52. 66 Ibid., pp. 50–1.
67 Ibid., p. 46. 68 Schimank, *Ingenieur,* pp. 52–3.

To be sure, a "double loyalty" to one's firm and one's profession characterized engineers in America and France, also professionalizing their occupation at this time against a backdrop of rapid economic change.[69]

The developments we have outlined above give rise to reflections on the nature of professionalization in engineering, however. It was the capitalist, free-market economy and its representatives who undermined the drive of the educational elitists in the VDI increasingly to redefine "engineer" as a man with a higher diploma or doctorate. (Unlike other professions, engineering did not have to deal with the question of female engineers before 1918.) But the notion of the engineer being a free professional, contracting out his labor and expertise, became preposterous in an era of big business enterprises, massive expansion of an unequal employee-company relationship, and the swamping of the labor market by lesser-educated technical middle-school graduates.

The obvious alternative to the "capitalist" or anyway free-market model was a bureaucratic one, and indeed the VDDI (and not only it) began to demand the opening of bureaucratic careers to engineers on the argument that technological knowledge was necessary to run a technological society. As one commentator complained in 1904, "The great technical progress of the nineteenth century was brought about by engineers. But in Germany the engineer is still banished from the state administration of technical work [e.g. railways, public enterprises, etc.]. The measures that govern our industry are conceived by jurists."[70]

For that matter, the bureaucratization of private industry, with the engineering elite at the helm, was an old idea that hardly needed to be revived in 1910. What was new in 1910 was the achievement of a certain educational status among a part of the engineers – that of an academically trained elite theoretically equal to the university graduates – without that status seeming to have the kind of guarantees and income that a bureaucratic ladder provided civil servants. The VDDI at least took up the tactic of trying to persuade both government and industry to grant such privileges to "academic" engineers. The graduate engineers in the BUTIB, although certainly not wishing to overturn the capitalist system, nevertheless sought more direct economic improvements by its unsuccessful union tactics.

All these ideas and alternatives lay about in 1914 and, as we shall see below, worked through the Weimar and National Socialist periods. But to many academically trained German engineers, whether in VDI, VDDI, or BUTIB, it

---

69 Rolf Torstendahl, "Engineers in Industry, 1850–1910: Professional Men and New Bureaucrats," in Carl G. Bernhard and Elizabeth Crawford, eds., *Science, Technology and Society in the Time of Alfred Nobel* (Oxford, 1982), pp. 263, 256–8.

70 Ludwig Bernhard, "Die Stellung der Ingenieure in der heutigen Staatswirtschaft," *Schmollers Jahrbuch* 28 (1904): 119. For an interesting contemporary view, see Ludwig Brinkmann, *Der Ingenieur* (Frankfurt, 1908), esp. pp. 75–80.

must have seemed increasingly clear that professional engineering associations alone, without the backing of the state, could hardly prevail against burgeoning German industry.

In the next chapter, we shall consider the professionalizing strategies of other groups who were less exposed to the free market of services and had by tradition been state employees in a direct or indirect sense. We may then be able to see if this alternative model was successful enough to justify the envious references of physicians to teachers or engineers to jurists.

9

Law-based professions, 1900–1918

As we saw in Chapter 8, the situation of such "free professions" as medicine, dentistry, chemistry, and engineering altered perceptibly with changes in the market for services, itself conditioned by such factors as demography, the rise of large-scale business, and social insurance legislation. The "freedom" of the "free professions," originally conceived in the liberal thought patterns of the 1860s and 1870s as liberation from bureaucratic control, appeared to take on a different meaning in the face of unequal "clienteles" such as large industry or the health-insurance funds. Words and sometimes behavior mimetic of organized proletarian labor appeared among the otherwise genteel professional organizations. The usually staid journal of the German Medical Association admonished its members in 1900 with words echoing the Communist Manifesto: "Physicians of Germany, unite! Organize yourselves! *'Si vis pacem para bellum'* [If you desire peace, prepare for war] is also valid for us."[1] Yet, it was not class warfare or the overthrow of the system that such groups preached and sought; instead they wished to use labor union and cartel techniques to strengthen their own bargaining position so as then to enter into a stable and equal partnership with the representatives of their "clients." In these struggles the state bureaucracy and legislature served more as tactical allies, at least incipiently, than as instigators of their own original programs of professionalization "from above."

Many of these generalizations hold true of the remaining professional groups in the period of 1900–18. One, that of practicing attorneys, could logically have been treated in the previous chapter along with the other "free" professions. But for reasons that will become apparent below, it is desirable to deal with them along with other juridically trained personnel. These latter, including judges, higher civil servants, and – increasingly – managers in the private sector struggled to redefine their traditional role, particularly vis-à-vis a state that already before 1918 was becoming more an intellectual abstraction than an object of self-identification. The "State" came increasingly to mean, in the critical

1 *Aerztliches Vereinsblatt* 27 (1900): 449.

language of these professionals, "them," the highest level decision-makers, rather than "we," the whole civil service. Long suppressed by the fiction of identity between the interests of the state and its servants, organization and open agitation for self-interest broke out among the latter, who comprised the majority of legal graduates.

Other state employees pressed their professional agendas with more or less success against ever-weakening resistance from the state itself. A few scant years after creating a national lobby, higher schoolteachers achieved their decades-old dream of equality with judges in status and remuneration. Elementary school teachers did not gain such status, since their educational qualifications were still subacademic, but they did make some gains in other areas, as did female teachers. Even university teachers got into the act, creating national organizations to press for their special interests.

As with the professions treated in Chapter 8, national professional organizations were often challenged by specialized groups, radical groups "for the promotion of economic interests" (a favorite slogan of the era), and transdisciplinary collective action groups (like BUTIB, discussed earlier). Also similarly, demarcations between "academic" and nonacademic sectors of the same profession began to emerge more clearly in many cases, with each sector tending to take a different path toward "raising the profession."

The proliferating number, vociferousness, and – quite often – influence of these professional groups in the last decades of the Wilhelminian empire contradict the idea of a state-determined "professionalization from above" in Germany. As if it were not enough to follow all those we have already encountered, we must also note stirrings of professionalization among businessmen, journalists, economists, and even actors and artists.

The newest aspiring professions in particular followed the pattern of their older brethren in looking to the state and its educational and certifying powers to regularize their position vis-à-vis stronger clienteles, raise educational qualifications and thereby claims to expertise and social standing, and harmonize differing standards in the various German states. But they often did so with modern lobbying techniques and a boldness that would have scandalized professional organizations thirty years before and very likely have brought the indignant wrath of the state bureaucracy down on them.

Yet the issue for new and old professions, for free and employed, was usually the same: to gain an unassailable and guaranteed status somewhere in the upper reaches of German society – unassailable by the rampant forces of industrial capitalism and guaranteed by the very state that employed many professionals.

1. ATTORNEYS

An excellent example of the professions' desire to use state power to increase or cement their position of advantage while insisting on the autonomy of the profession vis-à-vis the state was provided by the German attorneys. The period 1900–18 was relatively calm for the DAV, despite increasing concern over the growth of competition and its effect on lawyers' incomes. Surprisingly, the major representative group of German lawyers debated, but did not finally approve, artificial restrictions on the number of attorneys allowed to study or practice law (*numerus clausus*). Despite considerable discussion of educational reforms that would have made becoming a lawyer more laborious and expensive, there were no more than token changes proposed in this important area. There was general dissatisfaction with the state-mandated fee schedule and other income-related issues, but the attorneys never became so upset as to even suggest strikes or other less extreme tactics comparable to those of the physicians. Nevertheless, they obtained improvements in this area for themselves.

The bar had grown rapidly after the adoption of *freie Advokatur* and the *Reichsanwaltsordnung* in the 1870s. In absolute numbers, the number of practicing attorneys in Germany had increased between 1880 and 1900 from about 4,000 to nearly 7,000, or a 57 percent increase within twenty years. But between 1900 and 1913, the number had jumped to over 12,000, for a 55 percent increase in only thirteen years.[2] Although the number increased slightly in 1914, it had actually decreased to just 12,000 in 1919.[3] Such figures must be relativized by the admitted scarcity of lawyers before the 1870s and the growth of Germany's population, both absolute and litigating. The number of lawyers per 10,000 population increased from 1.3 in 1900 to 1.9, only a 46 percent increase per capital.[4] (By way of a current comparison, the ratio in the United States in 1980 was 25 lawyers per 10,000 population.)

Whether such statistics pointed to a serious crisis of overcrowding was then and remains now controversial. Some recent studies indicate a "crisis of qualifications" for professional careers,[5] but the changing structure and relationship to each other of the various components of the entire legal profession (including civil service and private economy) make such suggestions inconclusive. Although it is clear that the number of law graduates grew faster than the upper civil service or the bench, the numbers of which were kept within artificial limits, it remains unclear whether the "surplus" that went into the bar was seriously underemployed.

Other studies maintain that the bar still provided very good career possibilities before 1918.[6] And although most lawyers in Imperial Germany were more likely to complain about their lot than to praise it, enough improvement could be marked off between 1900 and 1914 to prevent approval of such drastic measures as the *numerus clausus* by the DAV. An undetermined but certainly grow-

2 Ostler, *Rechtsanwalt*, p. 60.   3 Ibid., p. 207.   4 Estimates based on ibid., p. 60.
5 Detlef K. Müller, et al., "Modellentwicklung zur Analyse von Krisenphasen im Verhältnis von Schulsystem und staatlichem Beschäftigungssystem," *Zeitschrift für Pädagogik, Beiheft* 14 (1977) 48–51, 65.
6 Rüschemeyer, *Lawyers*, p. 175.

ing number of lawyers was going into private service as *Privatbeamte*, as managers were sometimes called then. The market for lawyers' services grew along with the population and the increasing complexity of civil life, because the *Anwaltszwang* provision of the 1879 national civil trial code required that all parties in a trial be represented by a lawyer.

Thus, discontent with the economic situation of lawyers focused on two general solutions – raising fees and decreasing the numbers of attorneys competing for them. One 1911 survey indicated that 36 percent of all attorneys earned less than 3,000 marks yearly, and that 77 percent earned less than 6,000.[7] One might recall the median lifetime earnings of Prussian judges and schoolteachers mentioned in the last chapter, and by those standards German attorneys (particularly because so many of them were beginners) do not appear to have been earning notably worse incomes than other academic professionals.

Still, lawyers complained with other professionals that their fees were customarily (if not theoretically) limited to the schedules set by the Reichstag, that these had never been generous, and that price increases had already wiped out by 1900 a small increase in the schedules.[8] The DAV set up a commission to recommend an overhaul of fee schedules at its fifteenth national convention in 1901, and various regional attorneys' chambers made representations to the Reichstag in following years. As with other professional groups, the DAV found itself being challenged for inadequate lobbying in economic affairs by the foundation of a *Wirtschaftlicher Verband Deutscher Rechtsanwälte* (Economic League of German Attorneys, or WVDR) in 1907. The DAV wasted no time in responding to this challenge, debating fee schedules at its 1909 meeting and proposing modest increases. The national fee schedules were indeed increased in certain areas in 1909, and the Reichstag was approaching a complete revision at the outbreak of war. The accelerating inflation of the war finally forced some big-city lawyers' associations to approve stiff fee increases, a unilateral step later sanctioned by the DAV and not disallowed by the government.[9]

The dissatisfactions of many lawyers with their economic situation led to a palace revolt in the executive of the DAV in 1909, led by Hans Soldan, a founder of the Economic League. As happened in other organizations around the same time, the DAV was faced with centralization of control and the creation of a full-time staff with a hired business director, an innovation resisted by the old guard. After the national meeting of the DAV in 1909, however, the changes in personnel and statutes were carried through, making the DAV into a more streamlined and aggressive agency for the propagation and realization of the economic demands of large parts of its membership. It also signaled a challenge by local and state court attorneys to the traditional pattern of electing DAV leaders from the highest or *Reichsgericht* level.[10]

7 Ostler, "Werden," 36.   8 Ibid., 34–7.   9 Ibid.; Ostler, *Rechtsanwalt*, pp. 58–9.
10 Ostler, *Rechtsanwalt*, pp. 90–2.

One of the chief weapons envisioned by the young Turks in the DAV was *numerus clausus*. To be sure, the legal profession was virtually unanimous in rejecting any return to the state-controlled system that obtained before *freie Advokatur*, as votes of the DAV and the various Lawyers' Chambers showed.[11] But opinion remained divided on some other means of limiting access to the profession.

A poll by the Soldan's Economic Association published in 1911 indicated that 60 percent of the respondents favored some kind of limits (an equal percentage favored increasing educational requirements). But the national convention of the DAV in 1911 rejected any restrictions by an overwhelming majority.[12] Further polls and discussions revealed a certain tension between the massses of lawyers polled and the leaders in the DAV, who still constituted an undeniable elite.

But on measures of educational reform elites and economically threatened followers could presumably agree. The *Juristentag* debated adding intermediary examinations for law students in 1901, but turned them down. Nevertheless, adding an extra examination administered by professors was widely proposed as a solution both to student laziness and the surplus of trained lawyers.[13] More exams evidently appealed to the *Juristentag*, heavily influenced as it was by law professors, because such exams would increase their control of access to the profession.[14] In 1900 the *Juristentag* unanimously approved extension of law study to a minimum of seven semesters, the harmonization of legal curricula all over the Reich, and a reform of postgraduate practical training for entering the career of law in any of its branches, a proposal that would have legitimated a practicum in attorneys' offices as well as the traditional unpaid on-the-job training in the in administration and the courts.[15] The *Juristentag* also debated in 1911 adding mandatory courses in such fields as psychology and economics for law students, in a bid to bring lawyers' training into line with modern urban realities.[16]

For ordinary attorneys, similarly, the idea of a *praktisches Jahr* (practice year) somewhat comparable to the medical internship was widely discussed, particularly at the 1905 convention of the DAV. But the proposed *Praktikum* was set at two years, a serious delay for graduates eager to start their earning careers. It was opposed on grounds ranging from suspicion of a desire to create a cheap

11 Ibid., pp. 57, 65.; *Verhandlungen des XX. deutschen Anwaltstages zu Würzburg*, in *Juristische Wochenschrift*, 40 (1911), Zugabe zu Nr. 20, p. 50.

12 Ostler, *Rechtsanwalt*, p. 67.

13 See, for example, the reports of Professors Hiller and Rosin to the *Juristentag* in *Verhandlungen des 26. deutschen Juristentages*, 2 (1902), pp. 148–204 and 263–93; Henrich Gerland, *Die Reform des juristischen Studiums* (Bonn, 1911), p. 152.

14 Forty percent of the Standing Deputation, or board of directors, of the organization were professors in 1900: *Verhandlungen des 25. deutsche Juristentages* 3 (1900): xiii.

15 Olshausen, *Juristentag*, pp. 64–9.

16 Heinrich Gerland, "Ausbildung der Juristen," *Verhandlungen des 31. deutschen Juristentages* (1912): 894 ff.

pool of young scriveners for lawyers' offices to invidious comparisons with judges, who needed no similar preparation.[17]

In the face of the DAV's repeatedly stated opposition to *numerus clausus*, some lawyers began founding separate affiliations on a regional basis with the chief aim of pushing through some kind of limits on the number of practicing attorneys. Starting with the Rhenish-Westphalian Lawyers' Association, others were founded in Brandenburg, East Prussia, Upper Silesia, Saxony, Baden, and Bavaria. They continued to agitate throughout World War I for limits to access to the profession, although without breaking openly with the DAV. Their effectiveness was limited because they could not agree on the correct method for limiting access to the profession.[18]

Despite such signs of organizational fragility, the DAV continued to attract new members and to become by 1914 the unquestioned representative of most German practicing attorneys, encompassing some three-quarters of them. But the revolt of the years 1907–10 left many questions open and many members dissatisfied. The legal profession was still far from unified, as the failed attempt of the various state *Rechtsanwaltskammern* to persuade the Reichstag to create a national lawyers' chamber served to demonstrate.[19] Resentment of restrictions on the practice of law by lower-ranking lawyers attached to the *Amtsgericht* or *Landesgericht* drove a wedge between them and the more prosperous, prestigious attorneys in the higher courts (who could practice at all levels). The former were licensed to practice only before their local or regional court, where the value of civil-action cases (*Streitwert*) was usually lower and, consequently, the fees as well.

Still, it is too one-sided to say that the DAV had failed to extend the legal profession's control over its own affairs down to 1914 and that what professionalization took place was a "professionalization from above."[20] This might only be relatively true in contrast to France, Britain, or the U.S.A. But, as we have seen, by the end of the German Empire, the concept of professional autonomy associated with the ideology of liberalism of the 1860s and 1870s had been eclipsed by a new vision of the proper relationship between state and profession.

One aspect of the *numerus clausus* debate little discussed in public was anti-Semitism. A majority of Berlin lawyers on the eve of World War I was Jewish, as was about a quarter of the Prussian bar; nationally the Jewish component was about 15 percent. By contrast, only three to four percent of judges, and lower-level ones at that, were appointed in Prussia from among Jewish lawyers.[21] Thus keeping the bar open without readily manipulable means of excluding Jews was a vital preoccupation of its influential Jewish members, because other

17 Ostler, *Rechtsanwalt*, pp. 64–5.   18. Ibid.   19 Ostler, "Werden," 4.
20 Siegrist, "Gebremste Professionalisierung," 312.
21 Rüschemeyer, *Lawyers*, p. 177; Ernest Hamburger, *Juden im öffentlichen Leben Deutschlands* (Tübingen, 1968), p. 44.

branches of the legal community (civil service, bench) could be more readily filtered by discriminatory selection.[22]

The "commercialization of the bar" that was a code-word for anti-Semitic feeling had other aspects as well. As mentioned above, reformers such as Professor Heinrich Gerland believed legal education should be modernized to prepare lawyers better for administering the modern world. Indeed, we have also witnessed engineers and others complaining about the "jurist monopoly" in public administration. How could people schooled primarily in literary classics and formal law run a modern industrial society? But training in economics and other "realistic" subjects carried exactly the tinge of ungentlemanly practicality that had been so strenuously resisted by such established professions as law and medicine, as we saw in Chapter 5.

2. ECONOMISTS

This problem was illustrated well by another emerging professional group after 1900, that of economists. As far back as the mid-1880s economists had begun to argue for the recognition of the equality of their discipline with others such as law.[23] Two decades later the number and importance of "practical" economists had greatly multiplied. What was a *praktischer Volkswirt*? According to one definition in 1907, "anyone who makes economic policy in the broad sense, whether ex officio as a political official or high civil servant, or elected as a parliamentarian, member of a chamber of commerce or agriculture, or as a member of economic associations etc."[24]

One of the first priorities of the *Deutscher Volkswirtschaftlicher Verband* (German Economics Association, or DVV), founded in 1901, was to shape a reform agenda for the training of administrative elites. Beginning with lively discussions of individual questions about an economics "state examination" reminiscent of the recent similar discussion among chemists or the question of a special doctorate reminiscent of the engineers', the DVV went on to publish well-documented position papers on reform.[25] This *Verband* was not a scholarly organization comparable to, for example, the American Economics Association or the *Verein für Sozialpolitik* (Social Policy Association, or VFS), but rather "practicing economists" in the sense of managers. It later changed its name to *Reichsverband der Deutschen Volkswirte*, or RVDV. ("The term *Verband*, which I translate as "association," often came to replace the older term *Verein* after the

22 For a discussion of social discrimination against Jewish members of the legal profession, see Sigbert Feuchtwanger, *Die freien Berufe. Im Besonderen: Die Anwaltschaft* (Munich, 1922), pp. 165 ff.
23 See, for example, W. Hasbach, "Ueber eine andere Gestaltung des Studiums der Wirtschaftswissenschaften," *Schmollers Jahrbuch* 11 (1887): 587–94.
24 Edwin Krueger, "Der Beruf des praktischen Volkswirts," *Schmollers Jahrbuch* 31 (1907): 1,309.
25 See the issues of *Volkswirtschaftliche Blätter* from 1 (1901) through 7 (1907), as well as Deutscher Volkswirtschaftlicher Verband, *Die Vorbildung für den Beruf der volkswirtschaftlichen Fachbeamten* (Berlin, 1907).

new German Civil Code (BGB) came into effect in 1900: *Verein* came to be associated with registered, and usually strictly local, clubs and organizations.) The problem of defining the proper training of *Volkswirte* (economists) had never been addressed by governments. Should they go to universities and get degrees, on the model of civil servants? Or should they attend institutions with a more technologically open curriculum, such as technical colleges or even the *Handelshochschulen* (business schools) that were beginning to come into being around the turn of the century?[26] The first such schools included one founded in connection with the University of Leipzig and the Technical College of Aachen in 1898, and as separate business colleges in Cologne and Frankfurt (1902) and later in Berlin (1906). These institutions will be treated more fully in Chapter 10.

The Economics Association's publications included the results of a survey about the training of German managers, which showed how varied and incoherent it was. Despite discussions in the DVV and at the meetings of the VFS between 1907 and World War I, no firm consensus could be reached. One extreme group defended "assessorism," that is, they insisted that formal, academic legal education must continue as the bedrock of administrative training. The other extreme discounted "book learning" of the law and stressed practical knowledge and technology. As one analyst of the problem later put it: "The variegated nature of life misled people into underestimating the formal and general as a principle of education. Those were decades when the other extreme was emerging: the shallow expert mentality that still makes life such a joy today and undermines a proper reaction toward 'assessorism.' "[27]

3. CIVIL SERVANTS AS PROFESSIONALS

As for the "assessors," counselors, judges, and higher civil servants, who had throughout the nineteenth century enjoyed a privileged position in Germany, they too began to organize to promote their own professional interests after the turn of this century. Already at the foundation of the German Reich the Prussian statistician Ernst Engelberg calculated that the cost of educating a higher civil servant could no longer be recouped through his lifetime salary.[28] Bureaucratic salaries, particularly in the very highest levels, did not keep pace with inflation, let alone the kind of rewards increasingly available in the burgeoning private sector.[29] By 1900 the situation had deteriorated so badly that, according to statistics cited by the bureaucratic lobby, one could identify a trend toward

26 For an example of this kind of thinking, see Karl Thiess, "Hochschulbildung für Unternehmer," *Schmollers Jahrbuch* 38 (1914): 43–114.
27 Karl Pintschovius, *Volkswirte als Führer oder Fachbeamte. Eine sozialwissenschaftliche Untersuchung* (Munich, 1930), p. 45.
28 Hans Hattenhauer, *Geschichte des Beamtentums* (Cologne, 1980), p. 268.
29 Ibid.; Otto Most, "Zur Wirtschafts- und Sozialstatistik der höheren Beamten in Preussen," *Schmollers Jahrbuch* 39 (1915): 183.

the nonreproduction of bureaucrats, with higher quotas of bachelors, late marriages, marriages with no or fewer children, and the financial impossibility of bureaucrats funding their children's education: "bureaucratic families, rich in traditions, who had served the state through generations and carried on the spirit of the civil service, were bleeding to death as a source of future civil servants."[30]

This did not mean that the Prussian bureaucracy began more democratic recruiting, however, as evidence from Westphalia indicates: there 92 percent of the higher civil servants still came from upper-class families in the period 1900–18, the same figure as in 1835; and recruitment from high bureaucratic families had risen from 20 to 34 percent in the same period. In South Germany, upper-class recruitment was far lower and fairly constant around 60 percent.[31]

The contemporary cries of pauperization of the civil service, although not entirely fabricated, nevertheless must be relativized somewhat. Starting with the 1915 study by Most, successive investigations have tended to concentrate on the very highest levels of the civil service.[32] These levels, that is Prussian *Oberpräsidenten* and *Landräte* (provincial governors and district chiefs, two traditional preserves of the aristocracy) had undoubtedly slipped a bit in buying power between 1850 and 1910, because their salaries had increased only 32 percent in Prussia. But other civil servants had enjoyed increases from two up to two-and-a-half times the 1850 rate. This meant they virtually kept pace with general salary increases and inflation in Germany.[33]

Also, civil service salaries had been undergoing a general process of uniformization in the late nineteenth century, with salaries increasingly tied to rank and service-age principles rather than arbitrarily to this or that position. (One might recall here similar reforms already discussed in relationship to schoolteachers.) Lower civil servants had generally been better treated in salary increases than higher ones, presumably on the theory that the latter could dig into their family wealth (or that of their wives) to make ends meet. The most recent evidence confirms that, salaries aside, the secular trend from the mid-nineteenth century to 1914 was toward ever-greater recruitment of the civil service from the bourgeoisie and the professionalization of what had, in the *Vormärz* (pre-1848) period, still been a highly "feudal" service. One author goes so far as to maintain that the civil service was the most socially mobile group in prewar German society, principally because of the triumph of professional over aristocratic recruiting standards.[34]

30 Hattenhauer, *Beamtentums*, p. 270.
31 Hartmut Kaelble, *Soziale Mobilität und Chancengleichheit im 19. und 20. Jahrhundert* [Kritische Studien zur Geschichtswissenschaft, 55] (Göttingen, 1983), p. 50.
32 Hansjoachim Henning, *Die deutsche Beamtenschaft im 19. Jahrhundert. Zwischen Stand und Beruf* (Stuttgart, 1984), p. 10.
33 Horst Kübler, *Besoldung und Lebensunterhalt der unmittelbaren preussischen Staatsbeamten im 19. Jahrhundert* [Nüremberger Forschungsberichte, 6] (Nuremberg, 1979), p. 131.
34 Henning, *Beamtenschaft*, p. 153.

Nevertheless, it was among the lower civil servants where organizing drives took place first, for example, with the *Verband Mittlerer Reichspost-und Telegraphenbeamten* (Association of Middle-level Postal and Telegraph Officials, or VM-RTB, in 1890) or the *Deutscher Eisenbahnbeamtenverein* (German Railway Officials' Association, or DEBV, in 1891). Such organizations were looked on with great suspicion by governments at first and often had to restrict themselves to social and self-help (e.g. insurance) functions. The Postal and Telegraph Officials were forced, for example, to change their statutes in 1899 at the insistence of the Reich Secretary of Posts to include a loyalty declaration to the emperor.[35]

Such efforts to prevent, break or weaken bureaucrats' unions on the part of governments were increasingly undermined, however, by more tolerant interpretations of the "right of combination" (*Koalitionsrecht*), such as expressed in the debates over the new *Reichsvereinsgesetz* (Reich Association Law, 1908).[36]

In the wake of weakening government resistance and growing determination on the side of civil servants, some national organizations of university-trained administrators began to emerge around 1900, first with the *Deutscher Richterverein* (German Judges' Association, or DRV, in 1899), the *Deutscher Beamtenbund* (German Civil Servants' Association, or DBB, in 1906), as well as organizations of higher school and university teachers (to be treated later). Both the *Richterverein* and the *Beamtenbund* proved abortive, but more successful versions took root in 1909 and 1918, respectively. A plethora of other organizations representing nonuniversity-trained bureaucrats in various branches (even down to the level of a *Verband der Friedhofsbeamte Deutschlands* (Association of Cemetery Officials of Germany, or VFD, in 1903) came into being at the same time. And older organizations that had been essentially government-sanctioned bodies to coordinate self-help efforts, such as the *Verband Deutscher Beamtenvereine* (Association of German Officials' Associations, or VDBV, in 1875), were taken over by radicals or pushed into agitation for economic and status improvements by the success of the more aggressive, newer rivals.[37]

The first years of the new century witnessed a mounting debate about the role of bureaucracy in politics and the economy, as exemplified in the subject of the 1907 meeting of the *Verein für Sozialpolitik,* at which Johann Plenge suggested the creation of a special college for training leading economic managers.[38] As with technical professions, there were also attempts to found organizations that could successfully weld a united front of all *Beamte,* that is both state and "private" officials, irrespective of educational level, as in the

---

35 Wunder, *Bürokratie,* p. 100.   36 Hattenhauer, *Beamtentums,* p. 270.
37 Wunder, *Bürokratie,* p. 101.
38 Dieter Krüger, *Nationalökonomen im wilhelminischen Deutschland [Kritische Studien zur Geschichtswissenschaft,* 58] (Göttingen, 1983), pp. 102 ff. Also see Rüdiger vom Bruch, "Die Professionalisierung der akademisch gebildeten Volkswirte in Deutschland zu Beginn des 20. Jahrhunderts," in Karl-Ernst Jeismann, ed., *Bildung, Staat, Gesellschaft im 19. Jahrhundert. Mobiliserung und Disziplinierung* (Wiesbaden, 1988), pp. 361–79.

Bund der Festbesoldeten (impossible to translate, but literally "League of Regular Employees" or BDF, in 1909). In addition to the kinds of problems of internal disunity faced by the BUTIB, for example, the BDF's leaders faced punitive transfers and other signs of hostility from their civil service superiors.[39] It finally merged with the *Hansabund*, a sign of its failure, in 1913.[40]

Throughout all this activity, the higher civil service (the *Regierungsräte* or counselors of state in particular) remained generally aloof. Characteristically, the first *Deutscher Beamtenbund* (DBB), founded in 1906, emanated principally from municipal officials and did not succeed in uniting all public and private officials.[41] Its successor in name, refounded in 1918, was quite a different matter, as we shall see in Chapter 10. But the responses of governments to the universal issue enunciated by virtually all civil servants' organizations before World War I – that of inadequate salaries, and to a lesser degree the loosening of disciplinary rules to give them more security – proved far too little to dampen down disquiet: indeed, the BDF was founded as a direct reaction to "insufficient" salary increases in the 1909 Prussian Salary Reform.[42] As we shall see below, noncompensation for inflation and the collapse of the Hohenzollern monarchy were factors that opened the floodgates to agitation by upper civil servants in 1918.

One group of *Beamte* that did agitate for economic and status reforms before 1914 was that of judges (*Richter*). Although Prussian officialdom had successfully discouraged a Prussian judges' association throughout the late nineteenth century, other states had them, and a national *Deutscher Richterbund* (German Judges' League) was founded in 1909. The measure of judicial independence achieved by the German bench by the end of the nineteenth century, while still inadequate in the eyes of some judges, appeared to be both too much and to be exercised irresponsibly in the view of many outside critics. Particularly after 1900, waves of criticism of the courts washed through the German press, questioning the fairness of the bench. Not only did the socialists speak increasingly of "class justice," but even business interests complained of the clumsiness and slowness of German courts. The very idea that judges could discuss their concern about their salaries in public seemed an outrage to conservatives.[43]

To add to its isolation, the *Richterbund* let flare into the open a feud with the attorneys ("the born enemies of the bench") in its new journal, *Deutsche Richterzeitung*.[44] The judicial organization and its journal proclaimed the superiority of judge-dominated justice (precisely what was being criticized so roundly in Germany at the time) and in particular defended it as cheaper and quicker than when attorneys encouraged litigiousness or dragged out trials in-

39 Hattenhauer, *Beamtentums*, p. 280.
40 Andreas Kunz, *Civil Servants and the Politics of Inflation in Germany, 1914–1924* [*Veröffentlichungen der Historischen Kommission zu Berlin*, 66] (Berlin, 1986), p. 96.
41 Kulemann, *Berufsvereine*, pp. 42–5.   42 Wunder, *Bürokratie*, p. 101.
43 Hattenhauer, *Beamtentums*, 289–90.   44 Ostler, *Rechtsanwalt*, pp. 130–1.

definitely, presumably not to the disadvantage of their fee income. Some attorneys, however, were pressing for more lay representation on the bench (with "lay judges" as advisors), an idea that appalled the judiciary. And many judges, particularly during World War I, were eager to terminate the *Anwaltszwang* that required attorneys' presence in most courtroom situations.[45]

The judiciary also complained that its salaries were lower than those of men who, after the same education and on-the-job training, had gone into the administrative branch of the bureaucracy (*Verwaltungsdienst*); to make matters worse, the only group of state civil servants less well-paid than judges, the higher schoolteachers, were making inroads in the gap from the 1890s onward, as we have seen. The judges' complaints about lacking regular salary increases based on seniority were finally addressed by Prussia in 1908, but only years after similar reforms had been carried out for teachers, higher administrative officials, and even university professors.[46]

4. THE TEACHING PROFESSION

Even the latter group grew restive in the face of new realities. The rapid growth of German universities since 1870 had brought some distortions to the structure of their staffs: more and more of the teaching was being done by a growing army of *Nichtordinarien* (for example, "extraordinary" professors, *Dozenten* or instructors; laboratory assistants). Power and income was concentrated more and more in the hands of the full or "ordinary" professors, whose number had declined both as a portion of the teaching staff and in comparison to the student body since 1870. Furthermore, the proliferation of institutes and laboratories, in which the professor in charge often functioned as an autocrat, had by 1900 gone a long way toward overturning the "collegial" system of university self-government of the early nineteenth century. The growing influence and manipulation of cultural bureaucracies was symbolized by the "Althoff era" in Prussia, in which central policy-making took on a one-sided aspect that seemed to threaten academic freedom.[47]

The ordinary professors seemingly had little reason to found an organization to press for their economic betterment – they seem to have been relatively content. But a spate of academic "scandals" and perceived threats to academic freedom, as well as fear of the "bureaucratization" of the university, or its becoming just another "factory" (Harnack) impelled many German professors (especially

45 For discussions of this issue from the judges' viewpoint, see Richard Schmidt, *Die Richtervereine* (Berlin, 1911), pp. 52–67; from the attorneys', Ostler, *Rechtsanwalt*, pp. 129–39.
46 Wunder, *Bürokratie*, p. 103.
47 See McClelland, *State, Society*, pp. 258–87; Bernhard vom Brocke, "Hochschul- und Wissenschaftspolitik in Preussen und im Deutschen Kaiserreich 1882–1907: das 'System Althoff,' " in Peter Baumgart, ed., *Bildungspolitik in Preussen zur Zeit des Kaiserreichs* [*Preussen in der Geschichte*, 1] (Stuttgart, 1980), pp. 9–119; Rüdiger vom Bruch, "Universitätsreform als Soziale Bewegung," *Geschichte und Gesellschaft* 10 (1984): 72–91.

non-Prussian ones) to found the *Deutscher Hochschullehrertag* (German University Teachers Congress, or DHLT, in 1907). Its leading initiator, the liberal economist Lujo Brentano, and his allies were chiefly worried about academic freedom and the erosion of the university faculties' (i.e. ordinary professors') rights of self-government.[48]

Despite the high-minded rhetoric of the *Hochschullehrertag* down to the war years, its very hostility toward "bureaucratization" ran counter to the mounting demands of the lower-ranking university teachers, who saw in "bureaucratization" a useful lever against the "all-powerful" full professors. Although there was no national organization of the lower-ranking teachers, one could speak of a "movement" of local groups that wished precisely to regularize the relationship of the "nonordinary" university teachers and grant them more status, security, income, and power within their institutions. Certainly the annual meetings of German university professors were far from being or wanting to be a "professors' union."[49] The less privileged ranks of researchers and teachers certainly did not see it as such, but their discontent did not crystallize organizationally until after World War I.

If university teachers were still reluctant to organize for more than idealistic discussions of university reform (or indeed preservation against change), higher schoolteachers were not. The creation of the German Philologists' Association in 1903 (originally entitled *Vereinsverband Akademisch Gebildeter Lehrer Deutschlands*, or Association of Academically Trained Teachers' Associations of Germany) added a national roof for state *Gymnasium* teachers' organizations. It was from the beginning set up explicitly as an *Interessenvertretung* with special reference to questions of status in the bureaucratic hierarchy, salaries, and working conditions.[50] An additional impetus unquestionably was the losing battle of the "philologists" to retain the privileged position of classical *Gymnasium* education and the implementation by 1902 of the reforms decreed after the 1900 Imperial School Conference.

As we saw in Chapter 6, teachers of all kinds had made some progress in the first thirty years of the German Reich toward improvements in their salaries and working conditions. But the *Oberlehrer* (as *Gymnasium* teachers were routinely called around 1900) had still not achieved parity with the other university-educated civil servants, notably their reference group, the judges. As one commentator argued around the turn of the century, the *Oberlehrer* (along with physicians) had joined the working class in facing a "social question." Complaints about inadequate salaries and status had some justification, in the view of the statistician Franz Eulenburg. Not only did *Oberlehrer* have to study and wait for paying positions longer than ever before; "the classes from which a large part of school-pupils come have been rising." In other words, the status

48 Vom Bruch, "Universitätsreform" 81.
49 Hans Delbrück, "Eine Professorengewerkschaft?" *Preussische Jahrbücher* 129 (1907): 130.
50 Mellmann, *Philologenverbandes*, p. 93.

of pupils and teachers should correspond.[51] According to some estimates, *Oberlehrer* by 1900 had to study and prepare for their office for 6.5 years.[52]

The salary question was vocally discussed in the public press after 1900. Setting off this round was a book by Wilhelm Lexis, an advisor to the Prussian Education Ministry.[53] Vigorous attacks by *Oberlehrer* refuted the all too rosy picture presented by Lexis.[54] The teachers' basic argument was that they had to prepare for their profession as long, and make as many sacrifices, as judges; why should they not enjoy equal rank and salary?[55] Petitions and other forms of pressure brought some results. In the Prussian House of Representatives, for example, all parties joined in asking the government to grant the *Oberlehrer* equality with judges in 1907.[56]

Such constant agitation and pressure on parliamentary bodies applied by the DPV ended in success; in 1909 Prussia joined several other medium and smaller states (notably Bavaria, Baden, and Hesse) in making *Oberlehrer* equal to the lowest ranking judges in rank and salary. The 1909 budget provided for the same beginning salary for teachers (2,700 marks) but a higher housing subsidy; and triennial salary increases were steepened appreciably. After twenty-one years of service an *Oberlehrer* could expect to earn (including housing subsidy) up to 8,500 marks, compared with 6,000 in the previous year's budget.[57] Thus, demands of several decades were realized, it seems not coincidentally, within a few years after the national organization of the German *Gymnasium* teachers. Because the principle of salary increases according to periods of service had already been granted in the 1890s, the *Oberlehrer* were now firmly recognized as a part of the civil service, with a clear career ladder. As a final concession at the end of World War I, William II, who had mixed into school affairs more than any Prussian monarch, bestowed the title *Studienrat* on the *Oberlehrer*, an awkward-sounding title in English ("Counselor of Studies") but which contained the psychologically important rank of *Rat* just as in the higher administrative bureaucracy.

The higher teaching profession did not press, as did many other professional groups, for increased educational qualifications. As we have seen, their argument was that teachers already attended universities long enough to be compared to jurists, and that the unpaid training as a teaching aide also compared to the "assessor time" logged by trainees for the bench. To be sure, there were still occasional complaints to be read in the *Deutsches Philologenblatt*, for example a call for a *numerus clausus* and means testing for teachers because of overcrowding in the profession. One reader even noted ruefully in 1912 that lawyers were

51 Franz Eulenburg, "Zur Oberlehrerfrage," *Preussische Jahrbücher* 26 (1902): 195. This argument is repeated, also without hard evidence, more recently in Titze, "Umbildung," 110.
52 Richard Bünger, "Die Lage des höheren Lehrerstandes in Preussen," *Preussische Jahrbücher* 100 (1900): 462–3.
53 Lexis, *Besoldungsverhältnisse*, passim.   54 Bünger, "Lage," passim.   55 Ibid., p. 480.
56 Mellmann, *Philologenverbandes*, pp. 118–19.   57 Ibid., p. 140.

receiving a far higher share of the service medals doled out annually by William II![58] But the *Oberlehrer* seem to have been, on the eve of World War I, content with what they had achieved. One might agree with one recent critic who spoke deprecatingly of the *Oberlehrer* as "a profession that conformed" to the wishes of the imperialistic leadership of Germany; but one must add that such conformity had been purchased at the price of conceding the professionalizing demands of the teachers' association.[59]

Satisfaction with success also suffused the organization of teachers in "realistic" schools. The recognition of their equality with the *Gymnasium* in 1900 so pleased the *Realschulmännerverein* that some members called for the organization to dissolve at its 1902 national meeting, since it had accomplished its goals. Cooler heads prevailed against this whimsical notion, however: until the system of *Realschulen* was made homogeneous throughout the German states, the organization still had work cut out for it.[60]

In another area in which considerable reform took place after 1900, women's education, there were also clear repercussions for the professionalization of female teachers. The female teachers' organizations, as we saw in Chapter 6, tended to be more centered on mutual support (women teachers being required to maintain celibacy) than on such bread-and-butter issues as salaries, the central fixation of male teachers' organizations.[61] Part of the reason for this was the traditionally higher social class origins of female teachers, whose educational levels also did not vary as much as among male teachers. Less under the pressure of the female teachers' organizations than of larger feminist groups in Germany, the structure of women's education (including that of female teachers) began to change by the turn of the twentieth century.[62]

The central issue of interest for professionalization history in the reform of female education was the breaking open of higher education. Women had been allowed to prepare for and take the *Abitur* examination in conjunction with existing "Higher Girls' Schools" that through the 1890s were most comparable to the *Realschulen*. Women's groups called for the addition of three further years to these ten-year academies to give the female pupils a chance to learn the Latin they would need for the *Abitur* examination.

Once girls were allowed to become *Abitur* graduates from the 1890s on, the pressure mounted to grant them the access to university education that this diploma conferred on boys. Beginning with the state of Baden in 1900, by 1909 all German states, including a very unwilling Prussian government, followed suit on the theory that resistance would simply drive the women students to

---

58 *Deutsches Philologenblatt* 20 (1912): 151–3 and 87–8.   59 Titze, "Umbildung," 126.
60 Schmeding, *Schulwesens*, p. 182.   61 Gahlings, *Volksschullehrer*, pp. 68–9.
62 For an excellent account of the discussions surrounding these reforms, see James C. Albisetti, "The Reform of Female Education in Prussia, 1899–1908: A Study in Compromise and Containment," *German Studies Review* 8 (1985): 11–41.

attend universities in German states that allowed them to matriculate.[63] If women could now obtain the same teaching credentials as male philologists, the next question was obvious: was it not time to divide the girls' school system in Germany in ways comparable to the male school system? This question remained hanging during the remaining prewar era. The majority of teachers in girls' schools were still males, but all-girls' *Gymnasien* staffed by female philologists were becoming a thinkable alternative. (Only 15 percent of all elementary school teachers were female in Prussia in 1901, and they constituted the main group of all female teachers. But the numbers had risen to 21 percent by 1911.)[64]

The largest group of teachers in Germany remained male elementary instructors. As we have seen in Chapter 4, the Prussian salary reform of 1897 had made concessions to their most often heard complaint, that concerning salary. The reforms of 1908–9 in Prussia also affected them positively. These two reforms meant an average increase in real income to Prussian teachers of up to 50 percent for rural areas and at least 20 percent for urban areas. The average salary had been a little over 1,100 marks and 1,500 marks, respectively, in 1896; after the two reforms, the averages (unadjusted for inflation) were 2,150 and over 2,300 (rural and urban).[65] Although this compared favorably with incomes of ordinary workers in industry and trade, it was far less than *Oberlehrer* received, especially after the 1909 reform. From about that time, the DLV began to orient its salary demands on the higher schoolteachers for the first time.[66]

As we have now seen repeatedly, such demands were usually backed up with arguments based on comparable training for the exercise of the profession; and just before World War I, German elementary schoolteachers began to advance arguments why they, too, should attend universities. In Saxony, as in some other central and southern German states, regional teachers' associations petitioned the government in 1911 to allow graduates of teaching seminars to attend universities, although mandatory attendance by all teachers was not yet in the program.[67] By the end of World War I, the DLV made the creation of separate faculties to teacher education attached to German universities a part of its program.[68]

The DLV grew from a membership of some 83,000 in 1900 to 132,000 in 1914, a high degree of organization (75 percent) of all German elementary teachers, heavily Protestant and male.[69] Piecemeal reforms in the various German states had all but ended onerous secondary duties connected with the teaching office, such as serving as village church sexton. Prussia decreed that future hirings of teachers should normally be unconnected to parish duties,

63 Zinnecker, *Mädchenbildung*, p. 86.   64 Bölling, *Volksschullehrer und Politik*, p. 27.
65 Ibid., p. 24.   66 Ibid.   67 *Deutsches Philologen-Blatt* 20 (1912): 465 ff.
68 Bölling, *Volksschullehrer und Politik*, p. 169.
69 Pretzel, *Lehrervereins*, pp. 111–12; Bölling, *Volksschullehrer und Politik*, p. 36.

although the complete elimination of these was often not possible. Still, the trend lay in that direction, and even in the 1890s only about 22 percent of teaching positions were connected to extraneous duties.[70] The Prussian teacher salary law mentioned above also effectively freed teachers from direct dependence for salaries on the local governments that maintained the school, another large step toward autonomy for the elementary instructors.[71] Still, despite repeated requests by the DLV and smaller teachers' organizations, a clear status as "immediate" civil servant (*unmittelbarer Beamter*) comparable to that enjoyed by *Oberlehrer* was not achieved, neither under the empire nor the Weimar Republic.

The demands of schoolteachers for higher social standing were furthered by various means through the DLV. One of the most successful and surprising methods was to encourage (and even subsidize financially) *Einjährigfreiwillig* service by teacher seminary graduates, a possibility in Prussia after 1896. By 1912, nearly half the young teachers absolved their military obligation by voluntary service as *Einjährigfreiwilligen*.[72]

5. OTHER NEW PROFESSIONS

A number of other professions began organizing themselves or discussing claims to become academic professions in the last years of the German Empire. None of these achieved clarity about their status, but as indicators of a widespread social recognition of the importance of professional activity, they should at least be mentioned briefly. The profession of independent architect (as opposed to state-employed civil engineer or *Baubeamter*) was given a boost in 1902 by the introduction of a new degree, that of *Diplom-Architekt* (diploma architect), at the Berlin Technical College. The DATSCH occupied itself, inter alia, with the separate training program for architects in the last prewar years.[73] The *Bund Deutscher Architekten*, founded in 1903, emphasized the "artistic" quality of its members' work, and explicitly rejected either the "merely technical" or "entrepreneurial" side of building represented by the older *Verband Deutscher Architekten– und Ingenieurvereine*, or building contractors, respectively. By 1907 it had only four hundred members, however, and its major influence did not develop before the Weimar era.[74]

Another example might be found in sociology, a discipline with potential practical applications but as yet lacking even an academic curriculum. A German Sociological Congress was called for 1910 but, somewhat embarrassingly, found itself unable to agree on a definition of sociology![75] Conservative scholars

70 Christa Berg, *Die Okkupation der Schule*, pp. 172–3.   71 Ibid.
72 Bölling, *Volksschullehrer und Politik*, p. 26.
73 Bernhard Gaber, *Die Entwicklung des Berufsstandes der freischaffenden Architekten* (Essen, 1966), pp. 70–2.
74 Kulemann, *Berufsvereine*, pp. 179–80.
75 Walter Köhler, "Die wissenschaftliche Ergebnisse des Soziologentages," *Schmollers Jahrbuch* 36 (1912): 1,409–23.

like the historian Georg von Below denied any scientific character to sociology, and indeed even the first chairs in this field, set up right after World War I, were still "hyphenated" chairs, only partly in sociology.[76]

A contemporary study of journalists indicated that the chances for "academicizing" this occupation seemed slim: newspaper owners already complained that their writing staff contained too many overeducated people.[77] The answer, in the same observer's view, was a national journalists' association to protect and elevate the profession.[78]

6. CONCLUSION

As the German Empire plunged into the disaster of World War I, it had also largely concluded the process of formation of the modern professions and of their main representative organizations. Compared to forty or fifty years before, governments no longer suppressed professional organizations but rather negotiated with them. Rather than trying to insure survival by pretending to be merely scientific societies, many professional organizations by the end of the empire had openly adopted the economic and public lobbying methods so characteristic of an age of unions and cartels.

The more than four years of World War I caused a kind of suspension of normal activities for most professions, as males of service age (both professionals and their clients) went off to serve. There were many repercussions of this most "total" of mobilizations up to that time. The education of professional replacement cadres had to be modified or suspended; wartime standards were temporarily softened to hurry through their studies the small group of males who were still not drafted, so that they could replace those who had been sent to the front or killed. Universities were drained of both students and fighting-age teaching staff. All professional organizations heeded the government's call for national solidarity, sacrifice, and submission to the rigors of a centrally directed, authoritarian war economy. The economic dislocations of the war and rising prices probably had at least as much effect on the professionals as on the industrial workers, who chafed notably after 1916. But most professionals, like the rest of the middle class, held grimly to their loyalty to emperor and empire.

Overall the war may be said to have had a deleterious and retarding impact on the phenomenon of professionalization. Membership in many professional organizations declined slightly or held steady while so many professionals were

76 Georg von Below, "Soziologie als Lehrfach. Ein kritischer Beitrag zur Hochschulreform," *Schmollers Jahrbuch* 43 (1919): 1,271–322, polemicized against sociology as though it were tantamount to socialism. Also see Rüdiger vom Bruch, "Moderne Wissenschaftsgeschichte als Bildungs-, Sozial- und Disziplingeschichte," *Historische Zeitschrift* 242 (1986): 364.

77 Paul Stoklossa, "Der Arbeitsmarkt der Redakteure. Eine statistische Untersuchung," *Schmollers Jahrbuch* 35 (1911): 811.

78 Ibid., 306–7. For a sense of the desire for academic training of journalists mixed with extreme caution, see Martin Mohr, *Die Vorbildung der Journalisten* (Berlin, 1913), esp. p. 17.

involved as "amateurs" at the front. Demands for better working conditions seemed downright unpatriotic and were rarely posed by professionals, although as we have seen above, there were a few isolated complaints. Given the suspension of normal educational and examination patterns or their replacement by "emergency" measures, not even the level of certification already attained could be kept up. Medical examinations were at first reduced to only two days and the "practice year" dispensed with, producing a 7 percent increase in the number of licensed doctors in the first war year alone.[79] In the civil service, for example, half of all personnel was drafted, with the remaining half, returning pensioners, and other auxiliary personnel taking up the slack. By 1917, furthermore, inflation had effectively halved the buying power of "frozen" bureaucratic salaries.[80] The war, in effect, warped and suspended normal civic conditions upon which professionalization depended. One cannot even see any advantage to the "professional" officer corps, because so many of its members were swept away in combat and had to be replaced with reservists.

Still, these disruptions were perceived at the time as tolerable and short-term, as emergency measures that would not outlast the war and that posed no long-term threat to the achievements of the various professions. Speculation aside, it seems fair to say that the academic professions had attained sufficient stature and recognition by state and society before 1914 that their "professionalizing project" would have resumed in a normal postwar society. Such a society would have presupposed, however, either a German victory or at least an acceptably mild defeat.

The catastrophic loss of the war, the collapse of the Hohenzollern Empire, and the harsh "peacetime" era that followed, with all their other consequences, did create an entirely new situation for German professions, however. As we shall see in Chapter 10, most of the themes sounded up to now came to be restated after 1918, but in louder and more strident form, against backgrounds of heightened social and political dissonance.

79 Bergmann-Gorski, *Berufspolitik*, pp. 67–8.
80 Hans Fenske, *Bürokratie in Deutschland vom späten Kaiserreich bis zur Gegenwart* (Berlin, 1985). p. 23.

PART V

The Weimar era

10

~~~~~~

The "free" professions under Weimar

The models of modern professionalization developed in the Anglo-American world, as discussed in the introduction, present many serious shortcomings when applied outside that world of experience. One of the untested assumptions underlying them is a degree of political, economic and social stability that allows actors to carry out their roles consistently and over protracted time periods. If, to take one example, the American Medical Association was to exploit the argument of the superiority of school medicine in obtaining monopoly status for American licensed physicians, it needed stable and effective governments to squelch the quacks.

From 1918 to 1933, Germany lacked stable and effective governments comparable to those of America and Britain. The shifting multiparty coalitions of the Weimar Republic and the rapid change of cabinets implied a weak state constantly distracted by crises. Of course the old imperial administrative bureaucracy carried on, giving a certain continuity, but political imperatives from the parliament now had more weight, although they tended to cancel each other out over the long run.

In the face of this weak state, many historians have suggested, the influence of the *Verbände*, of corporate lobbies, unions, associations, and dozens of other types of groups reached new levels during the Weimar era. The professional associations were not least among those clamoring to achieve their own aims, in this case what one might term the completion of the professionalization agenda. Did they?

The economic problems of the Weimar Republic were massive and are vividly remembered even by people who do not know much else about the period. The massive postwar inflation culminated in late 1923, with its images of workers wheeling carts of billion-mark notes to the bakery for a loaf of bread and its more sinister reality of the economic ruin of large segments of the population, including especially the professional class. Five years of relative stability (1924–8) still did not bring a full economic recovery to prewar levels, and the Great Depression beginning in 1929 had a particularly devastating effect on Germany.

175

The "cures" for these economic crises, following the conventional and usually ineffective nostrums of the day, included emergency decrees that satisfied few and angered many, including professionals. The Weimar governments, saddled with huge foreign and domestic debts as a result of war, were rarely in a position to afford to implement innovations and reforms they had promised. High unemployment and taxes, coupled with low wages and living standards were characteristic of the epoch.

All major industrial societies and combatants experienced wrenching social adjustments in the wake of World War I; compared to the Anglo-American home of models of professionalization, however, Germany's were relatively more traumatic. Whatever the degree of persistence of its social influence, the German aristocracy suffered a blow in 1918 from which it never recovered, just as the industrial labor force had broken through as a factor that could not be bottled up or wished away. The continuing urbanization of Germany, the swift increase in "white collar" occupations as well as "blue collar" ones, and the relative decline of agriculture all contributed to shifts in the social structure of the country. The staggering loss of life, limb, and time that the war represented naturally had an impact on German society, ranging from encouraging women to enter the professional market to a "catch-up" boom in university enrollments in the years after the war (during which few had studied). Against a backdrop of democratic rhetoric about improving chances for social mobility, governments were reluctant to control massively superfluous numbers of students who would later become unemployed professionals. Students often played this desperate game, too, partly out of unquenchable hope that something would turn up and partly because being a student seemed marginally better than being an unemployed worker.

In addition to the political fragmentation of the Weimar era, other political factors weighed in the scales when professional matters were being decided. In a broad sense one might describe the aspirations of learned professions and the political left as generally incompatible. Most professions had been recruited from and trained to the level of Germany's imperial *Bildungsbürgertum*, or aspired to such a condition. The German political left, whether moderate like the Social Democratic Party (SPD) or more radical like the Independent SPD (USPD) and German Communist Party (KPD), were by inclination hostile to the claims of privilege, autonomy and elite status of the professional stratum of the bourgeoisie. In principle (if not always in practice), the left preferred state-run medicine, more lay participation in legal affairs, an end to such professions as pastor and officer, and the integration of all professional practitioners, organizationally and psychologically, into the broader party and union organizations maintained by the left.

Indeed, the left attempted to offer its alternative visions to professionals through its own organizations, either party-affiliated labor unions or, more typically, separate professional organizations that usually had strong ideological ties to political parties like the SPD. These groups were numerically quite small. Their significance lies in the fact that they attracted leftist members away from the mainstream professional organizations, thus weakening left political influence in them, and that their generally poor performance for their members served to reinforce the "nonpartisan" biases and tactics of the mainstream associations.

The political center and right were apparently far more congenial to the majority of German professionals, if only because the center and right were willing to recognize and agree with the agendas of professional groups. The Center Party (ZP) retained the loyalty of many Roman Catholic professionals, just as the People's Party (DVP) and Nationalists (DNVP) continued to attract the supporters of the former National Liberals and Conservatives, respectively. Even the Democratic Party (DDP) had, during its brief heyday, the support of considerable numbers of professionals (particularly schoolteachers). The Nationalist Party not only attracted many older professionals still unswayed in their monarchism, nationalism, and rejection of Germany's "humiliation" at Versailles; it also stood out in championing the professional classes, a role it could often afford, because it was so frequently in the opposition, unlike most other parties mentioned.

All professional groups continued the apolitical (or "suprapolitical") stance they had adopted before World War I. Professionals of all types were to be found in all parties, but no party could be said to have been the "party of professionals." Nor were professional groups heavily represented by Reichstag deputies. Given the shifting cabinets and the ultimate politics of deadlock in the Weimar experiment, it would have made little tactical sense for the professional groups to align themselves with any particular political faction. Nor should it come as any surprise that many university-educated professionals, who were recruited from or had just joined the *Bildungsbürgertum*, should sympathize more with the parties of the middle class than of the "proletariat" they were so desperately trying to avoid joining.

One party that had for many years a statistically negligible attraction for German professional groups or even individuals was Hitler's National Socialists (NSDAP). By the middle of the Depression, the Nazis had founded some of their typical special-interest groups for students, "jurists," physicians, and engineers, and by the very eve of the Nazi seizure of power, Nazi sympathizers could be found in growing numbers (but still as distinct minorities) in "apolitical" professional groups. Considering the fact that so many prominent Nazi leaders were members of the learned professions, it is surprising how limited was the appeal of National Socialism to the vast majority of professional people. As we shall see in Chapter 11, the appeal of success was overwhelming in the end. But during the 1920s and well into the Depression, the German professions on the whole resisted the siren call of fascism, even though it included the promise to deliver many of the changes demanded by the professions.

The Nazis themselves traded in ambiguity. Although they called for a restoration of the status of the professions, they also promoted an ideology that struck at the root of professional status. They thought in terms of all-inclusive occupational organizations (e.g. in medicine embracing everyone from bed-pan collectors to neurosurgeons) and pseudodemocratic *völkisch*[1] leveling, which made most academic professionals uncomfortable, without mentioning the Nazis' violence, crudity, and mistrust of all things intellectual. Last and not least, the Nazi program explicitly called for a purge of Jews (as well as women and political opponents) in the professions, a policy not calculated to win over the substantial and often influential minorities within them. What appeal the Nazis had for professional men appears to have been heavily concentrated on younger ones, those whose careers were distorted or blocked, often by the very "gerontocracy" of distinguished, wing-collared gentlemen who led the German professional groups.

One cannot reduce the demands of all professions in the Weimar era to one common denominator. There were still new professions, such as that of elementary schoolteachers and economists, for whom the establishment of tertiary-education requirements were a central concern. Others, such as doctors and lawyers, fought battles against inadequately certified practitioners carrying out tasks for which they were allegedly unqualified, in other words, battles for market monopolization. Many old professional demands remained on the table, such as those for a national Physicians' Code (*Aerzteordnung*) or national professional chambers (*Kammern*) for lawyers or engineers.

Yet, there was one common concern that overrode most others and pitted professional groups against state and society, sometimes even against each other: the concern about adequate incomes. This issue, which involved the whole complex of economic problems of the Weimar era, also linked up with questions of education, examination, and certification, as well the monopolization of markets, professional ethics, career ladders, and the autonomy – some alarmists even claimed further survival – of the learned professions. The "overcrowding" of the professions and the threat of even more by new waves of students, the fluctuation of demand for services, and other abnormalities in the "market" made professional occupations seem riskier and less remunerative than ever before.

To give here but one illustration, there were still about as many German attorneys practicing in 1918 as before the war. The number of civil cases (the backbone of the attorneys' practice) had shrunk during the war, however, if only because so many potential litigants were battling somewhere other than a courtroom. Even during the war, lawyers found that inflation was eating away at the value of their table-fixed fees, and unilaterally raised them in some cases. But

1 Impossible to translate in one word, *völkisch* ideology combined integral nationalism and racism to *include* all "Germans" or "Aryans" in a "people's community" while *excluding* "aliens" such as Jews.

they could not do this during the Weimar inflation, and emergency decrees (as in 1923) were simply unable to index their fees to the declining value of the *Reichsmark.* Thus most attorneys were working for fees that they were never paid, in real-money terms. As the postwar flood of new graduates entered the market, refusing to take cases remunerated in currency of dubious value could also result in losing clients to younger, hungrier competitors or to *Winkelkonsulenten* (paralegals). Even if the client was solvent and willing to pay the full fee at the outset of a case, the financial turbulence of the era could well leave him ruined or otherwise unable to pay. The amount of bill evasion in the Weimar era shocked contemporaries. If this were not enough, the Weimar governments reduced the number of legal transactions that required an attorney (*Anwaltszwang*) in the interest of simplified, popular justice, while increasing paperwork and labor costs drove up overhead for lawyers' offices. Yet, the attorneys, by most independent accounts, seem to have fared better than many professionals in a financial sense!

Despite such disincentives, students flocked to the bar as to other professions. Increasing the time and effort required to enter the academic professions may have had some impact on these waves of students, but not enough to balance supply and demand, both of which statisticians still learnedly calculated and projected, by 1930 with usually alarming predictions for the future. (They failed, of course, to predict the reintroduction of military service, Hitler's artificially stimulated prewar economy, and an actual shortage of young professional talent as a result of Hitler's drastic dismemberment of the student body in 1933.)

In addition to the constant economic problems faced by the professions in the Weimar era, one should mention the structural problems of remuneration. Although there were more professional people in this period than ever before, a smaller percentage of them were fully independent "free professionals." Although the number of lawyers increased, lawyers were still only a fraction of those trained in law; the majority went into the expanding civil service, business, or other careers as employees. The number of physicians also increased, but structural changes in the medical insurance system and other factors meant that very few physicians could sustain themselves solely from "private" patients. In other words, most German doctors were dependent on insurance funds or state jobs (e.g. in hospitals). Likewise the proportion of self-employed engineers and chemists fell as employment in a large company became the norm.

Do such structural trends mean a "deprofessionalization" of the learned occupations just as they were within sight of their "professionalizing" goals? This is a question properly raised by several recent studies of German professional groups, as we have already witnessed.[2] The question of whether employees

2 The works of J. F. Volrad Deneke, from *Die freien Berufe* (Stuttgart, 1956) to *Haben die freien Berufe noch eine Chance?* (Mainz, 1973), warn of the dangers to the "liberal professions" from state control and interference in the absolute autonomy of professional groups (Deneke particularly

(whether of the state or the private sector) can be considered true professionals hinges on the question of autonomy and rests principally on the experience of the English-speaking world. Perhaps it is sufficient to point to the current practice of the "free professions" in Britain or America, where large numbers – in many cases the majority – of doctors, lawyers, engineers, and chemists, to name only a few, are employees or dependent on insurance funds, government contracts, or other corporate patronage. Bureaucratization of professionals does not appear to have meant the destruction of the defining characteristics of professions. It has perhaps meant a loss in individual practitioner autonomy, but not necessarily of the autonomy of the profession as a group.

Similarly, one finds few cries of alarm in Weimar Germany about the decline of self-employed status. Anybody can be self-employed who is willing to starve. The central question was adequate compensation for employed and independent professionals alike.[3] In this sense, dependence on a health-insurance fund or a state job seemed preferable to the vagaries of self-employment in the economically turbulent interwar period.

1. THE MEDICAL PROFESSION

As in other professional fields, World War I brought a steep decline in certifications. Thanks to emergency waivers that made it easier to qualify, over 3,000 physicians were licensed in 1914, nearly three times the number of the last two peacetime years (or nearly five times in the case of women). During the rest of the war, certifications dropped as low as a third of prewar figures. By 1919, however, they were back to nearly double prewar levels, peaking at nearly 3,500 in 1920 and not falling below 2,000 (except for one year) until 1926.[4]

Throughout the prewar years of the twentieth century, the number of physicians per 100,000 population in Germany had hovered in the low 50s. By 1921 it lay around 60; by 1926, over 70; and by 1930, close to 80.[5] This meant roughly a doubling of the number of doctors per capita since the beginning of the 1890s and almost a tripling since the early 1870s. In urban areas the numbers were naturally much higher, despite improvement in medical care in the countryside. To be sure, some countries had more doctors per capita: Britain had over 100 per 100,000; the U.S.A, nearly 130 in 1925. Switzerland had

represented the views of physicians). That "deprofessionalization," or at least "professionalization from above," could be a danger posed by organized capitalism is a theme to be found in Hesse, *Berufe im Wandel*; Burchardt, "Professionalisierung"; Gispen, *New Profession, Old Order: Engineers and German Society, 1815–1914*. Johnson, "Academic, Proletarian, . . . "; and other works cited above.

3 Comments of this kind can be found in almost all contemporary publications about the professions, but for a sustained and lengthy argument (based on the author's own "theory of the economics of culture," as his subtitle proclaims), see Feuchtwanger, *Die freien Berufe*, esp. pt. 2.

4 Hochschulverwaltungen [before 1928: Prussia. Statistisches Landesamt], *Untersuchungen zur Lage der akademischen Berufe*, 1 (1932), *Bedarf und Nachwuchs an Aerzten*, p. 12.

5 Prinzing, *Handbuch*, p. 634.

about the same as Germany; France, with 60, somewhat less. European Russia had less than 20.[6] All countries with more physicians per capita were also economically in much sounder condition than Germany in the 1920s. But it is reasonable to assume that a ratio of 70:100,000 would have been acceptable for Germany under conditions of economic normality.

Despite the successes of organized medical resistance to the medical insurance funds on the eve on World War I, the DAeV and Hartmann League could hardly be said to be content to rest on past achievements. Struggles with the funds went on constantly, and physicians' strikes were again called, notably in 1920, again in 1924, and again in 1927–8. Constant changes in the insurance legislation had raised again the number of persons required to be insured, so that the vast majority of patients were now covered by the national health system. Physicians' strikes did not work as well as before the war. In many areas, the funds – now run by boards made up of two-thirds of representatives of the insured and one-third of employers – simply introduced their own ambulatory treatment systems, shutting out all medical personnel but their own employees. These, doctors complained, were often "unqualified," that is, they might be nurses or medical students.

Other measures imposed limits on the amount of prescriptions doctors could write. Further attempts to control costs by the funds led to required co-payments from the patients, and doctors complained that they were often unable to collect these, thus vitiating one of the advantages of the sickness-fund system in their eyes. Massive unemployment and financial distress during the Great Depression of course reduced the market for private patients at the same time that it vastly reduced membership in the sickness funds (which were tied to employment) and practically removed millions of Germans from all but charity medical care. The impact on physicians' incomes may be gathered from the decline in marks paid per fund member to physicians from 5.3 in the second quarter of 1930 to 3.9 in the first quarter of 1931.[7]

At this point the representatives of the funds and the physicians negotiated a reduction in physicians' fees commensurate with the diminished economic situation of the depression. An agreement of December 1931 brought the recognition by the funds of the principle of per-capita lump payments indexed to the insured's basic salary by the funds to the group of contracting physicians. This was reinforced by changes deriving from the emergency decree of December, 1931, which authorized the formation of local *Kassenärztliche Vereinigungen* (associations of sickness-fund doctors). These would distribute the lump sums and supervise medical practice – in itself a considerable step in medical self-government.[8] In addition, the same decree reorganized the insurance system so that patients had a limited choice of doctors instead of being forced to go to the one the funds chose – a long-standing demand of the medical profession.

6 Ibid., p. 637.   7 Hochschulverwaltungen, *Untersuchungen* 1 (1932), p. 34.   8 Ibid., 36.

Finally, limits already decreed in the 1923 crisis to restrict the number of new fund doctors that could practice in a given district were altered so that the number of insured people per physician was cut from 1,000 to 600. This measure in effect reduced the market protection of established physicians while not abolishing it. But it did not take care of the oversupply of physicians, either. Combined with a requirement that eligibility was tied to prior completion of a three-year residency (activity as an *Assistenzarzt*), a minimally protected market for the established fund physicians was purchased at the price of outsiders' chances, particularly of the thousands of medical neophytes (*Jungärzte*) emerging from the crowded medical faculties.

To be sure, these modest achievements by the DAeV and Hartmann League, while important in the long run, could not solve the immediate economic problems of a large segment of the medical profession. Virtually all authorities agree that there was a large fraction of German doctors who, even in the best years of the mid-1920s, were living in or near the level of destitution. A 1927 survey of only those doctors who paid the turnover tax (excluding those who were employed in institutions and those who had no practice at all for whatever reason) revealed that 17 percent had gross incomes of less than 5,000 marks (from which, it may be recalled, heavy overhead expenses had to be deducted). The great majority (58 percent) grossed between 5,000 and 20,000 marks (not a very helpful category), while 22 percent earned more than 20,000.[9] It may be assumed that the quarter or so of all physicians not included in this survey would bring all averages down considerably. One recent study calculates the average gross income of German doctors in the "good" year of 1928 at 12,000 marks, an "adequate, if not profligate" amount.[10]

The situation during the Depression was clearly much worse, thanks to a mounting oversupply of trained young doctors and the general economic downturn. As unable as everybody else in Germany to cure such economic catastrophes as inflations and depressions, the medical profession did make moves toward limiting the inflow of new physicians. One way of doing this was to increase requirements for licensing. At the very end of World War I, partly as a reaction to increases in both venereal disease and infant mortality brought on directly by the war, the fields of dermatology and pediatrics were made obligatory for the medical licensing examination.[11]

After the war, many physicians called for radical changes in the requirements for entering the profession. A national commission of representatives of medical faculties and the DAeV-Hartmann League was formed in 1920 to make recommendations. These included increasing the minimum study time to eleven semesters and the addition of otolaryngology and social medicine as required

9 Ibid., 33.
10 Michael Kater, "Physicians in Crisis at the End of the Weimar Republic," in Peter D. Stachura, ed., *Unemployment and the Great Depression in Weimar Germany* (Basingstoke, 1986), p. 60.
11 Bergmann-Gorski, *Berufspolitik*, p. 72.

examination fields. The state medical examination should be repeatable only once.[12] But warnings about the dire future of young physicians and increasing the requirements for licensing still did not discourage enough students. Despite five and a half years of required study (six including the semester to take the state examination), a further year of practical training, and (not required but increasingly the norm) one to three further years of residency to qualify for fund practice, students flooded the medical faculties starting in the second half of the 1920s. Having reached a postwar low point of about 7,700 in 1926, medical enrollments increased steadily thereafter almost to triple by 1931. Of these, significantly, almost a fifth were women.[13]

The medical profession was still discussing the idea of tightening examination procedures to serve as a filter during the depression. As one frustrated professor put it in 1931

Whoever enrolls today in any German university, assuming that he lives long enough and takes the required lectures and exercises, actually already has his license in his pocket. The number of those that cannot ultimately pass their *Physikum* [natural science intermediate] exam is very small. The man who fails the medical state examination is still waiting to be born.[14]

The German medical faculties unanimously endorsed a new policy of not allowing students who failed the examination to take it again.[15]

Although there were calls for a *numerus clausus* at the level of university enrollments, the DAeV could not agree to recommend such a step against academic freedom. Instead, as we have seen, it negotiated with the insurance funds and the government concerning limits on the number of doctors who could offer their services to health-insured patients. A growing minority undoubtedly favored some such drastic solution to the problem of overcrowding, however. The solution offered by the Nazis unquestionably held a measure of appeal for some German physicians. The National Socialists proposed to eliminate Jews and women from the field as well as to make drastic across-the-board reductions in the size of student bodies. Since women were coming to constitute 20 percent of the future medical profession and Jews (at least in Prussia) some 16 percent, their suppression promised to make a sizeable difference in market competition, especially in large urban areas.[16]

The chief organization of German medicine, the DAeV-*Hartmannbund*, had achieved by the 1920s a very high degree of organization of German doctors. By 1927, with over 45,000 members, the DAeV included 95 percent of all

12 Ibid., p. 80.   13 Hochschulverwaltungen, *Untersuchungen*, 1 (1932), p. 39.
14 Report of Professor Stiewe (Halle) to the German Medical Faculties Congress, 1931, as cited in Hochschulverwaltungen, *Untersuchungen*, 1 (1932), p. 43.
15 Ibid., p. 44.
16 On Jews in the professions before 1933, see Comité des delegations juives, ed., *Das Schwarzbuch. Tatsachen und Dokumente. Die Lage der Juden in Deutschland 1933* (Paris, 1934), p. 84.

German physicians.[17] Virtually all doctors belonged to the allied *Hartmannbund* because of its representative functions vis-à-vis the insurance funds.[18]

Yet, the DAeV-*Hartmannbund* had achieved many of the professional goals it had set out to promote at the beginning of the Hohenzollern Empire, including most items concerning preparation and certification, self-governing chambers in almost all German states, a practically unified medical profession, and considerable influence over government health policy and the insurance funds. What it could not do, and apparently did not unanimously wish to do, was destroy what was left of the principle of free access to the profession. Nor did it achieve a national Physicians' Code, but the principal hoped-for value of that, the prohibition of "quackery," was of decreasing importance with the rising and demonstrable therapeutic efficacy of "school" medicine.

As with regular physicians, the central problem for dentists in the Weimar era was tied to general economic malaise and an oversupply of practitioners. In many other ways, like the physicians, dentists were able to realize some more of their professionalizing demands. The VBDZAe leadership at the end of the war had appeared satisfied enough with the current educational requirements for dentistry to drag its feet in the face of proposals made by a *Dozentenvereinigung* (teachers' association) of dental instructors. The same *Abitur* as for physicians, but only seven semesters of university study, were the rule for dentists. In 1918, however, certification regulations were altered so that, by studying an additional semester, the dentist could qualify for a new degree, the *Dr. med. dent.* By the end of the 1920s, nearly 80 percent of all certified dentists in Prussia went on to take the doctorate, apparently for reasons of prestige.[19] As a rule, dentists also put in two to three years of residency before setting up a practice or qualifying for a salaried position in a clinic or hospital.

By the beginning of the Depression, the oversupply of dentists was forcing a reconsideration of training qualifications. The number of dentists certified in Germany almost doubled between 1900 (not quite 1,600) and 1910 (over 3,000), virtually ceased growing during the war, but more than doubled again by 1924 (about 7,500). By 1931 there were nearly 10,300 licensed dentists, with hundreds more coming out the pipeline of the clogged medical

17 Heinz Schmitt, *Entstehung und Wandlungen der Zielsetzungen, der Struktur und der Wirkungen der Berufsverbände*. [*Untersuchungen über Gruppen und Verbände*, 6] (Berlin, 1966), p. 38. Despite its title, this work is uncritical and highly sectoral in its treatment.
18 The disputes between the Hartmann League, which was closely affiliated with the DAeV, and the insurance funds, consequently also with socialist doctors who seceded in the late 1920s, has led some recent authors to paint it as virtually identical with the Nationalist party and, like that party, increasingly willing to drift into the Nazi orbit. One recent study went so far as to reduce the relationship between the DAeV/Hartmann League and the National Socialist Physicians League to one of "rivals, not adversaries," and to "prove" this by noting that all members of the latter also belonged to the former – as if virtually all German doctors did not. See Michael Kater, "The Nazi Physicians' League of 1929. Causes and Consequences," in Thomas Childers, ed., *The Formation of the Nazi Constituency, 1919–1933* (London, 1986), p. 160.
19 Hochschulverwaltungen, *Untersuchungen*, 2 (1932), *Bedarf und Nachwuchs an Zahnärzten*, p. 7.

schools. This represented a density of nearly fifteen dentists per 100,000 population.[20]

By 1929, the VBDZAe was passing a resolution asking for more clinical training and the extension of university study to nine semesters, which would practically have meant ten considering the high percentage of students who finished the doctorate.[21] But this demand was not realized, nor did the dentists' major organization call for a *numerus clausus*. They did complain about their rivals, the dental technicians, who were able to carry out many routine dental tasks at lower cost, thus making them attractive to private patients and insurance funds alike. These technicians grew in number, although not quite as rapidly, along with the dentist population, and there were a bit less than two of them for every German dentist. In the early 1920s the German Dental Association was able to influence policy only marginally, as when it consented to government decrees setting up special examinations for these technicians, a policy later viewed as a mistake.[22] In effect the dental technicians needed only a six to seven year combined apprenticeship to qualify for the state examinations, not the costly higher education and scientific training of the dentists.

The sickness funds were quick to exploit the fact that there were no fee schedules established for the technicians' work. In a 1924 agreement between the funds and the technicians' association, the latter guaranteed a 20 percent discount off the dentists' fee schedule for the same operation.[23] By 1928, a survey of estimated incomes for the two groups showed the result. Nearly 45 percent of technicians had incomes below 3,000 marks, but so did nearly 13 percent of the dentists. Although 70 percent of the technicians earned less than 5,000 marks, over 30 percent of the dentists did. The large majority of dentists (about 45 percent) earned between 5,000 and 12,000 marks in that "good year," a little over 20 percent above that.[24] The impact of the technicians can be deduced from the considerably lower average earning of dentists when compared to regular physicians.

Mounting dissatisfaction with the economic position of dentists led finally to upheavals in the organization of the profession. The economic lobbying organization of the dental profession (known after 1924 as *Reichsverband der Deutschen Zahnärzte*) had virtually taken over most professional activity from the older VBDZAe, and the even older Centralverein remained principally a scientific organization; all three fused finally in 1926. Just as the professionalization of dentistry lagged several decades behind that of regular medicine, so did the organizational efficiency and effectiveness of professional representation groups.

20 Ibid., pp. 8–9.
21 Fritz Schaeffer-Stuckert, *Geschichte des Zentral-Vereins Deutscher Zahnärzte, 1909–1934* (Munich 1934), p. 79.
22 Seefeld, *Zahnärzte*, pp. 85ff.   23 Hochschulverwaltungen, *Untersuchungen*, 2 (1932), p. 40.
24 Ibid., p. 36.

2. THE ENGINEERING PROFESSION

The formalization of two levels of licensed dental care practitioners during the Weimar era had its parallels, as we have already seen, before World War I for the engineering occupations. The VDI had indeed played a major role in shaping the network of secondary technical schools that now churned out "nonacademic" engineers who, somewhat analogously to dental technicians, could be hired to do the same work at lower pay, thus threatening the well-being of the "academics." This was a particularly difficult problem for academic engineers because more of them, too, were becoming employees as the German economy went through its various upheavals, including the "rationalization" movement in which large trusts and concerns swallowed smaller and independent companies. By 1928, a VDI survey showed that about two-thirds of its members were now employees; of the "independents," 12 percent were free consultants, the rest factory directors or manufacturers. The ratio of independent to employed VDI members was continuing to shrink, but, significantly, at a slower rate than before World War I.[25]

Meanwhile in the mid-1920s technical colleges and schools were delivering around 3,000 diploma engineers and 10,000 technical school graduates a year to the already oversaturated job market, a flood that could not be mastered even by such devices as the VDI's emergency placement and relief service.[26]

The VDI continued to receive competition from groups that had a broader and more engaged view of professional interests. The prewar BUTIB and the older *Deutscher Techniker-Verband* melded in 1919 into the *Bund der Technischen Angestellten und Beamten* (League of Technical Employees and Officials, or BUTAB), which had close ties to the socialist labor alliance *Allgemeiner Deutscher Gewerkschaftsbund* and the labor movement in general.[27] The *Reichsbund Deutscher Technik* (Reich League of German Technology, or RDT), espoused a politically active, if not necessarily unionlike, policy and the unification of all types of technicians irrespective of educational level. In the face of so much competition and its own hesitancy and uncertainty about what constituency to serve, the VDI ceased to grow as rapidly as before World War I. In fact it had fewer members (under 24,000) in 1920 than in 1914. And, although its membership grew to over 30,000 for the first time in 1928, the Depression pushed it below that level by 1932.[28]

25 Erwin Viefhaus, "Ingenieure in der Weimarer Republik: Bildungs-, Berufs- und Gesellschaftspolitik 1918 bis 1933," in Ludwig, *Technik, Ingenieure*, p. 301.
26 Ibid., pp. 334–5.
27 A counter-foundation, the *Verein deutscher Techniker*, or League of German Technicians (VDTe), distinct from the DTV, was helped to life by the nationalist *Handlungsgehilfen-Verband* as a self-consciously lower-middle-class organization, but it enjoyed little success. See Hortleder, *Gesellschaftsbild*, p. 70.
28 M.-L. Heuser and Wolfgang König, "Tabellarische Zusammenstellung zur Geschichte des VDI," in Ludwig, *Technik, Ingenieure*, pp. 560–1.

The VDI has been more or less severely criticized by recent historians of engineering for its "apolitical" stance and general fence-sitting during the Weimar era. But whatever the alleged failings of the leadership, the problem seems to stem at least in part from the still unresolved problem of what an "engineer" was. This problem had been increasingly resolved by other professions (e.g. by medicine, law, chemistry) thanks to their academic training and certification requirements. Consequently, a considerable amount of energy still went, during the Weimar period, into discussion of such matters as titles and their protection. The VDDI, stimulated by a decree in Austria restricting the title of engineer to academic graduates, began agitating for a similar step in Germany. Off and on throughout the 1920s, similar questions came up, introduced by the VDI's own members or raised by demands from other purely "academic" special associations like the VDDI (diploma engineers) or the VDAIV (architects and construction engineers). In the end, the VDI was drifting toward an "English" solution by the early 1930s, with a list of practitioners registered by some as yet undevised formula calculating educational level as well as experience. Throughout all these rancorous debates, the moderate leaders of the organization suggested the lame device of appending the letters "VDI" after one's name as a sign of engineering status, a rather Anglo-American self-help measure that failed to please the critics.[29]

This tendency of the VDI over the Weimar era to reflect more the wishes of academically trained engineers for a "closure toward below" presumably reflects the growing proportion of such engineers in the membership: about 55 percent of new members in 1926 were diploma engineers, and another 8 percent had studied several years at a technical college or university.[30] Yet, a majority of the older members had not enjoyed such higher educational qualifications and resented the idea that their experience was not supposed to be worth as much as "theoretical" training at a technical college.

The fact that the VDI heavily represented mechanical engineers (electrical, mining, and construction engineers having their own separate organizations) had meant since early on that it was associated intimately with manufacturing. The creation of rival organizations that were more "academically" exclusive (e.g. VDDI) or more inclusive and unionlike (e.g. BUTAB) left the VDI in an uncomfortable middle ground. Thus, it is no wonder the engineering community, including the VDI, was unable to reach unanimity about educational reform or self-disciplining bodies (chambers) in the 1920s any more than about titles. Caught between the desire to reform technical education in ways to make it less specialized and more flexible, on the one hand, and the financially strapped and often paralyzed German governments, on the other, the VDI and DATSCH, the cooperative committee of engineering societies for education, discussed proposals that proved to have little chance of realization. These ranged

29 Viefhaus, "Ingenierue," pp. 310–11.   30 Ibid., p. 312.

from steps toward integrating business and technical colleges to introducing teacher-education courses for the latter.

Although the enrollment boom in higher education was experienced somewhat less drastically in technical colleges than in universities, there was a significant "overproduction" of engineers for the conditions of the Depression. German industry complained that academic engineers were already overspecialized (not a new theme), so adding more specialized training or higher degree requirements did not appear a solution to managing the flood. Yet, attempts to introduce a "practical year," such as medical students had to complete, foundered on the disagreements of the differing kinds of engineers about what form it should take.[31]

The long-standing hope of the VDI to break more holes in the wall of the "jurists' monopoly," which had been raised anew during the 1918 revolution, proved disappointed by 1920, despite a few appointments by German cities and towns of engineers to high positions of responsibility. A decade later, a survey claimed that less than 6 percent of the 140,000 German engineers and architects were employees of the higher branches of the Reich government, that even city administration (where there was an obvious need for technical competence) had failed to open careers to engineers on a significant scale, and that only the state railways showed much improvement.[32]

3. THE CHEMICAL AND PHARMACOLOGICAL PROFESSIONS

The new profession most similar to engineering was chemistry, although there were far fewer chemists (about 11,000 in 1925), and they were more homogeneous in their training. But the problems of overproduction and unemployment plagued them just the same.

Thanks to the successful pressures of the VDC and the German chemistry professors, by the end of the 1920s a distinct, if not yet completely uniform, process for training chemists had emerged. A curriculum model had been worked out by the latter. Whether attending a university or a technical college, the chemist was expected to take certain courses, complete certain laboratory exercises, and take the *Verbandsexamen*, or the diploma examination (in technical colleges), both of which had come to resemble each other. Although the diploma could be used as a concluding degree, the *Verbandsexamen* was not, and those who passed either often went on to a doctorate. This process required a minimum of ten to twelve semesters of study (in fact, because of overcrowded university laboratories, usually much longer), placing it on a comparable level of difficulty and financial sacrifice with medicine.[33]

---

31 For a clear discussion of the very complex debates over educational reform in the 1920s, see Viefhaus, "Ingenieure," pp. 311–23.
32 Ibid., pp. 302–4.
33 Hochschulverwaltungen, *Untersuchungen*, 5 (1932), *Bedarf und Nachwuchs an Chemikern*, pp. 9–10.

The progressive tightening of requirements and the lengthening of study, along with the oversaturated market in industry, appear to have driven down the enrollments at higher educational institutions from a typical postwar boom high of 7,700 in 1923–4 to under 4,500 from 1926 through 1932. (By way of comparison, enrollments in chemistry in 1914 had been around 2,700).[34] Female students were much more visible in chemistry than engineering, where they were a tiny group. Women had comprised less than 1 percent of chemistry students in 1910; by 1930 their proportion had risen to over 12 percent. An index of the difficulties of chemistry as a learned profession was the fact that, as enrollments of new students sank, the numbers of those staying on for further postdoctoral work rose as high as 10 percent of all students.[35] Some estimated that there were only 250 new jobs a year for graduated chemists in German industry in the early 1930s, half as many places as needed.[36]

Thus, the German chemical profession had achieved, perhaps even over-achieved its objectives of professionalization via high educational and certification standards. International comparisons show German chemical training in a very flattering light.[37] Yet, as the VDC admitted even during World War I, when chemists were virtually war heroes for their successful efforts to synthesize substances Germany could no longer obtain in their natural form from abroad, public and government employment remained all but closed to them.[38] Chemists' incomes remained unsatisfactory, particularly considering the very long and arduous study they had to undergo.

Dissatisfaction with working conditions and incomes among chemists led to the creation in 1919 of an economic lobby to further their interests by "union" tactics. The *Bund der Angestellten Chemiker und Ingenieure* (League of Employed Chemists and Engineers, or BUDACI) went to work immediately on a national *Tarifvertrag* (framework contract) for academically trained employees of the chemical industry.[39] Endorsed by the VDC and accepted by the chemical industry, this "framework contract" completed the process begun before the war of defining the chemists' rights in terms of employment conditions, salary, share in inventions, *Karenz* and other matters for the first five years of employment. It was accepted by profession and industry and lasted even through the Hitler period.[40]

Having achieved the regulation of the profession via educational and certification channels and created a species of acceptable minimal standards at least for those chemists employed in industry, the VDC had reached some of its major goals by the early 1920s. It continued as a clearinghouse for information and offered such services to its members as job placement. By the end of the Weimar period, the VDC had grown from a membership somewhat over 5,000 during World War I to over 9,000, meaning that it encompassed 80 to

34 Ibid., p. 44.   35 Ibid.   36 Ibid., pp. 29, 57ff.
37 Ludwig Fritz Haber, *The Chemical Industry, 1900–1930. International Growth and Technological Change* (Oxford, 1971), pp. 38ff.
38 Ramstetter, "Chemiker," p. 312.   39 Ibid., pp. 321–2.   40 Ibid.

90 percent of all German academic chemists.[41] Nevertheless, the tendency of engineers and chemists to cooperate in striving for better working conditions in chemical plants was a sign of their growing interdependence in general, indicating that the needs of industry rather than the separate academic disciplinary boundaries of chemistry and engineering increasingly dictated the shape of the profession.

One profession dependent on chemical knowledge but which had still not become a full "academic" profession – pharmacy – might be mentioned briefly in this context. Even after examination changes in 1904, down through World War I it remained possible to become a pharmacist without achieving the *Abitur* and by a mixture of only four semesters of higher education and various apprenticelike training courses. The trend over the nineteenth century had clearly been toward less reliance on apprenticeship and more on "academic" training.[42] Changes in the examination system in 1921 prescribed the *Abitur* and four semesters of academic study; but in between came a two-year apprenticeship, a preliminary examination, and a one-year internship in a pharmacy. Only after formal study, a state examination, and two more "practical" years in a pharmacy or relevant university institute, could the pharmacist receive the license (called, as with medicine, *Approbation*).[43] The profession was further "academicized" in 1935 by increasing formal study requirements to six semesters and decreasing the final practical period by one year.

As with engineers and chemists, pharmacy became less a "free" profession as it became more an "academic" one: the ratio of employed to independent pharmacists became larger after the beginning of this century. In 1887 employees constituted only a quarter of all licensed pharmacists in Germany; by 1909 the proportion had reached 38 percent, where it hovered until the beginning of the Depression.[44] Nevertheless, the overall employment prospects appear to have been considerably better than in most other professions, with output coming close to matching openings even at the beginning of the Depression.[45]

At least as important for the shaping of the profession were questions of monopoly, local and national, which remained unsolved until the Nazi era and later. German law concerning pharmacies is too complex to warrant extensive discussion here, but suffice it to say that a mixed system of salable and unsalable ("concessioned") pharmacies came into being after 1894, with the partial result that although pharmacies were not treated like any other business, they were not necessarily protected from local competition. Nationally, the rise of industrial pharmaceuticals also appeared as a threat to an essentially preindustrial, indeed an ancient, craft. The medical insurance

41 Ibid.
42 Georg Edmund Dann, *Einführung in die Pharmaziegeschichte* (Stuttgart, 1975), pp. 51–3.
43 Hochschulverwaltungen, *Untersuchungen*, 4 (1932), *Bedarf und Nachwuchs an Apothekern*, p. 7.
44 Ibid., p. 8.   45 Ibid., p. 53.

funds contributed their part to the reduction of pharmacists' incomes and autonomy.[46]

Such competition, including practices introduced in the war such as hiring women "auxiliaries" who in fact continued to displace drafted males, hit the licensed pharmacists under age forty the hardest: whereas previously they could count on eventually moving up to run or own an apothecary shop, by the crisis of 1930 onward, if not earlier, they began to see their "employee" role as possibly permanent.

The strains and segmentations within the profession of pharmacy showed very clearly in its organizational structure. The old *Deutscher Apotheker-Verein* (German Apothecaries Association, or DApV, founded in 1872) in fact represented owners, not employees, of pharmacies, and it was more given to protecting property interests than forging some other basis for professional security.[47] That these property interests were still not adequately protected was the view of numerous small-town and rural pharmacists who founded what became a sort of Hartmann-League in 1907 (it nevertheless melded with the original DApV in 1923).[48] Among other professional associations, one, the *Verband Deutscher Apotheker* (Association of German Apothecaries) founded in 1910, became a union movement for employees and eventually joined the liberal labor union *Gewerkschaftsbund der Angestellten* in 1924.[49] It is an ironic comment on this organization that its leadership was constantly decimated by individual, if not collective, success: upon graduating from employee to owner status, such leaders of the DApV were required by their statutes to resign their office![50] The union membership, even in such a tame group as the Hirsch-Duncker unions, drove one significant group of members, which included the young pharmacist Gregor Strasser, to found yet another splinter group that failed within a year.[51]

Nevertheless, the major representatives of owners and employees were able to conclude a "framework contract" that became, after many challenges, generally a model for Germany after 1919, and in this sense the pharmacists' organizations did achieve a type of homongenization of working conditions (for those who were working). Apothecaries' chambers and honor courts were other signs of advancing professionalization through self-administration.[52]

It has been convenient to treat in this chapter the further development of the so-called free professions under Weimar conditions. All experienced continued growth in the number of practitioners, heightened competition and frustration over economic conditions, particularly among younger members of the profession. In all cases competitor organizations continued to foil the complete

46 Gerald Schröder, "Die 'Wiedergeburt' der Pharmazie 1933 bis 1934," in Hans Mehrtens and Steffen Richter, eds., *Naturwissenschaft, Technik und NS-Ideologie. Beiträge zur Wissenschaftsgeschichte des Dritten Reiches* (Frankfurt, 1980), pp. 166ff.
47 Adlung and Urdang, *Grundriss*, p. 241. 48 Ibid., pp. 224–5.
49 Schröder, "'Wiedergeburt, p. 168. 50 Adelung and Urdang, *Umriss*, p. 250.
51 Ibid., p. 252. 52 Ibid., pp. 251, 243.

unification of all practitioners under one roof. On the other hand, both the state and the private sector had come to regard the German professional organizations more as negotiating partners than threatening or (perhaps worse) ignorable lobbies. Educational and certification levels were in most cases considered adequate by the professions themselves, although these high standards failed to deter overcrowding. Nevertheless, no major organization representing the major "free" professions demanded artificial closure of access to its ranks.

As we shall see in Chapter 11, the bureaucratized professions showed similar evidence of increasing their organizational influence and achieving large parts of their program, but under the economic conditions of the Weimar era, clearly not their ideals of an appropriate standard of living for all practitioners. In the concluding chapter, we return to a comparative evaluation of the achievements and failures of both types of professions in the pre-Hitler period.

11

Professions based on law and pedagogy in the Weimar era

1. LAW-BASED PROFESSIONS

As we saw in Chapter 9, the market situation of attorneys by World War I was becoming sufficiently worrisome that some lawyers, although not the DAV, had begun to call for restrictions on admission to the profession. Having almost doubled (from 6,600 to 13,000) between 1899 and 1915, the number of attorneys in Germany remained relatively stable (under 13,000) until 1925, when it began to grow. By 1928 it had reached 15,500, and law enrollments were also rising, producing a pool of attorneys approaching 19,000 by 1935.[1] Despite some population growth, this meant an increase from 19 attorneys per 100,000 in 1919 to 24 per 100,000 in 1928.[2] At the same time, the field of activity for lawyers was being reduced by various measures, for example, by raising the income ceilings for those eligible to use the (lawyer-free) *Gewerbe- und Kaufmanngerichte*, special courts set up to settle disputes between employers and their employees. Similarly, new or reorganized courts such as the national Financial Court, Economic Court, and Administrative Court limited or excluded representation of parties by lawyers.[3] The tendency in Weimar was away from the older principle of *Anwaltszwang*. The bureaucrats claimed such streamlined justice was cheaper and faster for the people; attorneys claimed it weakened the rights of the parties.

One compulsory aspect of legal practice that remained from the old Reich was the fee schedules. These were made flexible during the great inflation of the early 1920s, but after stabilization fee schedules were reduced again by government decree, and severe limits were placed on large fees associated with large amounts in civil suits. The principle that fee schedules should be guidelines and not binding was pursued steadily, and unsuccessfully, by the DAV. Only in limited areas, such as persuading the state to remunerate attorneys for

1 Magnus, *Rechtswissenschaft*, app., "Bevölkerungszahlen und Anwaltszahlen"; Ostler, "Werden," p. 13.
2 Ostler, *Rechtsanwalt*, p. 207.   3 Ibid., pp. 163–4.

public-defender work, was the DAV successful in improving the economic well-being of attorneys.[4]

The result of all these market factors was the cry of "proletarianization" by the legal profession. Yet, during the few economically good years of the Weimar era, income surveys among lawyers do not make their lot appear any worse than that of many other professions. In 1928, one-third of German attorneys grossed no more than 10,000 marks per year.[5] At first glance, such figures seem high in comparison with the prewar situation. Then, a little over one-third of the attorneys earned less than 3,000 and 77 percent of them less than 6,000 marks.[6] But poststabilization Weimar marks still bought far less than prewar gold-standard marks had. To have stayed even with increases in the consumer price index, at least, would have meant that three-quarters of German attorneys, not one-third, should have grossed up to 10,000 marks in 1928.[7] After the full onset of the Depression in 1930, lawyers' incomes sank markedly: perhaps as much as 15 percent of the lawyers grossed less than 3,000 marks in 1931, a level considered "proletarian."[8]

Given the difficulties of the market for legal services, it is not surprising that the 1920s witnessed an intensification of certain kinds of specialization and diversification which in themselves raised questions about the nature of the bar. As early as 1920 the DAV convention discussed whether it was ethical for attorneys to claim "specialist" status.[9] As had been the case with physicians several decades before, conservatives felt claiming specialized knowledge to be a form of advertising, and unfair advertising at that. The notion of tax attorneys was beginning to have currency in big cities. The bar's honor court declared in 1923 that claiming such specialization constituted unfair competitive practices.[10]

There was similar debate about the *Syndikusanwalt*, a trained attorney who worked, full or part-time (as with a board of directors appointment), for industrial or commercial interests. Rather than viewing this as a welcome development and a new outlet for attorneys' talents, many viewed the commercial association as distasteful. One plan put forward by Rudolf Friedländer and others envisioned a division of the bar into a "courtroom" and a "business" division, the latter encompassing also the attorneys operating on the lowest (*Amt*) court level.[11] The Nazis were to play on this division among lawyers by prohibiting *Syndici* from appearing in court as a representative of organizations that employed them – certainly a blow to the development of the "corporate lawyer."[12]

4 Ibid., pp. 154–60.   5 Ibid., p. 208.   6 Ostler, "Werden," p. 36.

7 Estimate based on consumer–price indices in Deutsche Bundesbank, ed., *Deutsches Geld- und Bankwesen in Zahlen, 1876–1975* (Frankfurt, 1975), p. 7.

8 Ostler, *Rechtsanwalt*, p. 208.   9 Ibid., p. 162.   10 Ibid.

11 Sigbert Feuchtwanger, "Kultur und Wirtschaft," *Juristische Wochenschrift* 57 (1928): 2,768.

12 Ostler, *Rechtsanwalt*, p. 163; Rüschemeyer, *Lawyers*, pp. 179–80.

Such signs of differentiation and fluidity in the roles of legally trained professionals reflect the growing mismatch between German juridical training and the careers of those who went through it. It was tailored for a form of government that had ceased to exist and for an economic and social structure that was rapidly disappearing. Like most bureaucracies, the civil service had little reason to complain about the type of education which had produced its own positions. Many in business and the economics-related sectors of academia decried the outworn and narrow juridical training being perpetuated chiefly for the benefit of the bureaucracy. And the bar, as we have seen, was divided over the role of the legally trained in administration and business.

Increases in the amount or changes in the content of legal study did not appear as a panacea in the eyes of most attorneys. Nor did the option of a "practical year," a sort of internship between final examination and admission to the bar, win support from the DAV.[13] There were isolated calls for making law study more stringent and examinations harder, but the profession as a whole appears to have been satisfied with the current level of professional training.[14] The Nazis' national *Rechtsanwaltsordnung* of 1936 did introduce a four-year preadmission period, but this was almost purely a measure to discourage potential members of the bar, not to raise qualifications.[15]

The most serious discussions, and changes ultimately made, concerning juridical training and professional qualifications involved the technical and business application of law. Immediately after the war, the professional press was full of suggestions for improving law training by creating branches after a certain number of semesters of "foundations." The original impetus had been, among other concerns, the national homogenization of the training of judges, but since that training was also the same for lawyers and the presupposition for civil servants' later on-the-job training, the debate really was about all law education. Some reformers wanted to create a separate path for economists or at least divide law study up into a branch for those entering the "justice" system (future judges and attorneys) and those on their way to public or private administrative careers.[16] The DAV and the conference of German legal faculties were opposed to breaking up a unified foundation in legal education, although opinions differed about how long it should last (six semesters only, or eight?). And inevitably many warned that more prescriptions of required courses (*Studienordnungen*), set patterns to enter professions, and even more exigent ex-

---

13 Ostler, *Rechtsanwalt*, p. 214.
14 For a good example of calls for increasing quality controls on law students, see Rudolf Friedländer, *Der Arbeitspreis bei den freien Berufen unter besonderer Berücksichtigung der deutschen Rechtsanwaltschaft* (Munich, 1933), pp. 148ff.
15 Ostler, *Rechtsanwalt*, pp. 258ff.
16 See, for example, the comments of the Bonn law professor Ernst Zitelmann, "Die Vorbildung der Volkswirte und Juristen," *Schmollers Jahrbuch* 45 (1921): 305–11.

aminations would simply destroy academic freedom and produce a "practical experts' school."[17]

A special reason for reform came from the flood of students, particularly veterans, that suddenly burst into the faculties of law or "legal and state sciences," as some were called. These students were hoping to specialize in business-oriented law and economics. (Economics and sociology, which had only just become recognized as separate disciplines, were still usually housed in the law faculties.) This problem will be discussed separately below.

The other main consumer of law-trained professionals was the German civil service. Traditionally, those who did not enter the bar continued, after the first state examination common to all law students, as unpaid assessors, took another examination, and could then become referendars while they waited for a regularly salaried position. Some went into the "higher administration," although most entered the judicial service as judges or state attorneys. In Prussia at least, before World War I, these trainee civil servants were ruthlessly exploited, because they were often expected to function for years (sometimes a decade) in responsible capacities in lower courts or the state attorney's office with no regular salary. In Prussia the only way to restrict access to these antechambers of the civil service, before World War I, had been to require a *Vermögensnachweis*, or proof of the candidates' financial capacity, to get through all those poorly remunerated years of training and waiting. That requirement fell with the Hohenzollerns, which meant that there were even more candidates competing for fewer positions, an especially acute problem in the judicial bureaucracy.[18]

Many in the legal community, including the DAV, suggested some sort of controls on the creation of referendars (rather than a *numerus clausus* on all legal study).[19] The DAV presumed that the magnet drawing so many students into law was the slim chance of entering the ultimate security of a civil service position, no matter how many years of hungry waiting might be involved. The disappointed and rejected multitudes who did not make it could then, the DAV feared, still enter the bar.[20] Many non-Prussian ministries, not to mention Prussian ministries other than Justice, could often manipulate the access. But the Prussian government rejected in 1923 a bill supported by the organizations of judges and of assessors to give selectivity rights based on "professional qualifications" to the Justice Ministry: the fear of "political" criteria in appointments outweighed the fear of overcrowding among the *Anwärter* ("waiters").[21]

17 Ernst Heymann, "Die juristische Studienreform," *Schmollers Jahrbuch* 46 (1922): 161.
18 Thomas Kolbeck, *Juristenschwemmen. Untersuchungen über den juristischen Arbeitsmarkt im 19. und 20. Jahrhundert. [Rechtshistorische Reihe,* 3] (Frankfurt, 1978), pp. 104–106.
19 Ostler, *Rechtsanwalt,* p. 210.
20 See, for example, Feuchtwanger, *Berufe,* p. 149: "The free bar is becoming forced and degraded compared to the legally equal bench and is being endangered in its moral and intellectual status by the very freedom that is supposed to protect it. Admission limitations on the administration and the notary profession make this situation even worse."
21 Kolbeck, *Juristenschwemmen,* p. 107.

The number of regular positions for these "waiters" in Prussia underwent considerable fluctuation after World War I. Although there had been over 7,000 such positions for judges and state attorneys in 1915 (or over 18 per 100,000 population), reductions at the end of the war (primarily through the territorial diminution of Prussia at Versailles) led to around 6,700 in 1920 (still over 18:100,000). Further reductions had pared the number to just over 6,000 in 1925 (under 16:100,000). Numbers were on the rise again in 1930, however, when the government was able to restrict admissions to the "waiting" positions by resort to Brüning's new decree powers.[22]

The practice of keeping twice as many "waiters" in the unpaid antechambers to the profession of judge in Prussia is worthy of some further comment. The traditional argument of the government was that it was providing free training to candidates for regular salaried judgeships in return for their unseasoned labor. The requirement of independent financial means (still de facto if no longer de jure after 1918) limited the juridical profession to well-to-do families who could support sons through the long preparation and wait, well into their thirties and perhaps indefinitely, because a failed judge candidate found few other opportunities beckoning in midlife. Indeed, although most professional organizations in Weimar declared that professional qualifications alone should be the criteria for selecting judges from the pool of waiters, government inability (before 1930) to decide whom to entrust with that authority led to the defeat of purely meritocratic criteria. In fact a good deal of the day-to-day work of the courts was carried out by these "trainees," and it would have collapsed without them. They guaranteed Prussia a cheap, virtually free form of highly skilled labor (although some meager "expenses" were paid to some of them). Whatever the motives for retaining the old Prussian regime so long after 1918, and specifically for the justice system, it might be noted that this form of exploitation, which hindered professionalization of the bench in many senses (e.g. by resisting market-closure pressures), also served as a model for other branches of government and the private economic sector in dealing with would-be professionals. In terms of professionalization theory, this behavior might appear as the contrary of professionalization, with its haunting overtones of (or overture to?) Marx's idea of the "worker reserve army" needed by modern capitalism and institutionally realized in the chronic unemployment of the Weimar era. But the Prussian administration had followed this tactic long before industrial capitalism, or for that matter modern professions, had become major features of German life.

But there is another way to look at this phenomenon. If one grants that, for the juridical and indeed most of the administrative service, the entry level was not the state examination but rather the appointment to a secure salaried position as *Beamter*, with a respectable, life-long income and other benefits (in the

22 Ibid, pp. 124, 108.

Weimar era), then one might call the profession of judge or administrator the highest form of organized expert occupation in Germany. Certainly it was not the wretched assessors and referendars with whom German schoolteachers, lawyers, and even engineers and physicians, compared themselves, but the judges and other higher personnel of the state administration.

The perceived lack of success of judges in obtaining salary adjustments comparable to those of other civil servants was one of the factors triggering the foundation of the German Judges' League (DRB) in 1908 and certainly their Prussian affiliate in 1909, after many years of smoldering quiescence in the face of government disapproval of such professional organizations of state employees. But by this time judges, like many other professionals in state service, had defenders in parliament, and government ministers had to back off from threats of retaliation against judges who joined the DRB or its branches.[23]

Just as the chief impulse to the foundation of judges' professional groups had been financial, so did the worsening economic situation after 1918 bring a massive influx into them – virtually all judges and state attorneys joined their state association, with the DRB as a national forum. The chief object was reversing the financial losses to the profession from the 1920 national salary law and similar measures.[24] At first the notion of creating a comprehensive union that would include lower court employees was discussed, but the model of an academic professional body won out. Even the judges of the supreme court (*Reichsgericht*) joined the DRB out of pique with the government's salary reductions.

The DRB, or at least many German judges, were also repeatedly accused of conservatism and lukewarm feelings toward the new German democracy, at best. As one commentator put it, "The judges were accused of having exchanged the deficit in loyalty to the throne they had collected over the course of the nineteenth century for an even stronger conservative mentality."[25] Judges expressly loyal to the republic, including the Weimar Justice Minister Gustav Radbruch (SPD), founded the *Republikanischer Richterbund* (Republican Judges League, or RRB) in 1922. Composed chiefly of members close to the SPD, it was able to carry on a running criticism of "class justice" and the DRB, but not to attract the majority of German judges to its ranks, a symptom of the structural weaknesses of Weimar inherited with the virtually unpurged imperial bureaucracy. Yet another organization involving judges was the *Deutscher Juristenbund*, founded in 1919 to resist revolutionary changes in the legal system and including attorneys, administrative civil servants, and law professors as well as judges and state attorneys. Something like a permanently organized counterpart to the old *Juristentag*, it coordinated efforts by the various divisions of the legal community to maintain professional standards, as when it protested (along with the DAV) a Prussian government proposal to allow citizens without nor-

23 Carl von Frisching, *Die deutschen Richtervereinigungen* (Dissertation, Rechts- und Staatswissenschaftliche Fakultät, University of Freiburg/Br., 1936), pp. 6–7.
24 Ibid., pp. 10–11.   25 Hattenhauer, *Beamtentums*, p. 335.

mal legal training to sit for the state examination and, if passing it, become a judge – one more form of "American-style" democratization successfully resisted by the academically trained German professional organizations.[26] Like the old *Juristentag*, however, the *Juristenbund* was not designed to fight for the material interests of its membership.

Despite the DRB's refusal to join any labor unions in the immediate aftermath of the 1918 revolution, it had joined the *Deutscher Beamtenbund* (German Civil Servants League, or DBB), about which more later. As the DBB drifted closer to trade unionism, however, the DRB and the various regional judges' associations withdrew from it around 1922 and joined the *Reichsbund der Höheren Beamten* (National League of Higher Officials, or RHB). The appeals of the DRB and the regional associations for salary increases (or after 1930 against salary decreases), complaints that municipal civil servants were better paid, and similar economic grievances were overall similar to those of the RHB and will be treated below as a part of the discussion of civil service incomes.

German judges appeared to be generally satisfied with the existing educational and certification requirements for entering their profession, with some minor exceptions. The unification of those standards for all Germany was one objective, and the DRB approved of a 1930 agreement between the state and Reich governments on preparation for the bench. Frequent complaints echoed from the annual meetings of the judges about overemphasis on the theoretical and neglect of the practical training of future judges.[27]

Neither the DRB nor the DAV were particularly helpful to German women, who were pressing to become attorneys and judges after 1918. Indeed, although sex discrimination in the professions was implicitly wiped out in the Weimar constitution, it took until 1922 for enabling legislation to be passed allowing females to enter the bar and the bench. Between 1912 and 1919, one state after another had begun allowing them to take the legal state examination, but the next step was to enable them then to become assessors, referendars, attorneys, and judges. The DRB and (somewhat less vehemently) the DAV indeed opposed the Reichstag law opening all offices and legal professions to women.[28] Despite the continuing efforts of the tiny *Deutscher Juristinnenverein* (German Female Jurists Association) founded during World War I to pry open opportunities for women in the legal professions, very few women studied law. Even fewer went into the relatively open bar (eight of 3,000 lawyers in Berlin and four of 700 in Munich were estimates for the late 1920s), and perhaps only four women had become (very junior) acting judges in all of Germany in 1930.[29] At the time the Nazis took power and before sweeping women out of what offices they had been able to obtain, only 1.3 percent of German attorneys and

26 Frisching, *Richtervereinigungen*, p. 25.   27 Ibid., p. 35.
28 Deutscher Juristinnenbund, ed., *Juristinnen in Deutschland. Eine Dokumentation 1900–1984* (Munich, 1984), pp. 6 ff.
29 Ibid., p. 14.

0.3 percent of the judges in Germany were women (contrasted to nearly 9 percent of the physicians and over 30 percent of teachers). Many of the few judicial jobs they had were in traditionally "female" branches such as welfare and child protection.[30]

A final irony concerning women in elevated state positions was that the requirement of celibacy (which had been standard in the teaching profession in the empire), abolished by the Weimar constitution, was reintroduced in 1923 by the emergency "personnel reduction" ordinance: women bureaucrats, teachers, and other state employees could now be dismissed when they married, provided their means of subsistence as housewives was assured.[31] This means test was particularly easy if the husband was a state employee, too, because many women in fact met their spouses on the job. Thus, although women had gained a narrow ledge of equal formal access to civil service positions by 1922, they had lost their right to hold them and still become "double earners" through marriage — a social category (somewhat akin to the 1980s' "yuppies" in the U.S.A.) that was widely resented by the unemployed, and not merely by the Nazis.

However sadly one may look back on the struggles of professional women in the Weimar Republic, one cannot say that, aside from them, professional organizations of state employees were notably lacking in success in their lobbying efforts. This was true even though they were not able or willing to band together in a common front. The DBB, as mentioned above, began as a form of "suprapolitical" bureaucrats' representative organization with considerable membership from the middle and lower ranks of the civil service (including the postal and rail services), but it initially also contained the RHB and other groups representing academic professionals. The conservative RHB abandoned the DBB as too radical in the aftermath of the Kapp Putsch, when large parts of the upper civil service showed little enthusiasm for the general strike that the DBB joined to bring down the putschists. Yet, the DBB also declared its distaste for strike tactics in general during the 1922 railway strike, a decision that cost it a considerable number of members on the political left. These seceded to form the *Allgemeiner Deutscher Beamtenbund* (General German Civil Servants League, or ADB), which affiliated with the SPD's union movement. The DBB likewise ultimately drifted into an affiliation with the Catholic and liberal (Hirsch-Duncker) labor unions. The DBB, which had once counted over a million members (1920), sank in the mid-1920s and recovered by 1928. By comparison, the ADB sank from 354,000 members in 1924 to 171,000 in 1932. The RHB, which necessarily was smaller because it represented only higher civil servants, grew to about 100,000 members in 1924 and remained steadily at that level.[32]

To be sure, the entire gamut of civil servants contained very different views

30 Wunder, *Bürokratie*, p. 115.   31 Ibid.   32 Ibid., p. 125.

on what to consider a successful incomes policy. At the outset of the republic, when the interests of the left were more likely to be served, one of the chief achievements was the reduction of the number of salary classes in the civil service from 180 to 20. This also meant that the ratio between salaries of the lowest and highest ranks of the civil service changed from 1:8.6 to 1:4. Naturally, this relative halving of upper civil servants' salaries compared to the lowest clerks, whatever the merits of the latters' claims, did not look like a full victory to the academic professionals in state service, even if the 1920 and 1927 salary reforms raised all civil servants' salaries, and even though most observers considered the academically trained bureaucrats to be far better off than their colleagues in the free-market sector. The agitation of their representative organizations achieved by 1927 a change of the ratio back to 1:6.[33]

However much the academically trained civil servants in their various professional organizations might complain of their lot, it could have been much worse. Pressure from the bureaucratic lobby forced the inclusion in the Weimar constitution of a guarantee of the *wohlerworbene Rechte* ("vested rights") of the civil service, thus foiling the hopes of progressives and socialists to expand democratic control over the bureaucracy and end the "jurists' monopoly."[34] The practical tenure and independence of the judiciary was also anchored in the constitution. The even more radical idea of the independent SPD, to introduce elected civil servants, had even less of a chance. The senior civil service became more and more influential in the various organizations of bureaucrats by the late 1920s, too.[35] All this taken together would justify the judgment that the civil service professional organizations had reason to congratulate themselves a decade after the German revolution of 1918.

The deflationary policies of Brüning and his emergency decrees of 1930–1 diminished the influence of the judges, administrative civil servants, and other academically/legally trained professionals, ironically even though Brüning's cabinets were made up of bureaucratic experts. Salary cuts of 19 to 23 percent returned many parts of the civil service, which had finally reattained the levels of 1913 by 1927, back within the range of the previous low point of 1923. Appeals by professional groups to the supreme court to establish salaries as a "vested right" that could not be manipulated by decree were rejected.[36] Indeed, Brüning's determination in dealing with the civil-service lobby probably reflected a sense (remembering the 1927 pay award) that the bureaucrats had obtained too much influence in such matters. Reduction in forces through attrition and hiring freezes, as in the wake of the crisis of 1923–4 recurred under Brüning, causing additional hardship to young candidates for the civil service. The economic cuts, coming on the heels of the agitation over the Young

---

33 All figures are for final or maximum salary and benefits; from Hans Völter, "Die deutsche Beamtenbesoldung," in Wilhelm Gerloff, ed., *Die Beamtenbesoldung im modernen Staat [Schriften des Vereins für Sozialpolitik*, 184/1] (Munich, 1932), pp. 1–105.
34 Hattenhauer, *Beamtentums*, pp. 307–9.   35 Wunder, *Bürokratie*, p. 126.   36 Ibid.

Plan in 1929, began to drive some civil servants openly into the arms of the
political right: some made the argument that the bureaucracy, which had served
the new state in a nonpartisan way, was now being asked to shoulder a disproportionate share of the state's burdens, most bitterly that of paying for the "war
guilt lie."[37]

The contests between governments and civil servants' organizations over the
privileges, career ladders, qualifications, and rewards of employment of the bureaucracy in the 1920s is a fascinating subject which still lacks a definitive
treatment. That the contest was now played out openly before the public was a
sign of both political democratization and the particular dynamics of professionalization in Germany. The oldest modern profession, as it were, had now joined
the others in organizing to promote its own interests, but it had done so (like
the others) not as a closed caste, but rather along socioeconomic, functional and
even to some degree ideological lines. In fact, the civil service as a whole, all
million and a half members, was in no imaginable way a professional group
with common interests. Suffice it to say here, those groups with legal training
that formed the upper echelons of the civil service (administrative and judicial)
appear to have protected their own interests better than most others we have
examined in the Weimar era. (One should explicitly note here that we have yet
to examine whether this holds true for teachers, who were also civil servants of
a special type.)

Before moving on to teachers, however, it is necessary to dwell briefly on
another profession emerging in the first decades of the 1920s that also had some
roots and connections in higher legal training. The profession of *Volkswirt*, as
noted above, might under some circumstances require advanced education and
certification and thus come under the heading of a learned occupation. Many
aspects of economics and sociology were taught in law faculties, and the new
degrees of diploma or even doctorate in a combination of law and economics
became quite fashionable. At the same time, business schools were developing
from the less theoretical secondary type into tertiary institutions (such as the
Handelshochschulen of the Weimar era) or even becoming the nuclei of new universities (such as Frankfurt and Cologne, established at the end of the war).
Thus, the academically trained business expert was not strictly speaking another
legal professional, but part of the origins of this new type lay in legal traditions, so it may be reasonable to treat it here.

The clear model for *Handelshochschulen* to emulate was that of the *Technische
Hochschulen*, or technical colleges: obtaining the right to grant diplomas and

---

37 Hans Mommsen, *Beamtentum im Dritten Reich* (Stuttgart, 1966), p. 26. See also Kunz's more
recent treatment of the effect of the 1923–4 governmental cutbacks on public employees in
Civil Servants and the Politics of Inflation in Germany, as well as Jane Caplan, *Government without Administration. State and Civil Service in Weimar and Nazi Germany* (Oxford, 1988), especially chap. 2 and 3. Unfortunately, none of these works deals extensively with organizations of
professionals.

doctorates insured a kind of cachet that would upgrade the prestige of the entire institution. This became a more urgent necessity after the raising of Frankfurt and Cologne to Prussian universities (the original *Handelshochschulen* became their faculties of economic and social sciences), since business candidates could obtain doctorates there. Hence, several higher business schools (e.g. Berlin, Mannheim, Leipzig, Königsberg, and Nuremberg) were granted the right to award doctoral degrees between 1926 and 1929.[38]

German business education enjoys a very high international reputation in the literature on the subject.[39] No doubt much of its reputation can be attributed to its struggle to obtain academic respectability, the classic route, as we have seen, for "new" professions to establish themselves in Germany. This struggle was certainly not an easy one in the 1920s, when charges of shoddiness and of the innate incompatibility between the conflicting claims of materialistic affairs and the life of the mind abounded.

The postwar situation for economics and business schools of all types (for both university faculties offering economics courses as well as the *Handelshochschulen*) was one of greatly expanded enrollments. Since the field of economics (including business economics or *Betriebswirtschaftslehre*) had, like other academic disciplines, only a doctorate as a final degree, the large increase in students after the war also produced a great increase in doctorates. The resultant discussion about what sort of curriculum, minimum standards, and degrees were needed began with the 1920 meeting of the *Verein für Sozialpolitik* and produced numerous discussions in the academic press.[40] The central question was not the training of businessmen for the private sector, although that question necessarily sometimes impinged; it revolved rather around the question of proper training for the future civil servant who would be an expert in economic matters, for the *beamteter Volkswirt*.

Endless controversy ensued, with the RVDV warning against the decay of economics training into mere "vocationalism." A new degree was introduced in 1922–3, that of *Diplomvolkswirt*, or diploma economist. This was supposed to be a sensible intermediate degree, achievable after six semesters of university-level study and a state examination and comparable to that for engineers and businessmen (*Diplomkaufmann*). It was supposed also to reduce the enrollment pressures in economics doctoral programs. At the same time, pressures from the business schools continued, as noted above, until their right to grant doctorates was also recognized after 1926.

38 For a clear recent discussion of the history of business schools, see David F. Lindenfeld, "The Professionalization of Applied Economics: German Counterparts to Business Administration," in Cocks and Jarausch, *Professions*.
39 See, for example, Robert R. Locke, *The End of Practical Man. Entrepreneurship and Higher Education in Germany, France and Great Britain, 1880–1940* (Greenwich, Conn., 1984), esp. chap. 5.
40 For a useful summary of these discussions as they pertain to education for economics and civil service, see Pintschovius, *Volkswirte*, esp. pp. 56–111.

Regulation of the allowed channels for the new "profession" of economist was made difficult because of conflicts over what kind of training was best for what kind of "economist." As one commentator summarized the experience of the recent decade:

The study of economics in the postwar period degenerated into a scramble of the masses for the doctorate, especially the *Dr. rer. pol.*, in which jurisprudence was an obligatory examination field. Other doctorates, too, such as that of philosophy, were being taken by economists. On the other hand a purely academic degree was being devalued, just as on the other, a merely theoretical training in no way sufficed for a practical profession.[41]

The temporary outcome of these innovations was "a certain equilibrium between the universities and the business schools" in producing economists.[42] Unfortunately, the time period in which economics began to emerge with at least the outline of an educational and certification path, with established minimum requirements (six semesters of study), a diploma, and a doctorate available both in universities and business colleges, was very brief and remains somewhat poorly documented. Before the onset of the Great Depression and the Hitler regime, however, it is safe to say that many conflicts about the proper professional preparation of economically literate *Beamte* for public service or the private economy remained to be settled.

Ironically, the relative success of the RVDV's program for higher educational certification of the new profession led to its own organizational decline. Somewhat comparably to the VDI, its membership was unable to agree on whether it should continue being an organization open to all sorts of practitioners or become an exclusively "academic" one. By 1928 several competing "academic" associations had been set up, and the RVDV's membership began to decline accordingly. After several years of negotiations, these various groups (including one of female economists) joined in the *Akademischer Volkswirtebund* (Academic Economists League, or AVB) in 1932, which survived as a part of the National Socialist Jurists League (BNSDJ) after 1933, whereas the original RVDV, with declining membership, dissolved itself.[43]

To be sure, economics (under whatever name) has experienced great difficulty in establishing itself as a clearly profiled profession, or even a discipline, since at least the eighteenth century. In its German form of the 1920s, somewhere in a limbo between civil service and private enterprise, even its academic paths did not impress all observers. As one caustic critic of the unemployment crisis of academic professionals wrote in 1930, only a "parvenu-like delight in decorum" could explain why a bank teller should want to hold the title of *Dr. rer. pol.*[44]

41 W. F. Bruck, "Zur Reform des Bildungswesens der Juristen und Volkswirte," *Schmollers Jahrbuch* 52 (1928): 66.
42 Lindenfeld, "Professionalization of Applied Economics," 226.
43 Schmitt, *Entstehung*, pp. 226 ff.
44 Ferdinand Fried, "Die Spaltpilze," *Die Tat*, 21 (1929–30): 524.

To be sure, such harsh comments represented the view of radical rightist intellectuals, but they were not alone in their concern, only in their hope that disaffected professionals would help wreck the Weimar "system."

2. THE TEACHING PROFESSION

We may recall that the first great national mobilization of schoolteachers in modern German history coincided with the revolution of 1848. Some of the demands articulated then had still not been fully realized when the next revolution, that of 1918, came along. As we have also seen, however, many of the schoolteachers' demands had in fact been met in the last decades of the empire, with *Gymnasium* teachers having the most reason to feel satisfied and elementary teachers the least. The gap between these two groups, the attempts of the latter to close it and the resistance of the former to homogenization of the teaching profession constituted a major theme of the postwar period and reflected radically different visions for German society.

In republican Germany, it has often been said, it was difficult to find many republican university or higher schoolteachers. Even though the monopolies of *Gymnasium* and university over access to the academic professions had broken down, and the higher education institutions of Germany were swamped with students, German philologists still largely disdained their competitors in the practical schools, looked down on elementary schoolteachers, and clung to their associations with the "noble" tradition of German neohumanism as transmitted by university philology in the philosophical faculties.

Against this fundamentally elitist residue of pre-1918 thinking, elementary schoolteachers pressed for lessening the distinctions between primary and secondary education by various means. One proposal, the unitary school, had been discussed in 1848 (and would be again after World War II): all children would essentially attend one school type, thus eliminating the invidious distinctions between different types and "tracks" of schools. More promising and seemingly easier was the professionalizing reform of requiring tertiary education for all schoolteachers, including elementary ones. The traditional teachers' seminars, with their inferior status, lack of academic freedom, and consequently inferior-seeming professional certification came under severe attack from the DLV in the wake of the revolution.

At first it seemed they had achieved what they wanted. The Weimar constitution conceded in principle that academic training was necessary for elementary teachers, and adding new institutes or faculties to existing universities appeared the obvious solution.[45] The *Reichsschulkonferenz* of 1920 recommended against "pedagogical faculties" but for the addition of teachers' institutes to existing tertiary institutions, including technical colleges. This recommenda-

---

45 Helmut Kittel, *Die Entwicklung der Pädagogischen Hochschulen, 1926–1932* (Berlin, 1957), p. 42.

tion was taken as a great victory by the DLV.[46] The months dragged by, however, money was in short supply, and the Reichstag never passed the national enabling legislation implied in the constitution, preferring in the end to leave the problem of teacher training to the various states.[47]

One of the most prestigious educational reformers of the Weimar era, Eduard Spranger, also wrote a book against the idea of university-affiliated training on the theory that elementary education requires a special type of teacher for whom theoretical, academic education might be counterproductive. Spranger instead recommended separate-but-equal teachers' colleges (*Bildnerhochschulen*).[48] The outlines of this idea were gladly taken up by the Prussian education ministry; Carl H. Becker began calling for *Pädagogische Akademien* (pedagogical academies) which would take *Abiturienten* from the higher schools but give them only two years of further (and largely practical) training for the *Volksschule*. Becker's central argument was that the philosophical faculties at universities had not produced very outstanding teachers for higher schools, so why should anybody expect them to do better with elementary teachers?[49]

The Prussian Teachers' Association (a part of the DLV, but given the role of responding to Becker) agreed with the *Abitur* requirement and that philosophical faculties were not turning out superteachers. But in 1924 its board of directors unanimously demanded nonconfessional teacher-training institutes at universities, not separate "academies," a six-semester study requirement followed by an examination, a practical year, and a final licensing – in other words, a model comparable to that of other academic professions.[50] It seems fairly clear that the professional organizations of elementary teachers had no objection in principle to separate teachers' colleges, as long as they were equal to existing universities and technical colleges – a development which they, probably correctly, feared would never arrive. As they put their idea of equality, teachers' colleges would have to be set up in such a way as to make it normal for university professors to accept chairs at teachers' colleges and vice versa – an image very far removed from the realities of the Prussian "academies" when they were in fact set up.

The German elementary teachers continued to press for the evolution of these Prussian academies into "pedagogical colleges" by relocation in university towns, increase in the number of years of education, deemphasis of religious-confessional identity, the introduction of doctoral degrees, and dozens of other major and minor signs that would have made them more like universities and technical colleges. The university faculties, when polled about their views in 1919, had been split about whether to incorporate elementary teacher training

46 Bölling, *Volksschullehrer und Politik*, p. 170.   47 Ibid., pp. 61 ff.
48 Eduard Spranger, *Gedanken über Lehrerbildung* (Leipzig, 1920), pp. 40–4.
49 Carl H. Becker, *Die Pädadgogische Akademie im Aufbau unseres nationalen Bildungswesens* (Leipzig, 1926), p. 51.
50 Kittel, *Entwicklung*, p. 76.

themselves or consign it to separate teachers' colleges, but there had been little suggestion that, if separate, they should not have a constitution similar to the universities' own.[51] The financial crisis from 1930 onward in any case frustrated any real possibility of developing the Prussian teachers' colleges to the satisfaction of the teachers' association.

Instead, of the fifteen "pedagogical academies" created between 1926 and 1930 in Prussia, eight were closed by decree in 1931 as a savings measure (and because there was already massive unemployment among recent graduates). This was followed by a freeze on accepting new students in 1932, which brought on mass protests by the Prussian Teachers' Association.[52] Much as it had criticized the academies as being too little, closing their doors was hardly a victory.

Other states chose solutions to the elementary school teachers' demands for tertiary education that were more satisfying to the DLV. Saxony and Thuringia, both of which had left-wing governments in the early 1920s, fulfilled most of the DLV's ideas in 1922–3 after giving up hopes that a national law would be passed. New pedagogical institutes were set up at the state universities in Jena and Leipzig as well as the Saxon technical college in Dresden, with a six-semester minimum educational program. Other states, such as Hesse and Hamburg, followed suit.[53] To be sure, some states, like Bavaria, merely modified the old teacher seminar system; some, like Baden, made compromises – for example, only two years of study, loopholes to avoid the required *Abitur* as precondition, training colleges separate from the university, most colleges confessional and one not – that were rejected by the DLV as well as the Catholic Teachers' Association.[54]

Thus, the DLV's professionalizing demands, involving higher education for schoolteachers, encountered traditional resistance from conservative religious groups (Catholic as well as Protestant) concerning the "confessional" nature of training, the length of it, and qualifications for it that indicated more modest, traditional, and even authoritarian expectations of the schoolteachers' role. From those expectations, the teacher as supplementer of conservative family values, the DLV wished to break out into the promised land of autonomous professionalization, to the teacher as enlightener of the people. Even if the Weimar governments had had infinite funds at their disposal, the DLV's full program would therefore have been controversial in many German communities.

In fact, of course, fiscal limitations by governments did have much to do with the DLV falling short of convincing them that *Volksschullehrer* should be

51 Ibid., pp. 306–7.
52 Harald Scholtz and Elmar Stranz, "Nationalsozialistische Einflussnahmen auf die Lehrerbildung," in Manfred Heinemann, ed., *Erziehung und Schulung im Dritten Reich* [*Veröffentlichungen der Historischen Kommission der Deutschen Gesellschaft für Erziehungswissenschaft*, 4,1 and 4,2] (Stuttgart, 1980), vol. 2, p. 111.
53 Bölling, *Volksschullehrer und Politik*, pp. 179–80.   54 Ibid., p. 183

finally raised to full equality with other academic professions. Even Saxony, Thuringia, and Hamburg, which paid their academically trained teachers more than those trained under the old system, did not pay them as much as *Gymnasium* teachers; in other states that had upgraded the teacher training less significantly, there was practically no difference between salaries paid to the old seminary and the new "academy" graduates.[55]

The elementary schoolteachers had raised their sights on salaries with the 1918 revolution. In keeping with the 1920 Reich framework salary law for the civil service, they asked for elementary school salaries to be placed in the ninth of thirteen newly created categories, just behind that of the tenth, where the "upper" civil service began. This would have placed them only one rung below *Gymnasium* teachers and at about 90 percent of the latters' basic salary of 8,400 to 12,600 marks.[56] Prussia instead enacted a complicated salary law for teachers that provided for career raises from the seventh to eighth group and the possibility of promotion into the ninth as school principals (rectors). This meant they began with 69 percent of a *Gymnasium* teacher's basic salary but could move up to 90 percent of it.[57] All these changes, in Prussia and elsewhere, became relatively meaningless during the great inflation through 1923, however, from which their income suffered greatly (real income down to half that of 1913). In the mid-1920s, thanks to further changes, *Volksschullehrer* only made on average 60 percent of what a *Gymnasium* teacher did. More changes in 1927–8 improved the situation a bit but made it vary from state to state. In Prussia, base salaries were pegged between 2,800 and 5,000 marks (compared with 4,400 to 8,400 for the higher schoolteachers). Principals and other administrators, however, were rewarded with steep salary supplements, which tended to cause resentment among the ordinary *Volksschullehrer*.[58]

By the end of 1931, as a result of repeated emergency decrees, schoolteachers in Prussia had found their salaries cut from a minimum of 19.5 percent up to nearly 29 percent. Both higher and lower schoolteachers were asked to make the smallest sacrifice, but the largest was reserved for elementary teachers in their first two years of employment.[59] Massive dismissals and forced retirements in 1932 also affected the youngest elementary teachers most severely. Not surprisingly, many of these teachers quit the DLV.[60]

The creation of a unified teaching profession, or at least a common educational basis for elementary teachers, eluded the DLV, the largest German teachers' organization, with the failure of the Reichstag to pass a national teacher education law in 1923. Although teachers all over Germany were required to show higher educational achievements by the end of the 1920s than under the empire, the dissimilarities in the various states' teacher-training laws were even greater than had been the case before 1918. To be sure, then the DLV had acted

55 Ibid., p. 187.   56 Ibid., p. 29.   57 Ibid.   58 Ibid., pp. 30–1.
59 Ibid., p. 200.   60 Ibid., p. 202.

as a kind of alternative socializing agency to the increasingly despised state teacher seminars, particularly in its further education courses.[61]

Failing to obtain clear equality with the other learned professions, did the elementary schoolteachers make up in organization what they still lacked in credentials? As with other professions we have examined, the *Volksschullehrer* were also pushed and pulled by old and new options for social action and organization. The rival associations for Protestant, Catholic, and female teachers continued to exist, as did separate organizations for *Gymnasium* and *Realschule* schoolmasters. With the advent of the republic, the worst fear of nineteenth-century German education ministers became a clear possibility – the teachers' union.

The leadership of the DLV insisted even more strongly than before on the "professional" nature of the organization and tended to look warily at labor unions; but the DLV was not above streamlining its internal machinery to achieve more of the discipline and power it perceived as an advantage of unions.[62] After the civil servants' strike that helped end the Kapp Putsch in 1920, the question of the DLV's relationship to the DBB and to strikes other than a Kapp-style rescue operation for the republic produced much debate at the annual DLV convention. Despite pressure from leftist members (e.g. the Saxon Teachers' Association), the majority voted to exclude the strike weapon in salary questions.[63] Nevertheless, the DLV officially called itself a "professional union" (*Berufsgewerkshaft*) so as to gain recognition as a negotiating partner with government, and it called upon its members to resign from competing "unions" (such as the Catholic and – more likely candidates for dual membership – Protestant teachers' associations).[64] Most other, smaller teachers' associations also joined the DBB as the "bureaucrats' union" responsible for direct negotiations with government. An exception was the female Catholic teachers' association, VKDLn. And more politically activist teachers joined such small unions as the *Gewerkschaft Deutscher Volksschullehrer* (Union of German Elementary Teachers, founded in 1919 and renamed *Freie Lehrergewerkschaft Deutschlands*, or Free Teachers' Union of Germany, in 1928) or the *Verein Sozialistischer Lehrer und Lehrerinnen* (Socialist Teachers' Association, founded in 1919).[65]

Female teachers did join the DLV at the same time they belonged to the ADLnV, but the divisions of sexual politics continued to effect the elementary teaching profession through the Weimar era. In fact, partly thanks to wartime teacher shortages and the official end to the celibacy requirement, a growing proportion of *Volksschullehrer* were women. Whereas at the beginning of the century women had constituted only 15 percent of the 147,000 elementary teachers in Germany, by 1921 the figure had risen to a quarter (of 196,000), a percentage women generally retained until the Hitler era.[66] About 86 percent of women teachers were organized in the ADLV or the Catholic VKDLn at the

61 Kittel, *Entwicklung*, p. 31.   62 Bölling, *Volksschullehrer und Politik*, p. 94.
63 Ibid., p. 100.   64 Ibid., pp. 101–3.   65 Gahlings, *Volksschullehrer*, pp. 70 ff.
66 Bölling, *Volksschullehrer und Politik*, p. 27.

beginning of the 1930s, although some held membership in the DLV as well. The latter organization could claim only 78 percent of all teachers (irrespective of religious affiliation or sex) as its members.[67]

If women did not make even more progress in improving their share of the teaching positions, it may have had to do principally with the fluctuations in the absolute number of teachers over the 1920s. Beginning in 1921, the drastic drop in school-entering population caused by wartime birthrate decline (added to fiscal austerity) meant teacher reductions (from a high of 196,000 in 1921 to 187,000 in 1926). Despite a valiant and successful struggle by German governments to improve teacher/pupil ratios and recovery of enrollments, there were still only 190,000 elementary schoolteaching jobs in Germany in 1931–2.[68] The practical reintroduction of celibacy through the back door of the 1923 "personnel reduction" decree mentioned earlier (forcing female teachers who married to leave the civil service unless they could prove their husband was indigent) continued under the Nazis' campaign against "double earners" in the work force.[69]

Even the differences in teachers' salaries and the growing perception of the rank and file of the DLV that ordinary classroom teachers had little voice in the organization contributed to tensions within the DLV as the Weimar era wore on. Country teachers were given subsidies to keep them down on the farm, which teachers in large urban areas (incidentally disproportionately women), facing higher living costs, resented. Elementary schoolteachers with administrative duties, for example principals and vice-principals, were also given subsidies. Because the teacher-organization leaderships consisted heavily of such school administrators (63 percent of the board of directors of the Prussian Schoolteachers' Association in 1927, for example), their acquiescence in government layoffs and salary reductions in the Great Depression made them appear aloof from the concerns of the rank and file.[70] By 1932 there were also over 15,000 mostly newly minted candidates for elementary school jobs in Prussia alone, the so-called *Junglehrer*, who had little prospects of a job.[71] In a situation where even the employed were drawing salaries comparable to factory workers, the discouragement and suspicion of the unemployed with the DLV and other teachers' organizations festered. But even the old were affected: Prussia in 1931 ordered the forced retirement of all teachers sixty-two and older. The supine response of the teachers' organizations caused a wave of member resignations.[72] The revolutionary era had ended, not with the full triumph of the *Volksschullehrer* as a full academic

67 Ibid.; Gahlings, *Volksschullehrer*, p. 74.   68 Bölling, *Volksschullehrer und Politik*, p. 27.
69 Wunder, *Bürokratie*, p. 115.
70 Wilfried Breyvogel, "Die staatliche Schul- und Lehrerpolitik 1928–32 und die Lehrervereine als Interessenorgane der Volksschullehrer," in Manfred Heinemann, ed., *Sozialisation und Bildungswesen in der Weimarer Republik* (Stuttgart, 1976), pp. 284 ff.
71 Bölling, *Volksschullehrer und Politik*, p. 29.
72 Breyvogel, "Schul- und Lehrerpolitik," p. 287.

professional, but with the proletarianization of this predominantly lower-middle-class group.

Despite their ideological and pedagogical differences, however, the various German teachers' organizations were able to agree on many things (hence their cooperation with the DBB on salary and working-condition matters) and occasionally act together, as when they generated a common nationwide protest to save teacher-training establishments from further Depression-driven cuts in 1932.[73] Like other professional organizations, the DLV tried to maintain a stance "above the parties," although its membership was more likely to gravitate to the political middle and left than most others and, until the grave disappointments at the hands of Weimar cabinets piled up higher and higher, to support the republic. But the closeness of elementary-school teaching to its clientele, the federal and religious structure of schooling, and the very permeation of every level and place in Germany by the *Volksschule* constituted centrifugal forces that impeded dramatic organizational triumphs by the teachers' associations.

Needless to add, elementary schoolteachers hardly received any help from the instructors in higher schools. Much more vehemently than the philosophical faculties of the universities, which were sometimes willing to entertain the idea of training *Volksschullehrer*, the German philologists rejected the idea out of hand in the Weimar era. Similarly the German Philologists' Association protested the granting of the title *Studienrat* ("counselor of studies," one of the more awkward attempts to extrapolate from the bureaucratic *Hofrat* and similar titles) to such nonacademically trained teachers as singing and drawing masters who might be hired by higher schools.[74] For the philologists, firmly stuck in the self-protecting mentality of nineteenth-century pedagogical elitism, only classical philology could serve as a proper "scientific" curriculum for the higher schools and basis for the other professions; only university-trained philologists could teach such a curriculum; and any other views were mere "demagogy" and fashionable clap-trap.

Such views were readily compatible with a deep nostalgia for the "good old days" of the empire and a corresponding mistrust of the Weimar Republic, including its attempts to reform the school system with such democratic concepts as the unitary school. Most politically active DPV members were close to Stresemann's German People's Party (DVP), but the second largest group belonged to the Nationalists (DNVP). About one-third of the politically active members were, however, committed to the parties of the "Weimar Coalition," Center (ZP), Democrats (DDP), and Socialists (SPD).[75] Under these

73 Gahlings, *Volksschullehrer*, p. 71.
74 Franz Hamburger, *Lehrer zwischen Kaiser und Führer. Der deutsche Philologenverband in der Weimarer Republik. Eine Untersuchung der Lehrerorganisationen* (Dissertation, Philosophische Fakultät, University of Heidelberg, 1974), pp. 69–70.
75 Ibid., p. 105.

circumstances, an officially nonpartisan stance was logical. A tacit alliance with the right wing of the Center Party, the DVP, and the DNVP was also logical, however, as these parties tended to press actively for the interests close to the hearts of the philologists. The KPD's attitude to the DPV was not designed to win friends among *Gymnasium* teachers, the "class enemy"; typically, the KPD dismissed the DPV program as "nationalistic belching."[76]

The German Philologists Association adopted that name in 1921, but it remained steadfastly the "association of academically trained teachers of Germany," its previous title. It evinced hostility to female higher schoolteachers, who therefore founded their own small *Verband Akademisch Gebildeter Lehrerinnen*. Its position on training and certification for the career of higher schoolteacher was not that it needed improvement, but that it should remain as exclusive as possible.

Nevertheless, these worshipers of ancient Greece and Rome did have one agendum for change: they militated constantly for improvements in their bureaucratic status and salaries. Having achieved bureaucratic parity with judges of the lowest courts, they sought to inaugurate new rungs for promotion into even higher rank and salary levels. Indeed, one of the main reasons for reorganizing and renaming the association in 1921 was to enhance its fighting potential in the arena of salaries.[77] The typical *Gymnasium* teacher's salaries were mentioned above in the discussion of elementary schoolteachers. As with other professions in state service, the incomes of employed *Philologen* fluctuated with government adjustments and cutbacks. As with all other professions, the personnel policies of late Weimar governments in the face of the Great Depression caused a sharp worsening of the fate of young, beginning practitioners as well as hardship for the established *Studienräte*.

Nevertheless, the DPV was organizationally rather successful. With 31,000 members in 1926, it encompassed virtually all its chosen body of practitioners (male *Gymnasium* teachers), was able to build political bridges to the center-to-right parties in the parliament, where it did effective lobbying, and had the ear of government ministries.[78] It was closely allied with the *Reichsbund der Höheren Beamten*, which even elected a philologist as its chairman in 1932.[79] Its influence was strong enough to frustrate many would-be reformers of the German school system, resist the elementary teachers' attempts at equality, and hold to a minimum the number of females teaching in the higher schools. This may seem to be a sad record by progressive standards; but it is a record of considerable realization of the profession's own aims, defensive, negative, and anachronistic as these may appear.

76 Ibid., p. 106.   77 Ibid., pp. 200 ff.
78 Ibid., pp. 142–7; Reinhold Schairer, *Die akademische Berufsnot. Tatsachen und Auswege* (Jena, 1932), p. 29.
79 Hamburger, *Lehrer*, p. 88.

3. DOKTOREN OHNE BROT

As the Great Depression still approached what we now know to have been its nadir, in 1932, the neoconservative periodical *Die Tat* estimated the current crop of unemployed academics at 70,000, predicted 140,000 by 1934, and maintained that the entirety of *employed* professionals in Germany amounted to 350,000.[80] A somewhat more sober account published the same year argued that there were really only 330,000 "academic" professional jobs in Germany, far fewer than the 400,000 estimated by Gertrud Bäumer; and that at current rates of production by higher educational institutions, there would soon be a million candidates for those one-third million positions.[81]

One commentary from the radical intellectual right deserves extensive quotation here, to give a sense of the arguments and a flavor of the fear and frustration undoubtedly felt by many professionals themselves:

These few but significant selected groups [engineers, chemists, economists, physicians, civil servants, Gymnasium teachers], which can give an idea about most of the others [learned professions], shows how academics today, after four or five years of higher education and a more or less long waiting period for a position, can slip into jobs that initially produce a monthly income of about 400 marks. Of course, a family can live on that. But how? The worker, with his 200–300 marks a month, lives in a modest apartment, in modest clothes, and from good but simple food. Travel and cultural needs can be obtained from his party or his union. The [professional] class we are talking about here . . . cannot live too simply, is not allowed to dress cheaply, and must fulfill its cultural needs as a matter of necessity. Therefore it scrimps on food. . . . Between the thoroughly well-organized masses of labor and capital stand these human beings, who under pressure from these two massive millstones are beginning to dissolve and ferment like bacteria, until one day the bubbling pot will spill over.[82]

It is ironic that the modern German learned professions and their representative groups had achieved so much of their programs over nearly a century, with high levels of education and certification, a species of homogeneity within professions and often clear career ladders, their recognition by government and society as negotiating partners, widely admired (and even feared) levels of technical mastery and skill, ethical codes and self-policing machinery, in many cases a considerable degree of professional autonomy (despite trends toward bureaucratization) and market control, only to be ground down in unemployment or at least economic distress brought on by the complex of economic and social maladjustments of Germany in the postwar period.

80 Friedrich Maetzel, "Doktoren ohne Brot," *Die Tat* 23 (1931–2): 1,005.
81 Schairer, *Berufsnot*, pp. 5, 28. The feminist leader and Democratic party Reichstag deputy Gertrud Bäumer was also a ministerial counselor for educational matters in the national Interior Ministry during the Weimar years.
82 Fried, "Spaltpilze," p. 528.

Many authors, especially recent ones, have rightly injected such terms as "deprofessionalization," "proletarianization," "the end of the liberal professions," "crisis of the professions," and many others into the debate about 1918–33. But how justified are we in accepting them at full value? In the next chapter, after surveying what happened to the professions after 1933, we return for a fuller consideration of this question.

PART VI

The fate of professions
under and after fascism

12

Collaboration, coordination,
and professionalism

The fate and redefined role of learned professions under German fascism deserve a much fuller treatment than is possible in this broader history. Difficulties with sources remain formidable, although as this work goes to press there is hope that "openness" may also embrace some remaining German archives. The resurgence of autonomous professional groups and their development since the Nazi dictatorship will have to remain a topic for planned future publications by this author.

Nevertheless, one cannot fail to indicate in a few broad strokes how the major German learned professions fared under the beginnings of fascist rule. After the Nazi "seizure of power" at the end of January 1933, the policy of "coordination" *(Gleichschaltung)* of major institutions in German society became a chief instrument of the consolidation of National Socialist control. The learned professions were also a victim (and to a certain degree the willing collaborators) in this process. It went forward at different paces, with varying degrees of thoroughness, but certainly by the end of the 1930s every last vestige of independence had, at least nominally, been stripped from the major professional groups, most already within the first year or two of the "national revolution." Thus, the 1930s constitute a logical closing place for this book. The process of formation of autonomous national professional groups and the process of modern professionalization had, with the swift strokes of the German dictatorship, seemingly been thrown on the rubbish heap of history, along with so many other traditional institutions and ideas loathed by that professional manqué, Adolf Hitler.

The specifics of professions under fascism are still largely unresearched, although many excellent monographs and articles have begun appearing, and even more are in the offing for the near future. Naturally, the fact of coordination and cooperation with the Nazis has not left the professional organizations any less burdened with the "unmastered past" than other groups, which has undoubtedly complicated and often hindered objective research into postwar professional developments and even access to relevant document.

217

1. COORDINATION AND THE PROFESSIONS

Just how readily did German professional groups flock to the National Socialist movement? As one recent study concluded, "The German professions welcomed the National Socialist seizure of power with restrained enthusiasm."[1] Some other studies of voting behavior have recently sought to challenge the equation of fascism with the "lower middle class" by showing how the very upper middle class to which professionals supposedly belonged also voted, in some instances, for the Nazis.[2] Still other authors have pointed to noisy, if admittedly small, National Socialist organizations for professionals that predated the "seizure of power" and thus seem to prove a special susceptibility of such groups for Nazism.[3]

The difficulty with such claims is that they tend to personify group behavior and to treat large groups (or even social strata) as if they had a single will. The reality of professions' reactions to National Socialism and the seizure of power was more nuanced than uniform. Looking at all German professions together, we have noted that their memberships spanned the political gamut from far left to far right, although the KPD and the NSDAP were at first little represented. Insofar as many could still be called members of the *Bildungsbürgertum,* academic professionals certainly tended to be more nationalist and conservative than, for example, industrial workers, and certain professional groups (such as the DAeV or the DRB) contained high percentages of sympathizers with the DNVP or at least the DVP.[4] And there were individual members who joined the Nazi party in the crisis years of the Weimar Republic. Nevertheless, had the Nazis been so strong, they could have taken over the professional organizations from within, rather than having to wait for the triumph of their party at the pinnacle of government in 1933. It must be emphasized that if a large percentage of German academic professionals sympathized with the Nazis before 1933, they were uncharacteristically docile and incompetent in capturing leadership of their respective professional organizations. It was the power of the Nazi state after 1933 to break and intimidate societal organizations that was decisive.

The fact that a number of prominent Nazi leaders were professionals by training might tempt one to think of *pars pro toto.* One can mention, as a small

1 Konrad H. Jarausch, "The Perils of Professionalization: Lawyers, Teachers and Engineers in Nazi Germany," *German Studies Review* 9 (1986): 109.
2 Richard Hamilton, *Who Voted for Hitler?* (Princeton, 1982); Thomas Childers, *The Nazi Voter* (Chapel Hill, 1983), passim.
3 See, for example, Michael Kater, "Hitler's Early Doctors: Nazi Physicians in Predepression Germany," *Journal of Modern History* 59 (1987): 25–52; idem, "Medizin und Mediziner im Dritten Reich," *Historische Zeitschrift* 244 (1987): 299–352; idem, "Physicians in Crisis," in Stachura, *Unemployment,* 49–77; and idem, "Professionalization and Socialization of Physicians in Wilhelmine and Weimar Germany," *Journal of Contemporary History* 20 (1985): 677–701.
4 Michael Kater, "Nazi Physicians League," states, " . . . A great majority of practitioners sympathized strongly with the nationalist Right. . . . " (p. 151).

sample, the Ph.D. Germanist Goebbels, professional officers such as Goering and Heydrich, the chemist Ley, the apothecary Gregor Strasser, the diploma-agriculturalist Himmler, the elementary schoolteacher Streicher, the engineer Feder, or the architect Speer. Hitler's own lifelong interest in art and architecture stemmed, as is well known, from his youthful hope of entering one of those professions. But none of these leaders evinced much interest in the professional drive of their respective groups, abandoning careers in them for politics or at most agitating for the Nazification of the professions. Like many men who went through the experience of World War I and the difficulties for the professions in the Weimar era, their personal and political aims were largely incompatible with those of the larger professional organizations.

Furthermore, the "national revolution" propagated by the NSDAP was not a slogan unique to it by 1933. The Nationalist party, we should recall, entered the Hitler cabinet and gave the Nazis the Reichstag votes they needed to pass the dictatorial Enabling Law of March 1933. Many of the early decrees affecting the professions, such as that on the "Restoration of the Professional Civil Service," contained elements borrowed from the nationalist right and the professional groups themselves. One can blame those professionals who welcomed such "solutions" as shortsighted, an affliction that was epidemic at the time, or call the Nazis opportunistic. But to think of all professional groups as going over enthusiastically to the Nazis is a distortion of the known historical record so far.

Lack of stiff and determined resistance by the professional groups' leaderships, on the other hand, cannot be denied. Tired, used-up, and often helpless in the face of the economic misery of their members, the leaders of most professional groups shared the outlook of many other Europeans caught in the grip of the Great Depression. In some cases their memberships were dwindling or divided about what policies to follow. Younger members appear to have been particularly alienated and perhaps desperate enough to believe in radical solutions. Survival of their organizations, rather than sudden answers to intractable problems both political and economic, appears to have become the chief aim of most professional leaders by 1933.[5]

The failure of the leadership to achieve that aim became more and more obvious in the first year or two of National Socialist rule, although in the first weeks and months it may have been less easily predictable. Not that there was any genuine choice, but the Nazi government at least initially held out the carrot of further "professionalization" in addition to the stick of compulsion. As we shall see below, even when these promises were occasionally fulfilled, the content of reform was largely perverted by the loss of professional autonomy

5 For a further discussion of the collective behavior of professional organizations in the crisis of Weimar and the Nazi seizure of power, see Charles E. McClelland, "Escape from Freedom? Reflections on German Professionalization, 1870–1933," in Michael Burrage and Rolf Torstendahl, eds., *The Formation of Professions* (London, 1990), pp. 97–113.

exacted by the regime. Achieving a national medical code (a demand of German doctors since the 1870s), for example, meant little if the NSDAP controlled the medical profession.

The destruction of autonomous professional groups did not, formally or practically, mean there were no professions in Nazi Germany. As we have seen, professionalization had also gone forward in the nineteenth century under conditions of considerable official constraint and control. No doubt many German practitioners (and even some of their organizational leaders) entered the "national revolution" of 1933 with the hope that willing cooperation would insure the advance of professionalization. Some of these hopes (e.g. restricting competition, increasing income) were realized in part or for a short time. Yet, these signs of further professionalization (or "reprofessionalization") should properly be seen as tactical concessions prior to the hardening of National Socialist control and the onset of the Nazi strategy of militarization and totalitarianization of German and European society.

It is also important to disaggregate several generalizations about the professions before and after 1933. With the large-scale purge of Jews, "non-Aryans," women, and liberal or leftist practitioners, the professions were not identical groups over time. Among the nonpurged majority, one must also be aware of a distinction between conservative and nationalist supporters (at least initially) of the "national awakening" and convinced Nazis. One must also carefully distinguish, in some cases, between overlapping but not necessarily identical phenomena, such as "scientific" biological determinism on the one hand and Nazi racism and genocidal intentions on the other. If many German doctors endorsed the eugenics movement before 1933, for example, so did many of their American and British colleagues, without fascism or a Holocaust resulting in those countries. Because eugenics and racism have some common ancestors and are both discredited today, it has seemed tempting to argue that the German medical profession was particularly pro-Nazi because it was particularly eugenicist. Yet, careful historical analysis must insist on more compelling evidence than this to characterize the German medical profession as a whole as genocidal. A more fruitful approach might be to explain the failure of the National Socialists to subvert completely the traditional values of a large number of professional practitioners, perhaps even the large majority, and the continuation of those values into the period after the regime's bloody end in 1945.

Prior to early 1933, the Nazis' role in the major academic professions had been restricted to forming a fifth column inside existing professional groups or, in a few other cases, rival groups outside of them, but none was able to take over leadership of any profession. Some organizations had significant subgroups targeted by the Nazis in their memberships (e.g. Jews in the DAV and DAeV, women in teaching and other professional organizations, and socialist, liberal, or Catholic members in many others). There was no single pattern of "coordination." Some organizations simply dissolved themselves, others were taken over by Nazi party special-interest groups, still others were dealt with in ad hoc ways. There was a little resistance, but not much.

The largest group of academic professionals fell into the Nazis' realm of manipulation with the "seizure of power" itself: as the constitutionally appointed government, the Nazi-Nationalist coalition cabinet directly controlled not only the Reich civil service but, thanks to Chancellor Papen's coup d'état in 1932, that of the overwhelmingly largest state, Prussia. Despite some inroads among the civil service, by the end of 1932 the Nazis had evidently not been able to attract any significantly greater ratio of them than their representation in the general population.[6] The restoration of the professional civil service law meant the elimination of Jews, liberal, and leftist opponents of the regime, and large numbers of women, while the education decree drastically reduced the number of students in institutions of higher learning, again with Jews and women being especially harshly victimized.

Instead of the Nazis infiltrating the civil service at all ranks, however, the civil service flocked to join the party: 81 percent of the new members joining between 30 January (the day of Hitler's appointment as chancellor) and 1 May (when joining was suddenly made more difficult) were officials of one level or another. The League of National Socialist Jurists (NSJB) rocketed from under 1,500 to 80,000 members in the course of the year.[7] The DBB was incorporated into the Nazi party in early 1934, and all other representative bodies of legally trained professionals were either dissolved or "coordinated." Nevertheless, debate continues to this day about how thoroughly the NSDAP was able to suppress the independence of the civil service, bench, and bar. Even within the Nazi movement, such individuals as Frick and Hess struggled with each other and with many other party officials, as well as the party's own "professional" groups and the Labor Front, over control of the state apparatus, a struggle that went on largely unresolved through the 1930s.[8]

Just as the Nazis needed some control over the civil service to consolidate their immediate authority (and thus had to meet at least some of the bureaucrats' professional goals), so their future control impelled coming to terms with teachers, a large part of the state bureaucracy. For the *Volksschullehrer*, the Nazis offered the achievement of *their* professional objective of university-level training and an end to the status differences between them and higher schoolteachers. The Prussian pedagogical academies were renamed *Hochschulen für Lehrerbildung* (teacher-training colleges) in 1933 and generalized to the whole Reich by 1937.[9] But as was so often the case in the confusion of Nazi policies, the ultimate goal of academic professionalization was never reached: manpower shortages caused in part by Germany's economic recovery and later by its military

6 See Jane Caplan, "Speaking the Nazi Language: The Nazi Party and the Civil Service Vote in the Weimar Republic," in Childers, *Nazi Constituency*, esp. p. 198.
7 Wunder, *Bürokratie*, p. 140.   8 Mommsen, *Beamtentum*, pp. 32ff.
9 Scholz and Stranz, "Einflussnahmen," pp. 112–115.

The fate of professions under fascism

buildup created a deficit of trained teachers and thus prevented the full academicization of the elementary schoolteaching profession. By 1940, Hitler had ordered in effect short-training courses for such teachers, and, inevitably, despite the mysogynist intent of Nazi legislation, most of the new "instant" teachers were women.[10]

The DLV had already begun to fear serious defections, especially from young and unemployed teachers, as early as 1931, and it made the typical solidarity declarations in 1933, hoping to save its independence; but by May 1933, it was integrated into the *Deutsche Erziehergemeinschaft* (German Educators Community) under the leadership of the Nazi Teachers' League (NSLB).[11] Although Nazi members of the DLV may have been proportionately higher for this occupational group than some others, the evidence indicates that the DLV, despite some infiltration efforts by the Nazis, continued to hold itself aloof from the NSDAP until 1933.[12] Indeed, before 1933, the Nazis' Teachers' League only managed to attract some 6,000 members (compared to the DLV's nearly 150,000).[13]

Curiously, the largest professional organization of higher schoolteachers was able to hold onto its independence a bit longer. The DPV "refused to be swallowed by [the National Socialist Teachers League], this mass organization of their intellectual or social inferiors."[14] By joining the new German Teachers Community, the leadership of the DPV evidently hoped to maintain its autonomy under the "merely nominal" political control of Hans Schemm's NSLB.[15] This strategy ultimately failed, despite the "firm assurances" of the Nazis in 1933. Membership in the DPV and support for its journal *Deutsches Philologenblatt* declined, and the organization dissolved in 1936.[16]

The story of the representative groups of the "free" professions was marked by the same overall outline, although the ultimate disposition varied from case to case. Somewhat like the higher schoolteachers, the attorneys allowed themselves to be misled into approving the organizational integration of the DAV into the BNSDJ or Nazi Jurists League as a mere "umbrella." By December 1933, however, the DAV was no more. At first the DAV had attempted to protect its Jewish members but yielded to their "resignations for the good of the organization" by May of 1933.[17] Corporate integration into the BNSDJ was made more attractive to the lawyers through the promise that this step would save them from having to join the Nazi party individually. By the end of September the Nazis changed the DAV's statutes to eliminate Jews from membership.[18] The Lawyers Chambers were also purged and "coordinated" in the course of

---

10 Ibid., p. 117.   11 Bölling, *Volksschullehrer und Politik*, pp. 203–8.   12 Ibid., p. 209.
13 Breyvogel, "Schul- und Lehrerpolitik," p. 289.   14 Jarausch, "Perils," 111.
15 Johannes Erger, "Lehrer und Nationalsozialismus. Von den tranditionellen Lehrerverbänden zum Nationalsozialistischen Lehrerbund (NSLB)," in Heinemann, *Erziehung und Schulwesen im 3. Reich*, vol. 2, pp. 227–8.
16 Deutscher Philologen-Verband, *Achtzig Jahre Deutscher Philologen-Verband* (Düsseldorf, 1984), p. 25.
17 Ostler, *Rechtsanwalt*, pp. 230ff.   18 Ibid., p. 233.

1933. The DAV's influential journal, *Juristische Wochenschrift*, was first "Arya-nized," then taken over by Nazis, and finally even its name disappeared by 1941.[19] Nevertheless, the process of Nazification of the bar went on slowly: as late as 1937 a third of the Berlin attorneys were still "non-Aryan," and about 70 percent of similar attorneys in Prussian cities remained on the job.[20]

As for the small number of female attorneys, none were admitted to the bar after 1936 (although it was not made specifically illegal), and women attorneys as well as judges were driven out of sight if not forced out of the courts completely. By 1937, when a new law dissolved all organizations of civil servants and officers of the courts, no female attorneys' organization existed to dissolve.[21]

Ironically, the lawyers did finally get a national Lawyers Chamber (*Reichs-rechtsanwaltskammer*, 1935) and a new national Lawyers Code (*Reichsrechtsan-waltsordnung*, 1936). The major change in this was to restrict access to the profession: training and certification were the same as for judges, that is, im-plying a "trial year" in the courts plus three years of virtually unpaid work as an assessor. Naturally, Jews, women, political opponents, and certain other types of people uncongenial to the Nazis were also effectively excluded.[22] The result of purges and the new code was a shrinkage in the number of attorneys from about 19,500 in early 1933 to a little over 16,000 during the first months of World War II.[23] The average salaries for attorneys are calculated to have risen from 6,500 marks in 1933 to 11,000 by 1938.[24]

Another professional group that was a particular target of Nazi coordination was the whole medical profession (including dentists and pharmacists), which had a high proportion of Jewish practitioners. Also, obsessed as they were with biological matters (virtually *the* characteristic that set Nazism off from other "fascist" movements), they were especially keen, as Michael Kater nicely phrased it, to control the German medical profession so as to turn the family doctor into "a kind of bio-political block warden" of the regime.[25]

As with the lawyers, the National Socialists went forward on various fronts, Nazifying the national and regional medical associations and physicians' cham-bers by the summer of 1933, force-retiring Jews and leftists from all public medical offices, encouraging medical personnel to join the National Socialist Physicians' League (NSDAeB) as well as the NSDAP directly, and reorganizing the whole medical system with a national *Reichsärzteordnung* and a *Reichsärztekam-mer* which, however, were no more than mechanisms for Nazi control, not the autonomous bodies for which physicians had been agitating for decades. As with the legal community, however, internecine feuding among such Nazi medical

19 Ibid., p. 237.
20 Kenneth C. H. Willig, "The Bar in the Third Reich," *American Journal of Legal History* 20 (1976): 5.
21 Deutscher Juristinnenbund, *Juristinnen*, pp. 16–17.   22 Ibid., pp. 258–9.
23 Ibid., pp. 269–70.   24 Ibid., p. 275.   25 Kater, "Medizin und Mediziner," 307.

leaders as Gerhard Wagner and Leonardo Conti prevented a fully effective implementation of all the National Socialists' ideas.[26]

Through intimidation (the DAeV-Hartmannbund asked its own Jewish and leftist leaders to resign from office in the spring of 1933 in the hope of keeping a shred of independence) and legislation the Nazis slowly achieved the virtual elimination of Jews from medical practice in Germany by the beginning of World War II. Such steps included prohibiting Jews from being newly empaneled by medical insurance funds, followed by the elimination of existing Jewish members first from the public funds, then from the private ones; boycotts; and ultimately the measures of September 1938. These basically left only a few "non-Aryan" physicians around to treat the diminishing Jewish population. The proportion of Jewish doctors before the Nazi takeover was estimated at between 15 and 17 percent, and 90 percent of these practitioners had been forced out of their profession by 1938, leaving only 700 "treaters of the sick" (even their title of *Arzt* had been revoked). The impact was uneven, however, because "non-Aryan" doctors had been heavily concentrated in the cities and made up large minorities in many municipalities (and a majority in Berlin).[27]

Nazi control of the insurance funds, not just of the doctors' and dentists' organizations, was clearly an important mechanism for throttling "undesirable" doctors. Thus, the *Kassenärztliche Vereinigung Deutschlands* (Insurance Fund Physicians Association of Germany, or KVD) was created in August 1933. It embraced the 80 percent of all doctors in panel practice and acted as their agent vis-à-vis the sickness funds. The latter were also reorganized to destroy socialist influence and reduce the voice of the insured, while fees were adjusted in the doctor's favor. Jealousy of the power of the Minister of Labor, whose bailiwick included the KVD, induced Wagner to trump with the Reich Physicians' Chamber, which regulated all doctors centrally.[28] The Reich Physicians Code (RAeO) of late 1935 provided for the dissolution of the DAeV/Hartmannbund the following spring, and after being subsumed by the German Women's Front, the *Bund Deutscher Aerztinnen* was also dissolved in 1936.[29]

Female doctors were not, however, reduced in number as was the fate of so many of their colleagues in other professions. In fact, the number of doctors generally continued to rise – from 55,000 in 1935 through 59,000 in 1939 to almost 80,000 in 1944. Much of this growth had more to do with territorial annexations than improvements in the doctor/population ratio, though, which actually shrank from about 1:1350 to 1:1540 between 1933 and 1943.[30] Female doctors as a fraction of all physicians increased from a little over six to nearly ten percent between 1932 and 1939, and rose to one-eighth by the

26 Ibid., p. 306.
27 W. F. Kümmel, "Die Ausschaltung rassisch und politisch missliebiger Aerzte," in Fridolf Kudlien, ed., *Aerzte im Nationalsozialismus* (Cologne, 1985), p. 76. See also Stephan Leibfried and Florian Tennstedt, "Sozialpolitik und Berufsverbote im Jahre 1933," *Zeitschrift für Sozialreform* 25 (1979): 129–53 and 211–38, especially for the fate of leftist doctors.
28 Kater, "Medizin und Medziner," 307.   29 Ibid., p. 324.   30 Ibid., p. 304.

war year 1942 (of course, most of these women were relegated to dependent medical jobs).[31]

More doctors joined the Nazi party than any other professional group overall after 1933. Estimates as high as 50 percent (and not lower than 39 percent) have recently appeared.[32] Why this was so is still controversial. Although it is difficult to determine exactly to what extent German doctors benefited economically from the new order, they evidently did benefit from it: economic recovery alone, coupled with diminished competition on a per-capita basis would have improved the overall position of the surviving physicians. According at least to tax-based reports, the average taxable income of German physicians rose from a low of 9,300 marks a year in 1933 to nearly 15,000 in 1938, incidentally putting them ahead of attorneys for the first time.[33] Conditions were less and less pleasant for young doctors, however, whose educational standards sank and who were more and more trained to be the kind of military surgeons so many had to become in World War II.[34]

The Nazis operated with dentists and apothecaries in ways similar to the physicians. Jews were purged, independent professional organizations were coordinated (there was even a Reich Dental Führer), and certain long-standing demands were addressed by way of holding out a carrot. The dentists, for example, were promised a regulation of competition from dental technicians. The Nazis also halted the growth of both dentists and technicians, if not in absolute numbers, at least as a per-capita figure. The same was true of the numbers of licensed apothecaries.[35] The training system for apothecaries was changed in 1935 to extend formal university training to six years (after the *Abitur* and a two-year apprenticeship in a pharmacy), to reduce the following "practice" time to one year, and to limit the number of new pharmacists by limiting the number of apprentices. The number of the latter allowed each year was decreed by the Minister of the Interior.[36] Thus, for all intents and purposes, pharmacy had become a full academic profession, with a *numerus clausus*, only under the National Socialist regime. But the new Nazi leadership of the *Standesgemeinschaft* (professional community) of German pharmacists otherwise failed to achieve many of their economic objectives, such as limiting the role of big pharmaceutical factories, because the latter had great influence at high levels of the NSDAP.[37]

The coordination of the engineering and chemical professions took slightly different forms from the ones discussed above. The cultural antimodernism of

31 Ibid., pp. 317–18.
32 Ibid., p. 311; and Georg Lilienthal, "Der Nationalsozialistische Deutsche Aerztebund," in Kudlien, *Aerzte*, p. 117. The lower figure is arrived at by factoring out dentists, pharmacists, etc.
33 Walter Wuttke-Gronberg, ed., *Medizin im Nationalsozialismus. Ein Arbeitsbuch* (Tübingen, 1980), p. 347.
34 Kater, "Medizin und Mediziner," 340ff.   35 Stürzbecher, "Versorgung," p. 251.
36 Adelung and Urdang, *Grundriss*, pp. 144–5.   37 Schröder, " 'Wiedergeburt,' " pp. 172–5.

the National Socialist leaders, as has often been remarked, did not include hostility to certain aspects of technology and applied science. The Nazis needed technicians in a way they did not need (or in any case appreciate) lawyers, bureaucrats, or even doctors. Thus, the party's own organizations, meant to compete with and subvert such "academic" and "elitist" professional organizations as the VDI or VDC, wound up being shunted aside in a peculiar alliance between the party leadership and the old-line organizations.

The *Kampfbund Deutscher Architekten und Ingenieure* (Fighting League of German Architects and Engineers, or KDAI) and the *Ingenieur-Technische Abteilung* (Engineering-Technical Department) of the NSDAP, already in existence in 1931, maneuvered to take control of the VDI. But Gottfried Feder, the "leader" of the KDAI and one of the most senior Nazis, fell increasingly out of favor with Hitler. As the VDI rushed to "Aryanize" its leadership in the spring of 1933, Feder evidently encountered orders from Hitler not to change the VDI radically (e.g. rob it of its character as a largely "academic" professional association). The major change, after negotiations, was that predominantly Nazis were "elected" to the board of directors of the VDI in May 1933.[38]

The VDI was forced to join with the smaller engineering associations (e.g. VDE, VDEh) in a *Reichsgemeinschaft der Technisch-Wissenschaftlichen Arbeit* (Reich Community of Technical-scientific Work, or RTA) but also managed to wriggle out of the grasp of Robert Ley's German Labor Front (DAF). Despite the forced resignation of "non-Aryan" and other members uncongenial to the Nazis (between one and two thousand a year between 1933 and 1936), the VDI resumed its overall growth by 1935 (just under 34,000 members) to reach a wartime peak in 1944 of 60,000.[39] Such figures became increasingly meaningless by 1937, however, after the VDI's members were collectively forced to join the Nazis' League of German Technicians (NSBDT).[40] As a sign of the relative disfavor of purely academically based professional organizations, the VDDI, which resisted joining the NSBDT and even tried to use legal action against the Nazis, finally dissolved itself entirely in 1939.[41]

The fate of the VDC ran largely parallel to that of the engineering associations. The organization became more and more a shell, although its membership continued to grow from over 9,000 in 1933 to 11,500 by the time of its demise in 1945, including "annexed" colleagues from Austria.[42]

Nevertheless, despite the obvious and long-range "deprofessionalization" of the technological professions, most signs indicate that opportunities for well-paid work increased as competition (e.g. the halving of the number of technical college students) decreased in the period before the war.[43] By the eve of the war, shortages of technically educated professionals and a marked deterioration

38 Karl-Heinz Ludwig, "Der VDI als Gegenstand der Parteipolitik 1933 bis 1945," in Ludwig, *Technik, Ingenieure . . .* , pp. 408–11.
39 Ibid., pp. 417, 561.   40 Ibid., pp. 420–1.   41 Ludwig, *Dritten Reich*, p. 140.
42 Ramstetter, "Chemiker," p. 322.   43 Jarausch, "Perils," 122.

of the training of new graduates were beginning to tell in engineering and chemistry as well as many other fields.[44]

Such tendencies before and during World War II — including the virtual closing of higher educational institutions at the end — point to the erosion of qualification and training for the professions under German fascism. One can thus readily agree with Konrad Jarausch's assessment that, in the long run, National Socialism meant not the "reprofessionalization" but the "deprofessionalization" of most academically based occupations.[45] The short-term economic gains purchased for some groups, e.g. physicians and lawyers, by the end of the 1930s cannot be seen in peacetime isolation from the ultimate effects of Nazi aggression, with the inevitably devastating effects on all professions. It is also difficult to imagine that a successful outcome of the war for the Nazis would have meant a return to even the status quo ante bellum for the German professions. Whatever peacetime privileges and immunities the professions still enjoyed were guaranteed partly by the Nazis' disorganization, distractedness on other domestic fronts, or even caution, combined as well with a certain protectiveness of the status quo by conservative bureaucrats and other powerful interest groups. The erosion of all these factors was palpable as the war progressed and totalitarian techniques and interventions multiplied. The undermining of the authority of the traditional officer corps, of the bureaucracy and its remaining scruples about the "rule of law," no matter how perverted, or the jerky and inefficient use of technologically trained professionals in the war effort may serve as examples of these trends.

The apology for a Nazi regime that "did some good things" before 1939 and then went "off the tracks" thereafter may still even today enjoy some credit with ignorant people or unregenerate Nazis, but it has been refuted by decades of historical scholarship. Seen over the entire career of the twelve years of Nazism in power, the effect on professions and the professionalization project of the past was almost wholly negative and destructive. Even if some professional groups as a whole witnessed some short-term relief from intense competition or low incomes, as with physicians and lawyers, this cannot be regarded as unambiguous evidence of steps toward market monopolization. For it was the Nazi party hierarchy that effectively dominated the market, not the professions, their organizations, nor even their own relatively ineffectual "brown" leadership.

National Socialism may have made tactical alliances with willing collaborators in the professions, but the overall trend of Nazi ideology and, ultimately, practice, was hostile to most central goals of modern professionalism, such as autonomy, self-regulation, and respect for formalized educational credentials. There were some professionalizing projects supported by the Nazis, such as the new field of psychotherapy, but these were usually matters of expediency.[46]

44 Ibid., 123.   45 Ibid., 122.
46 Geoffrey Cocks, *Psychotherapy in the Third Reich. The Göring Institute* (New York, 1985), esp. chap. 5.

Such gains as professionals made, such as increased average income in some cases, were the result of other Nazi policies, such as purges of Jews, restrictions on university study, and shortages of expert personnel in the wake of war production, not of a concerted policy of professions.

On the other hand, German fascism did not use its authority to bind the professions into a new "bureaucratic" submission to the state, the often-cited alternative to professionalization in a market setting. Although using the state apparatus it had captured to manipulate access to the professions, successively restricting and then facilitating such access, it did not fully bureaucratize the professions themselves. Instead the National Socialist party attempted to impose its xenophobic and racist ideas, and above all its claim to totalitarian control. Such attempts appear to have a mixed record of success. Certainly their efforts to create a "pure German" physics or mathematics were negative, fruitless and even counterproductive.[47] The belief in amateur "genius" on Hitler's part and the *Führerprinzip* based on charisma merely reflected the deep contempt of Nazi sentiment for hard-won expertise and its application in a fearless, autonomous way. The aim of the *Volksgemeinschaft* was not intended to produce a democratic community of political equals with unequal skills and rewards, but a homogenized mass of "coordinated" followers led unquestioningly by a party-created "elite." The Nazis' own ideas about elite training, judging by the party training schools *(Napolas)* and the SS training programs were, however, hardly compatible with current notions of professional training.

Nazi nihilism toward professional ethics also led to such perversions as horrible medical experiments on humans, chemists perfecting poisons for the "final solution," lawyers throwing away normative legal standards in the "People's Courts," armed forces officers colluding in mass murder of civilians, and countless other crimes. It is improbable that the majority of professionally trained people in the Third Reich participated personally in these crimes, despite encouragement from the hostile Nazi attitude toward traditional professional ethics. (We shall perhaps never have complete evidence to back or refute such a guess.) The disposition of German professional personnel before and even during World War II, keeping the home front running and serving the direct manpower needs of the *Wehrmacht,* meant there was relatively little opportunity for most of them to participate in activities that ran directly counter to these ethics. Most engineers built military projects, not gas chambers. Thus, in the end moralist questions about the German professionals' collective behavior can only be answered with moralist methods of argument.

It is of course impossible to predict the ultimate fate of what was left of professionalism in Germany had the "thousand-year Reich" lasted considerably longer than its twelve-year term. Nor should one downplay the willingness of large numbers of professional people to collaborate with the Nazi regime even

47 Alan Beyerchen, *Scientists under Hitler: Politics and the Physics Community in the Third Reich* (New Haven, Conn., 1977), chaps. 7–10.

in its waning and most brutal days. As events turned out, there remained enough of a basis in personnel and professionalization concepts after 1945 to return to the pre-1933 situation. The post-1945 situation was of course different in many ways: growing economic prosperity, a relatively decentralized state, widespread acceptance of a "social market economy" (Erhard), and Allied policies all created a more favorable milieu for the reestablished professional groups in West Germany.

There is no linear necessity for the growth and success of the drive of academically trained experts toward professionalization. The fragility of the enterprise in the face of authoritarian regimes, social and economic crises, wars, and more secular changes in conditions should need no further elaboration here.

2. POSTWAR RECOVERY

The destruction of Nazism in Germany by Allied Forces opened new opportunities after 1945. Especially in the areas that became the Federal Republic of Germany, most of the organizations I have described sprang up again, sometimes with name changes that were meant to be obvious continuators under different constitutional circumstances. Unfortunately for historians, these groups often maintain a kind of triple-monkey attitude toward the "unmastered past" of the Third Reich. Someday the history of professions in post-World War II Germany may be written (and this author hopes to make a contribution to it), but cooperation from professional organizations is uneven and delicate. The fact that numerous postwar figures in professional groups had a possibly tainted past explains much of the reticence. The need to rebuild essential professional services, the porousness of Allied "denazification" procedures, and the subsequent Cold War all help explain why there are many presumed skeletons buried in the files.

Yet, it is fair to say that the various West German professional groups rejected the Nazis' solutions to the crises of the professions and reverted to the situation existing at the end of the Weimar Republic. Professional organizations are again partners with the state and are, if anything, more powerful than they were at their peak in the 1920s. The aims of most such groups for full professional status have largely been met. By all the standards of professionalization set out in Chapter 2 of this book, academic professionals have achieved more of their demands than ever before in German history.

The structure of professional training and employment is in many ways more "steered" in the Federal Republic than ever before, too. *Numerus clausus,* resisted by the state down to the Hitler era, and not always demanded by the professions themselves, has become a common feature in certain areas, notably medicine. As a result of informal steering mechanisms, serious unemployment of trained professionals has been largely restricted to a few areas, such as teachers from time to time. Yet, those teachers who have achieved employment in the almost completely state-dominated school system are university trained and highly paid.

Thus, the development of the professions in the relatively liberal "social market economy" of postwar West Germany has been marked more by heightened cooperation between state organs and professional groups than by the clear triumph of the latter. As in any contemporary industrial society, there is never any lack of grumping by professionals about their lot, but by almost any measure it is far better than anything the professions experienced before. If many professionals are employees rather than members of the "free professions," this does not appear to have affected their privileges, social standing, and incomes nearly as much as the so-called deprofessionalization trends of the period before 1933 might have led one to expect. Only those who, by definition, describe such occupations as nonprofessional can deny the large-scale achievement of most professionalization goals through a process of corporate harmonization with the government in West Germany since 1945. Whether this is "good" or "bad" is largely a matter of ideological and political standpoint, but hardly a phenomenon to be denied.

The postwar situation in East Germany was largely dictated by the Soviet model of professions, which precludes the sort of autonomous organizations about which this work has been concerned. Given the secrecy and opaqueness that surrounded so much of life in the German Democratic Republic, a situation that is only now changing, it is difficult to draw any firm conclusions. There is little reason to believe, however, that the level of expert training and competence of East German professionals is far below that of their West German confreres. The submergence of an autonomous role for professional groups under the dominance of a single party for four decades may have distorted the course of professionalization in the German Democratic Republic even more than the dozen years of National Socialist rule. Yet, in the wake of recent "reform" efforts there as elsewhere in the "Soviet bloc," one cannot help remarking the prominence of professional cadres in the newly formed "democratic opposition," nor the resurgence of strong interest in autonomous professional life since the end of 1989.

13

∿∿∿∿∿∿∿∿∿∿∿∿∿∿∿∿∿∿∿∿∿∿∿

Conclusion

The rise of modern learned professions and their representative organizations in Germany did not follow the same patterns as in the English-speaking world any more than German history paralleled that of England or the United States. Nor can one convincingly argue that professionalization in Germany took a "special path," despite the clearly closer ties between professional groups and public authority (as elsewhere on the European continent). We might now reflect on comparisons and contrasts by way of conclusion. Having begun this book with questions about how modern professions come into being and develop, and having then surveyed the empirical realities of various professional groups and associations in Germany, we may now reflect further on the correspondence of that experience to, and divergence from, major social science conceptions of professionalization.

A first question concerns the degree to which occupations became modern and professionalized in Germany. Certainly, by one measurement, the creation of large and powerful professional organizations, the process began in the German states only shortly before the middle of the nineteenth century but, owing to persistent government mistrust, effectively only in the 1860s and 1870s. The early bureaucratization of so many occupations, not only in administration and justice, but in medicine, teaching, and the clergy, was in some ways an alternative to modern, independent, professional organizations; certainly determining standards for recruitment and training were set principally by the state through its virtual monopoly over the educational system. Starting in the 1860s, however, a trend toward deregulation of professions began as a part of the liberal era, making medicine, dentistry, and lawyering into "free" professions, and these quickly organized national associations around 1870, predated chiefly by another "free" and relatively new profession, the engineers.

The modernity of these professions lay in their combination of rigorous and long-lasting education for a single lifelong occupation, less and less alloyed (as had been still common at the turn of the nineteenth century) with secondary or tertiary occupations. With the rapid differentiation and growth of the

231

professions (of course more rapid in some than others, and happening at different times), career ladders or stages also began to emerge, adding another characteristic of modernity. And the definitive acceptance of *Wissenschaft* as the basis of learned professions was a final factor in differentiating modern from earlier professional training.

That engineering, chemistry, and teaching emerged as new "professionalized" occupations had much to do with the process of scientificization in the nineteenth century, a process that also affected such older learned professions as medicine and law. As knowledge and technique multiplied and came to be based more and more on abstractions, higher education came to play a more and more central role in the creation of professional cadres. It was no longer enough to be "learned" in the classics to enter the "learned professions," but now it was required to have a *wissenschaftlich* training. Themselves shaped through such training, followed by state examinations and certification, more and more professional men pressed their organizations to raise the scientific rigor (and by implication duration and cost) of qualifying education. In areas of curricular and licensing reform, modern professional organizations, with their high component of professorial members, collaborated with governments and the educational system to "raise the standards of the profession," as the phrase went from the late nineteenth century onward. German professional organizations' record in achieving over the long run their educational and certification requests was a good one, even if one of the aims – to make the occupation more exclusive and thereby reduce competition – rarely was achieved.

Considering the fact that there was no genuine political structure one could even call "Germany" before unification, the German professional organizations also carried out a large measure of uniformization and mental nationalization of professional practice, even in cases where the federal states retained ultimate legal competence over their activities. This alone was no small achievement, considering the relative ease with which comparable professional organizations in France, Britain, and America found a standard political framework in place for them to work with. Indeed, if one accepts Larson's argument that learned professions in Britain and America actually manipulated political institutions to reinforce their own professionalizing projects, the accomplishment of a higher degree of uniformity in standards is an even more remarkable achievement in Germany because of the relatively long-lasting resistance of political authorities there to such pressure-group tactics. The discussion of nationally applicable guidelines and their broad acceptance as goals by most professional organizations indicates that they were willing to work toward the elimination of widely differing standards that in effect protected the special rights of practitioners in this or that German state.

Thus, most German professional organizations reacted to expanding competition with grudging acceptance and rarely, if ever, called for artificial limits on access to the education system (such as *numerus clausus*), except during the height of the Great Depression. In this sense modern German professional organizations might be accused of weakness, having failed to hammer through some mechanisms designed to foster market "monopoly on services." The squeeze of competition, however, appears to have affected mostly the youngest, less qualified, and more marginal members of the professions, rather than the older, more established ones who tended to dominate professional associations (as we saw with attempts to establish professional "unions" after 1900).

Indeed, the creation of high educational and certification standards at the insistence of the leaders of Germany's major professional organizations should have guaranteed a measure of market control, if not monopoly, which has rarely been achieved in fact by any modern learned profession (including such organizations as the American Medical Association, frequently cited and even more frequently implicit in allusions to "successful" professionalization). But the ironic fact of German educational history was that German higher education was more "inclusive" in the late nineteenth and early twentieth centuries than that of most other countries.[1] Access to professional qualifications was cheaper than in England or America, for example, because of large state subsidies, and as long as Germany's economy was expanding rapidly, more and more professionals were needed. Thus, any "failure" to impose strict market monopoly by German professional groups should be blamed on their general satisfaction with the ones they were achieving. Oversupply and economic difficulties, as in the 1920s and early 1930s, were more signs of the weakness of the general economy (when professional study always appears more attractive) than of the professions.

By another traditional measure of professionalization, autonomy, German learned occupations surely achieved a high degree of success over the century leading up to the Hitler era, although it was neither universal nor even. Lawyers and doctors achieved their freedom from state control and their demands of self-governing disciplinary bodies *(Kammern),* and the medical association (Hartmann-Bund/DAeV) also won important victories in its struggle with insurance funds. Teachers achieved a different sort of autonomy, that is from close or arbitrary supervision by local church authorities or from interference by parents, even though such autonomy (again ironically) had to be purchased with a higher degree of bureaucratization of the profession. The creation of secure career ladders for the teaching profession presumably meant more to it than, for example, the "freedom" of physicians and lawyers: because education in Germany was overwhelmingly public, and the teaching profession preferred it that way, autonomy had to be found within the parameters of bureaucratic rights and privileges, which of course also guaranteed a "market monopoly."

The situation of such industrially oriented new professions as engineering and chemistry appears not to have changed toward more autonomy, at least not by

1 See Fritz K. Ringer, *Education and Society in Modern Europe* (Bloomington, Ind., 1979), pp. 152 and 229, for comparisons of percentages of youth cohorts entering German, French, and British university-level institutions in the late nineteenth and early twentieth centuries.

the measurement of the percentage of practitioners who worked for themselves. An irony in these fields, but especially in engineering, lay in the parallel improvement of higher educational qualifications along with the expansion of employment positions for technical trainees emerging from secondary institutes. Attempts to create "technicians' unions" before World War I reflected the resulting further division of technically oriented occupations along such lines as higher or secondary educational qualifications. The autonomy of engineers and chemists, even those with the highest qualifications, was undoubtedly restricted to some degree by the nature of "practicing" in large corporations as employees, even when highly paid and privileged. Nevertheless, such organizations as the VDI and the VDC did manage to gain acceptance for certain rights of professionals that had not existed before about 1900, as in the area of patents or *Karenz*. The engineering profession, both much larger and more variegated than that of chemistry, is difficult to generalize about. The VDI down to the beginning of the Hitler period never achieved the same standing as a *learned-professional* organization as, say, the DAeV or even the VDC, because many of its members were still self-taught engineers. The VDI, in other words, was as much an *occupational* as a *professional* association, which muddies the waters concerning the degree of autonomy of all its membership. A more exclusive professional engineering association, such as the VDDI, would be a more likely exemplar for testing the question of autonomy, but not enough is known about its success to make any safe hypotheses. Other engineering-related breakaway groups, such as the VDEh, consisting of 80 percent entrepreneurs, clearly had their own financial interests in mind, rather than the professionalization of the occupation. It remains difficult to exclude them from all scrutiny on this account, however, and this shows the difficulty of empirical approaches to professional groups.

Aside from entrepreneurial groups, as they professionalized, did the German learned occupations grow wealthier? A privileged economic and social position is another of the often proposed indices of the success of the "professionalizing project." The evidence points fairly clearly toward such success in the case of schoolteachers over the entire period under review. But it is more difficult to establish such a clear trend for most other professions taken as a whole. Certainly in the relatively backward and poor country that preindustrial Germany was, and considering the catastrophic economic consequences of both World War I and the Great Depression, such a measurement might even be misleading as a sign of successful professionalization in this particular time frame. The general prosperity enjoyed by professionals in the Federal Republic of Germany under what might be called "normal conditions of comparativity" would argue strongly for the long-term success of professional organizations in establishing their members' rights to higher incomes and social respect than most other occupations. On some occasions, clearly, German professional organizations were able materially to improve their members' momentary economic position, as with the physicians' victory over the sickness funds prior to World War I.

In another sense, however, the measurement of economic privilege may also be misplaced in German society as it was constituted before 1933. This has something to do with the peculiarity of a "corporate" social mentality, which will be discussed below. Whatever the increasing role of money and wealth in twentieth-century social values, the earlier high value assigned to education (and correspondingly low one to money) reinforced the prestige of professional expertise. This was undoubtedly one of the reasons German professional groups were so eager to tie qualifications to the *Abitur* and university-level education (for certainly less traditional methods of training were thinkable). As long as the qualifications for membership in the learned professions and the *Bildungsbürgertum* were largely congruent, then the "social status" goal of the professionalizing project was largely achieved, at least as long as membership in that social group was more highly prized than membership in the newly wealthy circles of industry and commerce. With the rapid expansion of higher education in the twentieth century, the recruitment of academic professionals from other strata of the bourgeoisie and the economic and social decline of the old *Bildungsbürgertum*, the social prestige of the academic professions had to be based increasingly on claims to expertise.

As for altruism or a public-service ethic, as well as codes of ethics or other mechanisms for protecting that ethic, it is worth noting that most German professional organizations claimed such for themselves. It is also more likely that the *Kammern* set up for the legal, medical, and other professions did more to regulate unfair competition than to protect the public. One is tempted to say that the controversy over altruism as central to professionalization is a false one. A service occupation, such as most professions are, must by definition serve the public, and whether it serves well or poorly is perhaps not provably a function of the good or bad intentions of its members.

Certainly the history of modern German professions and their representative organizations shows that pure, high-minded altruism was never the main driving force behind organization and lobbying. Indeed, as we have seen, the tendency was for organizations to begin with declarations of high-minded ("scientific") purposes and, once established, to go over more and more openly to an everyday practice of "interest politics." But that same history also indicates that the favorite lever for "raising the profession" was increasing educational and certification qualifications, which in turn produced an unarguably first-rate professional corps in all fields of service to the public by the beginning of this century. Thus, by heavily emphasizing one attribute of professionalization more than was historically common in the English-speaking world, German professional groups indirectly contributed to the public welfare.

Such a point must be considered when approaching the critics of "functionalist" theory of professions, those who espouse a "power" or "critical" interpretation. Power over the market in professional services (e.g. monopolization) is the presumed chief (and perhaps only) real goal of the "professionalizing project." Yet, the German experience seems not to support this theory, which like so many suffers from its narrow origin in Anglo-American experience. German professional organizations did request that the state support higher standards of admission to the profession and in the long run received such state sanction, but the result was not to vastly enhance the professionals' incomes. (The German states were, by the way, carrying out their role as assigned in "critical" models, that of protecting, not opposing, the professional drive toward monopoly.) Nor, as we have seen, did German professional groups usually call for restrictions on numbers of people entering the occupation by restricting access, *as long as* those candidates met valid standards. Open-market competition was chosen by most professions, although some (and parts of several others), such as teaching, actively promoted the bureaucratization of their careers, expecting improvements in working conditions and greater professional standards through that route. Thus, by a "functionalist" definition (validation of professions through expertise), German professions carried out a "professionalizing project"; yet in their cooperation with the state, they were behaving according to a "critical" definition; and with the result that they failed in their "critical" mission, maximizing incomes by choking off "production of producers" of professional services.

It would seem equally plausible to argue, from the German experience we have examined, that German professional groups did what they were supposed to do (at least in part) by both "functionalist" and "critical" definitions. If the qualification system appeared at times to "produce too many producers," it may have been because there were too few consumers, or that they were not the right kind to fit Anglo-American models. The creation and expansion of mandatory health insurance after the 1880s, at first having little impact, came to create a whole new mass market for health-care services as well as lower per-capita fees for doctors. Yet, as we have seen, the German medical profession did not oppose socialized medicine, only certain features regarded as unfair. By the standards of the American Medical Association, this may appear to be a total failure of the German profession's efficacy. But viewed in terms of the tradition of cooperation between state and profession in Germany, it does not appear as a form of deprofessionalization, but as an opportunity to expand the market for medical services.

The issue of "deprofessionalization" has been touched on in other contexts in this work, as well. No doubt the rise of new classes of "technicians" without higher educational qualifications (especially in engineering and applied technology fields) and working for less pay under less secure conditions may plausibly be viewed as a sign of deprofessionalization in a given occupational area. Yet, nobody would assert that the American medical or dental occupations have been deprofessionalized because of the existence of paramedical personnel or dental technicians. Nor, comparing German and American engineering, can one say that either has been particularly successful in creating a monolithic professional organization capable of dominating the market for services. Indeed, organizational differentiation and competition on a *universal* level appear as much a part of the development of modern professions as the attenuation of rivalries among professionals on a *local* level. The multiplication of professional organizations, representing different specialties and differing levels of educational qualification (e.g. "academic" and "technical" or "shop" and "school" orientations in engineering and applied science), do not appear to offer clear evidence of a failure of professionalization or of "deprofessionalization." Instead, they merely show that growth in such occupations has been faster in occupational sectors of engineering and science that are not at the time able to follow the professionalization project as fully as members of the academically trained sectors. One might call these rapidly growing twentieth-century groups "semiprofessional" or "proto-professional," but even these terms are of debatable use. Some authors argue that these cadres, though less well trained, paid, and more likely to be employees of large firms, are also products of a kind of professionalization.[2] They have also been more susceptible to unionization attempts, as we saw in the German case. But their existence would only be equatable to a "deprofessionalization" of an entire occupational category (e.g. engineering) if they undid or reversed the professionalizing achievements of the older or more academically oriented subgroups within it.

Another threat perceived by some authors, particularly regarding the German experience, has been that posed to the autonomy of professions to create their own standards. Whether as "professionalization from above" or as "the construction of occupations" (*Berufskonstruktion*), German professions have sometimes been depicted as fundamentally different from Anglo-American ones because of the role of forces outside the occupational practitioners themselves in shaping the standards of the professional group.

As we have seen, the German state always had some direct or indirect hand in shaping the professions, even though it withdrew increasingly from regulation and unilateral impositions after the 1860s. But state power was never completely withdrawn from the realm of the professions, nor did the latter generally perceive such total withdrawal as being in their own interest. A state that was willing to subsidize professional education could hardly be asked to be indifferent to its structure. The same might be said of the private market for services. As we have seen, it was again the engineering and applied-science occupations in which the interests of the employers appear to have exerted considerable influence (e.g. in the creation of the *Verbandsexamen* for chemists). Yet, on further reflection, the market for services usually has some impact on the shape of professionalization, even if it happens to be organized into capitalist industry. Similar influences might be discerned in the "market" organized by the sickness funds. Did the funds (even before checked by concerted action by the medical profession) however "construct" the medical profession or impose

2 Douglas Klegon, "The Sociology of Professions. An Emerging Perspective," *Sociology of Work and Occupations* 5 (1978): 275.

"professionalization from above"? Only from a liberal-market perspective, in other words from a traditional Anglo-American bias, could one make the apposition of professionalization "from within" (successful manipulation of the market by group) and "from above" (domination of forces external to the group). Unless German professionalization was not "real," it must be seen as occurring on a field where negotiation with market forces, not a fantastic "triumph" over them, represented historic facts, just as it often seems to have in Anglo-American facticity, if not in theory. Momentary historical deviations from ideal types should not be overly worrisome to theorists, either, as long as theory can allow for the "evitability" in all trends and shifts in the goals of professional groups over long periods of development (e.g. from 1850 to 1990). Thus, such theoretical attempts to differentiate German professional development from that of other countries based on "occupation construction" or "professionalization from above" really seem to reduce to statements that German professions were organized under different circumstances from those of some (if by no means all) other countries.

For it is precisely the premise of this work that the rise of modern professions did develop differently in Germany from that in other, particularly more liberal-market countries such a Britain, the United States, and Switzerland, at least until after World War II. (Adjustments in the relationship between independent professional practitioners and political and social institutions in Britain and, less rapidly and dramatically, the United States clearly shifted in the direction of the German model after 1945.) The reason for the emergence of this German model of professionalization was not so much that professions were feeble or negligible; or that the process of professionalization was stunted from birth or "doomed." Rather, it is because professionalization went on at a different (often indeed faster) pace, under clearly different social, economic, and political conditions (not to mention attitudinal ones). Largely members of the *Bildungsbürgertum*, German professionals tended to share a social vision more attuned to corporatist, *ständisch* thought than the swiftly changing urban and industrial realities growing up around them.

Although it was widespread and fashionable as late as the 1930s, corporatist social philosophy also succumbed along with the defeat of European fascist and authoritarian regimes, which had tried to exploit (if not really implement) corporatist ideas. Similarly, the term *Stand* – meaning a profession – failed to survive National Socialist rhetoric, which had sullied a previously respectable word. Insofar as older generations of German professionals thought of themselves in "corporatist" (as opposed to "pressure group") terms, they were adopting contemporary, not socially reactionary or "feudal" ideas. The mentality of the *Bildungsbürgertum*, not merely that of professionals, was conditioned by elite pride in being cultivated and knowledgeable, but also by an awareness of the need to cooperate with the state and its institutions, which provided the essential recognition and support for elite status. In other words, to fight successfully against "state interference" in their autonomy (a part of the "functionalist" view of the role of professions) or to "capture the state" for their own use and manipulation (the role assigned in many "power" analyses) would have neither been possible nor desirable for German professions. Interaction with the state, particularly with the educational system (many of whose leading figures also played important roles in professional organizations) was the model German professionalizing strategy. (So as not to awaken echoes of arguments about "special paths" in German history, let it be noted that it was also modal for many other societies, too.)

As we noted in the early chapters of this book, modern German professions emerged not so much from a guild-based form of protectionism as from a more recent bureaucratized form of authority and protection. Medicine and the law, both archetypical "free" professions in most Anglo-American models, were in fact subject to state regulation in most parts of Germany in the early nineteenth century. The guild tradition, insofar as it had survived or recovered slightly from the Smithian economic liberalization of the Napoleonic era, had long since ceased to have much relevance to the organizational forms of learned professions. Liberated from such strict regulation in the reforms of the 1860s and 1870s, German professional organizations began to develop more in parallel with their Anglo-American counterparts, but never without traces of their former close association with public authority. Nor did such "new" professions as engineering and chemistry find any conflict in containing in their organizational ranks representatives of the very private authority (industry) that provided an increasing percentage of the employment for their members.

The civil service itself, having provided many models for the organization of professions, also broke out of the confines of pure "professionalization from above" and began to organize its own lobbying organizations around the turn of the twentieth century. Nothing illustrates the mutability of "professionalizing models" more than this emulation by the putative former "model group" of the successful tactics of the so-called "free" professions (as well as the successful tactics of such quasicivil servants as schoolteachers). The weakness of such abstractions as "professional groups" manipulating "the state" for their own benefit becomes evident when one looks at the evolution of professional organizations of civil servants in Germany – they were the living incorporation of "the state" and yet found it impossible to manipulate "the state" to their satisfaction. Stepping into the "private" sphere of lobbying seemed to many members of the upper civil service the only way to improve their professional position. Only members of the clergy and military officers, though both certainly professionalized "from above" in that their training and certification requirements increased over the time period we have been examining, failed to lobby loudly and effectively for their professional self-improvement, although both groups had representative organizations by the 1920s. Perhaps rebellious priests and mutinous officers are harder to imagine in German history than self-assertive bureaucrats; but professional associations of military officers and clergy comparable to those in medicine or law have not been a notable feature of the history of professions in other countries, either.

The professionalization of clergy and the military through a chain of command or a hierarchy raises the question of elites within the professions. Just as synods, the Vatican, or the general staff has more to say about the qualifications for entry into careers within the priesthood or the officer corps, certain groups within each profession exercised a disproportionate influence on its entry and career requirements. As we have seen, in the newer, applied-science professions such as chemistry and engineering, the elites tended to be drawn from successful practitioners in the private sector and higher education. Local elites in the medical profession tended to dominate the local medical associations, which in turn shaped the policies of the DAeV. In the national bar association, practitioners in the *Reichsgericht* or the *Oberlandesgerichte* tended to set the standards, rather than the attorneys practicing in the lowest courts (e.g. *Amtsgericht*). The larger, better-organized, and older a professional organization became, the less likely were the interests (particularly of the material interests) of the youngest, most vulnerable, or least well-educated and certified members of the profession to dominate the concerns of the association.

Thus, the rise of modern professions was also accompanied by the phenomenon of the elites in learned occupations attempting to impose discipline on those who would enter it – a function carried out by civil authorities under bureaucratic despotism or by guilds in local trades before the late nineteenth century. These same elites almost always pressed for increases in the educational and certification requirements for membership in the profession, arguably a self-serving goal for the members of the leadership themselves active in higher educational establishment.

Yet, there were limits to the justifiability of raising educational and certification requirements, and most professional associations, engineers and lower schoolteachers being exceptions, appear to have reached plateaus beyond which they did not push very much by the 1920s – precisely a time when the threat of overcrowding should logically have increased their agitation for raising standards.

This observation raises the problem of the role of education in professionalization: is its level of requirements set by the independent requirements of science or knowledge in the field, by the need for a determinable quantity and quality of advanced expertise? Or is the knowledge, or at least the certification of knowledge, for professions indeterminate, arbitrary, and a function of struggles for power or social prestige? It is difficult to defend either of these extreme views on the basis of German professionalization. Clearly, the requirement to submit to some form of classical school education (to obtain the *Abitur*) was a residue of the traditional assignment of social status through the agency of an arcane (classics-oriented) and exclusive body of knowledge, without much convincing evidence that such preknowlege made for better or worse professional practitioners. The outcry among German physicians in the late nineteenth century concerning weakening the classics requirements for entry into medical study is a case in point. On the other hand, it is hard to deny that the revolution in science and the explosion of knowledge in general required a more complex, more rigorously organized, and longer lasting "apprenticeship" for the modern professions than could be provided by traditional master-pupil relationships. Higher education and certification systems delivered this training more cheaply and efficiently. The fact that German learned professions and universities emerged in the modern form almost concurrently was also no coincidence.

The advantages of the German system of training members of the learned professions were clear enough to warrant considerable emulation abroad, even in the United States, where German methods had a particularly deep impact on legal, medical, and engineering education. The close cooperation between the professoriate and the leading elites of German professions has been noted repeatedly in this book. The professoriate's influence doubtless had certain ineluctable shaping influences upon German professional development. Not only in the most obvious form of shaping curriculum and helping determine examination standards, but in indirect ways, too, the interests of the professoriate ran counter to some of the "natural" interests of the professional groups in which they served. For example, because a good part of the income of professors (particularly the more famous and influential ones) derived from student lecture fees (over and above their nominal salary), it lay in the economic self-interest of the professoriate to maximize the size of the student body, rather than to restrict the pool of future practitioners. By the same token, it was also in their interests to increase the number of recommended or required courses in each professional curriculum.

The effect of these self-interests was to make professional study more arduous, but also to make it relatively accessible to a growing percentage of the German population. Thus, one factor of German professionalization – the mutual interest of the professoriate and professional leadership elites in higher educational standards for the professions – raised standards but did not make access more socially exclusive, but the opposite. This is not to say that German professions were open to all strata of German society: very few children of peasants or laborers could afford the costs (including foregone income) of even subsidized education. But the children of the commercial and industrial classes increasingly could and did.[3]

The increasingly critical "oversupply" of professionals resulting at times in the twentieth century, whether in hard reality or in the fears of the professionals themselves, no doubt undermined the ability of many professional groups to achieve what they regarded as an adequate overall income or a strong negotiat-

3 Ringer, *Education and Society*, p. 93.

ing position vis-à-vis clients and employers. But, as we have also seen, this problem seems to have been caused at least as much by the dislocations of the German economy (especially in the 1920s and 1930s) as by an absolute "over-supply" – far more professionals per capita have achieved satisfying incomes in the prosperous Federal Republic than the far fewer per capita were able to under the Weimar Republic.

In the last analysis, the problem does not appear to be that German learned occupations did not successfully undergo professionalization over the past century and a half; or that they cannot properly be called professions; or they failed to overwhelm the authoritarian and bureaucratic traditions of the traditional German states (let alone stand up to the dynamics of the brief Hitler era); or that they were not in charge of the economic and social conditions that deprived their members or satisfying working conditions during certain phases of history. The problem rests principally with their history not conforming to that of the Anglo-American world, the experience of which has informed so much of the theory of modern professions and professionalization.

Their development was not unilinear or foreordained, although long-term trends can be perceived. The setback of the Hitler period (and of Soviet-model professions in the German Democratic Republic) show fully that no professionalization process is irresistible or even particularly powerful, but is rather dependent on the historical conditions of the moment. The German experience demonstrates the danger of thinking about professions in rigid categories. It seems to show that professionalization and bureaucratization can coexist (a lesson that other countries' history also demonstrates), that professional autonomy and public control (such as the German medical insurance funds) are not mutually exclusive, and that professionalization and the public interest need not always be in conflict.

Nor should we overlook the fact that the German historical experience of professionalization included alternatives that might again arise, such as rigid state control (as in most of the traditional learned occupations before the mid-nineteenth century and, to a different degree, under the GDR regime) or the destruction of autonomy through "coordination" (as under the National Socialist regime). Whether the technology of the future will make professions obsolete, more necessary than ever, or even grant them a frightening degree of control over everyday life are questions debated (inconclusively) today by social scientists. As there seems to have been no inevitability in the past, however, to predict the future would be folly. If the German experience teaches us anything about professionalization in the European/Atlantic world, it is, indeed, to be sparing with sharply formulated categories and generalizations. It might be said that this is one of the delights and frustrations of studying central European history in general.

A word about sources

Publishing constraints today have discouraged the inclusion here of a full bib-
liography. The chapter footnotes indicate most of the important sources on the
subject, however.

This work is built mostly on printed sources, such as the published debates
and news of the professional organizations themselves, or published parliamentary debates or government decrees. Each major professional organization had
at least one periodical publication, such as the *Aerztliches Vereinsblatt* for the
medical association or the *Juristische Wochenschrift* for the lawyers' organization.
Most of these records are extant somewhere in libraries, but their provenance is
very checkered and often requires immense patience to find. No single library
in the world contains them all. I used the Bavarian State Library and its interlibrary loan system for the most part; assiduous checking in other libraries
revealed that the German interlibrary loan system had found most of what is
still extant. The Library of Congress and such excellent collections as the
Berkeley, Stanford, and New York Public systems, as well as many smaller
libraries in the United States, often contain fragments not available anywhere in
German sister libraries.

As difficult as collecting these printed sources was, the availability of archival
sources was much more problematical. Whatever the final verdict of debates
among military historians about the effect of bombing raids of the British and
American Air Forces on German war production, they were certainly effective in
destroying most of the records of German professional organizations. Most or
all of the pre-1945 records of the major German organizations of lawyers, physicians, dentists, apothecaries, chemists, engineers, architects, and teachers
were lost. These records had been largely centralized in large German cities by
the time of the Weimar Republic – in Berlin, Leipzig, or other major centers.
What survived is usually not interesting for this sort of study. Even private
records, taken by retiring officials of professional organizations, appear to have
been destroyed for the most part in the chaos of World War II. Those that
remain and were made available to me say little about decision-making. Most

positions in German professional organizations were run before the Hitler period as honorific offices.

The records from the other side of a partnership, from that of the individual states or the Reich government, are equally elusive or thin. I have examined the archival records of most of the West German states and some parts of the Reich government records now housed in West Berlin. I was also able to consult the relevant records of the Prussian education ministry now reposing in Merseburg, in the former GDR, several times in the 1970s, and recall no major documents relevant to this study that have not been reprinted or published in some form. My requests to use these same original documents for this study were refused by the Archival Administration of the German Democratic Republic. A formal complaint about this from myself, the U.S. State Department, the American Historical Association, and the National Archives of the United States remained "under study" for over seven years by the GDR, until its disappearance as a state.

The likelihood of new, undiscovered primary materials relevant to this study in the former GDR archives, however, is small. Not only my own microfilms from GDR archives but also those generously made available to me by colleagues in Western Europe and the United States indicate no clear patterns of interactions between professional groups and Reich government offices. This generalization might not hold for the period after 1918, for which the GDR always refused me (and most Western scholars) access.

The scantness of materials in state archives that I have been able to consult (principally the *Geheimes Staatsarchiv Dahlem, Bundesarchiv Koblenz,* and the Bavarian, Baden-Württemberg, Hessian, and Lower Saxon State Archives) convinced me that most relationships between government and professional organizations were carried out on an informal basis in any case. The point of professionals having a national representation was to insure that such contacts were established. In this work I have been frustrated in looking for clear, written agreements. I have operated on the principle that the pattern I have often found documented might carry over to those I have not. In the long run, that interaction followed the pattern of (1) stated wish; (2) negotiation; (3) frustrated wish; (4) ultimate partial success. Governments do not make policy without input. I have concluded from the archival material that I have seen that, over the long pull, governments did take that input from professional organizations more and more seriously, and that successful lobbying is rarely well-documented in government sources.

Given this situation of sources, direct cause-and-effect negotiation sequences cannot be expected, but chiefly the long-term trends evident from decades of pressure from professional organizations (as recorded in their own literature) and government actions in the form of changing laws, decrees, and policies which, fortunately, are still left to the researcher despite the destruction or witholding of so much.

Index

248 Index

184, 185; economists, 160, 162, 202–4;
elementary, 111; engineers, 66, 68, 91,
93, 115, 124, 149, 187, 234; judges,
199; legal, 40, 42, 58, 59, 87, 109,
121–3, 159, 195; liberal, 15; medical, 40,
42, 55–7, 80, 82, 183; Nazi, 228; physicians, 135, 138, 142, 182; preprofessional,
107, 108, 111, 114, 116; teachers, 46,
62, 100, 102–4, 126, 154, 166, 188,
205, 206, 207, 208; technical, 47, 68,
108, 149, 236; women, 167–8
Eichhorn, J. A., 61
Einheitsschule (unitary school), 63, 205, 211
Einjährig-Freiwillige, see officers, reserve
Enabling Law (1933), 219
Engelberg, Ernst, 160
engineers, 3, 16, 17, 22, 24, 25, 45, 53,
65–6, 67, 68, 74–7, 91, 92, 93, 96,
97, 108, 110, 113, 115, 118, 123–6,
131, 132, 146, 148–53, 159, 179, 180,
186, 187, 190, 198, 203, 213, 225,
227, 228, 231, 232, 233, 234, 236,
237, 239, 240; early organizing efforts,
65; Nazi, 177, 226
England, 5, 7, 16, 19, 21–5, 31–33, 35, 36,
41, 48, 58, 59, 66, 158, 175, 180, 231–
3, 238
Enlightenment, 32, 33, 61
Erhard, Ludwig, 229
ethics, professional, 14, 16, 25, 39, 43, 57,
77, 84, 85, 134, 178, 213, 228, 235;
apothecaries, 191; attorneys, 87, 194;
chemists, 147; dentists, 143; physicians,
83, 84, 135, 140, 142
eugenics, 220
Eulenburg, Franz, 165
examinations, 14, 16–18, 20–22, 25–7, 34,
35, 37–9, 102, 107, 109, 112, 116, 118,
120, 127, 171, 178, 197, 232, 241;
apothecaries, 190; chemists, 115, 188;
civil service, 199; commissions, 59, 122;
dentists, 143, 185; economists, 159, 203,
204; legal, 40, 42, 58, 59, 91, 121–3,
157, 195–6; physicians, 55, 112, 119,
137, 182, 183; teachers, 46, 64, 102,
103, 126, 206

faculties, university, 33, 110, 112; legal, 40,
81, 196, 202; medical, 81, 119, 136,
143, 182–4; pedagogical, 168, 205; philosophical, 44, 69, 81, 126, 205, 206, 211;
social science, 203; theological, 44, 126;
Falk, Adalbert, 98, 112
Feder, Gottfried, 219, 226
Federal Republic, 229, 230, 234, 242
fees, *see* income

Fischer, Ferdinand, 96
Fortbildung. see education, continuing, 127
France, 5, 16, 26, 33, 41, 48, 54, 59, 98,
124, 151, 158, 181, 232
Frankfurt National Assembly, 52
Frederick III, 54
freedom, academic, 34
Freidson, Eliot, 14, 18, 21, 26
Freie Lehrergewerkschaft Deutschlands, 209
Frick, Wilhelm, 221
Friedländer, Rudolf, 194
Friedman, Milton, 244

Gadamer, H. G., 8
GDR (German Democratic Republic), 230, 242
Gerland, Heinrich, 159
German Democratic Republic, *see* GDR
German Empire, 36, 54, 73, 75, 108, 244
Germanic Confederation, 36, 37, 49
Gewerkschaftsbund der Angestellten, 191
Gleichschaltung ("Coordination"), 217, 221,
222, 223, 225, 242
Gneist, Rudolf von, 59, 60, 122, 123
Goebbels, Josef, 219
Goering, Hermann, 219
Grashof, Franz, 67, 68, 115, 124
groups, professional, *see* associations,
professional
Gymnasium, 33, 36, 37, 45–7, 56, 62–4, 69,
79, 97, 101–4, 108, 111–13, 123, 126,
139, 165–8, 205, 208, 209, 212

Hamburg, 57, 207, 208
Handelshochschulen. see schools, business
Hansabund. see BDF
Harnack, Adolf von, 164
Hartmann League, *see* VAeWI
Hartmann, Hermann, 138
Heckscher, Wilhelm, 70
Hegel, G. W. F., 7
herbalists, 18, 55
Hess, Rudolf, 221
Hesse, 49, 83, 105, 166, 207
Hesse, H. A., 144
Heydrich, Reinhard, 219
Himmler, Heinrich, 219
Hitler, Adolf, 3, 7, 177, 179, 192, 204, 217,
221, 222, 226, 228
Hofmann, A. W., 95
Holborn, Hajo, 4
Holocaust, 220, 228
Holy Roman Empire, 36, 37
hospitals, 179, 184
Hughes, E. C., 13
Humboldt, Wilhelm von, 4
Hungary, 26
hypnotists, 18